Adolf Hitler's fanatical thirst for empire, the courageous resistance it provokes, and the titanic battles that ravaged a continent are now brought to breathtaking life in this remarkable new series by noted historian Edwin P. Hoyt. Here is the unforgettable story of World War Two in the European theater—a detailed, dramatic and astonishing military chronicle of victory and defeat in the brutal struggle between the forces of freedom and tyranny.

VOLUME ONE

B L I T Z K R I E G

VOLUME ONE

WAR IN EUROPE

BLITZKRIEG

EDWIN P. HOYT

AVON BOOKS ◆ NEW YORK

WAR IN EUROPE VOLUME ONE: BLITZKRIEG is an original publication of Avon Books. This work has never before appeared in book form.

AVON BOOKS
A division of
The Hearst Corporation
1350 Avenue of the Americas
New York, New York 10019

Copyright © 1991 by Edwin P. Hoyt
Published by arrangement with the author
Library of Congress Catalog Card Number: 91-91799
ISBN: 0-380-76155-6

First Avon Books Printing: September 1991

AVON TRADEMARK REG. U.S. PAT. OFF. AND IN OTHER COUNTRIES, MARCA REGISTRADA, HECHO EN U.S.A.

Printed in the U.S.A.

RA   10 9 8 7 6 5 4 3 2 1

CONTENTS

CHAPTER 1

The Roots of War

Anyone seeking an explanation for the root cause of the Second World War need look no further than the Versailles Treaty that ended World War I. In the clauses of the treaty, and particularly in the mind-set of the Allied politicians who imposed the treaty on Germany, the desire for vengeance overcame common sense. The result was an imposed penance so heavy, so unfair, and so savage that its result was quite the opposite of what the Allied leaders wanted. They wanted peace in the future ever after, and they made sure that they would have war within twenty years.

Those leaders—the results of their counsels deny them the title of "statesmen," although the world accorded it to them in their own time—were so imbued with rage and the demand for retribution that they ignored the economic realities of a defeated enemy. A comparison between the Treaty of Versailles and the treaties that ended World War II, and a look at the world a half century after that Second World War, show the difference clearly. Mankind can learn from experience, and the generosity shown the defeated enemy of World War II by the Western Allies created a world in which those defeated enemies were able to arise, with the help of their erstwhile opponents of the battlefield, and rebuild

1

totally shattered economies. The great difference was in the attitude of the peacemakers, who in the 1940s showed a compassion that was totally absent in the treatment of the Germans after World War I.

World War I was the result of struggles for power in Europe and the world that had been building for half a century. Within weeks of its beginning the struggle developed into a wrestling match between titans, neither of whom could secure and maintain the advantage necessary for victory. After four seesaw years of war, both European factions were virtually exhausted, and the difference was in the new blood poured into the struggle by the United States. In the summer of 1918 the Germans launched a new offensive. It began on July 15, 1918, and it failed, largely because the German reserves had vanished in the bloodshed of four years. On August 18, the German military leader General Von Ludendorff made this appraisal:

"August 8 was the black day of the German Army in the history of the war . . . It put the decline of our fighting power beyond all doubt . . . The war must be ended."

The German high command then altered its war aims. Knowing they could no longer hope to win, they fought thereafter to wear down the Allies and achieve a stalemate.

The Allies began an offensive of their own. They attacked at Chateau Thierry and west of the Argonne. At the end of September 1918, General Ludendorff began seeking peace with the Allies, and Prince Max, the chancellor, made an appeal for an armistice to President Wilson of the United States, even as the Allies were launching a renewed offensive that broke through the German Hindenburg line.

Meanwhile Austria, which was Germany's principal ally, collapsed and signed a separate peace on November 3, 1918. The German armies fought on, partly because the plea to America was answered by a virtual request for "unconditional surrender." But on the German home front, the German fleet mutinied, revolution broke out, the kaiser abdicated, a republic was formed, and the military situation became impossible, although the German army was intact. So at 5:00 A.M. on November 11, 1918, in French Marshal Foch's railway carriage on a side spur in the forest of Compiègne, the Germans signed an armistice. It was observed by both sides and the war ended.

The German soldiers marched home as heroes. No one told the people of Germany that they had lost the war. They believed the armistice had been the result of exhaustion by both sides, and it was months before they learned the truth. When they did learn the truth, during the negotiations at Versailles, their bitterness against their leaders was extreme, and it became one of the major reasons for the rise of Hitler and Nazism in Germany.

The Versailles Treaty arose out of the Fourteen Points enunciated by American President Woodrow Wilson, in the winter of 1918. A look at them indicates the basic problems of Europe and its colonies that led to World War II.

1. Open covenants of peace, openly arrived at.
2. Freedom of the sea, except when abrogated by international action.
3. Removal of artificial trade barriers among nations.
4. Sweeping reductions in national armaments.
5. An absolutely impartial adjustment of colonial claims.
6. The evacuation of and self-determination of Russia.
7. The evacuation of and restoration of Belgium.
8. The return of Alsace-Lorraine to France.
9. Readjustment of Italy's boundaries along the lines of nationality.
10. Autonomy for the subject peoples of Austro-Hungary.
11. International guarantees for the integrity of Rumania, Serbia, and Montenegro.

12. Autonomy for the subject peoples of the Ottoman Empire, and free passage for all nations through the Dardanelles.
13. Establishment of an independent Poland with access to the sea.
14. A general association of nations "formed under specific covenants for the purpose of affording mutual guarantees of political independence and territorial integrity to great and small nations alike."

After President Wilson enunciated these Fourteen Points in a speech in January 1918, the ideas spread quickly across the world, and in Germany were the basis of the undermining of the German will to continue the war. By October 1918 the Fourteen Points had been accepted by the German government as the basis for peace negotiations. But France and Britain accepted only with two major reservations. They excluded the "freedom of the seas" point on Britain's insistence, and on French insistence they demanded compensation from Germany for all damage done to the civilian population of the Allied states and their property by German aggression.

These two radical changes were communicated by President Wilson to the German government early in November. The German government obviously found them hard to swallow, particularly the latter, which would give a blank check to the Allies, but the internal situation in Germany was by then so desperate that the government in effect yielded by getting in touch with French Marshal Foch, and accepting the terms he set down for an armistice. The question of reparations, which might have blown the whole armistice sky-high, was sideslipped in some murky diplomatic language that really left the matter up in the air.

The heart of the Versailles Treaty was the first part of the treaty. It established a League of Nations, which guaranteed the independence and territorial integrity of all the nations. This League was to supervise the fate of the former German colonies, which had been split up into "mandates" given to the supervision of established states with an eye to the eventual freedom of the territories, but no specific promises or timetables. As a part of the punitive action that developed rapidly at Versailles, Germany was not invited into the League of Nations at the time. This was significant, particularly because of the resentments this sort of treatment set up in Germany.

The League also had the responsibility to supervise the trade in arms with developing countries, where there was obviously field for conflict and revolution, and to encourage the general reduction of armaments by all nations. The Western world at that point, 1919, was throughly sick of conflict and hoped they had, as some Americans put it, "made the world safe for democracy." The League had other—and much more fertile—fields of action, in the matters of human labor and world public health, where nationalism and politics made less of a difference.

The stated purpose of the League of Nations was to prevent war, and the process involved arbitration among nations and delay of military action in the hope of conciliation. There was provision of international economic sanctions against aggressor nations, which was supposed to bring potential aggressors to heel by hurting their economy if they did not heed the international will.

The League of Nations was to be governed by a council and an assembly. The council was to consist of the victor nations of World War I: Britain, France, the United States, Italy, and Japan, as permanent members, holding a majority of the votes, and thus able to control the actions of the council. All member nations would have seats in the assembly.

Two other bodies were established by the treaty, a Permanent Court of International Justice, at the Hague, the Netherlands, to which any aggrieved nation might apply for judicial restraint against the actions of another, and the International Labor Office, which was to supervise the welfare of the world's workers.

The League also had the responsibility for supervising the government of the Saar industrial basin, and the Free City of Danzig, which were taken away from German control. The League was also to supervise continued German disarmament, which was stipulated in the treaty.

Parts two and three of the Treaty of Versailles stripped Germany of much of her territory. Belgium acquired the districts of Eupen, Moresnet, and Malmédy, taken as compensation of damages done to Belgium by the German occupation. Luxembourg became independent. The Saar basin was governed by the League, but its rich coal mines were ceded to France, in compensation for German damages to French coal mines during the occupation of Northern France. This situation was to persist for fifteen years, at which time a plebiscite would be held and the people of the Saar would choose their own way: union with France, union with Germany, or continued internationalization.

Alsace and Lorraine were both ceded to France, in compensation for general German damages, which meant that Germany lost and France gained two million citizens, most of them bilingual, and some of them bicultural.

Under the treaty, the Rhine River, the great waterway and sometimes border of Germany, was demilitarized. The left bank was to have no military installations, and the right bank's demilitarization would extend fifty kilometers from the river, which meant that all the forts were to be torn down, and no permanent defense erected. Germany, then, would have no defenses of its borders.

In the north of Germany, the Germans lost northern Schleswig to Denmark, after a plebiscite. This territory had been disputed since the days of Bismarck's empire building.

One of the most painful, and indeed irritating, territorial losses was that in the Baltic, where West Prussia and most of the province of Poznan were given to Poland, creating a "corridor" which separated German territory into two parts, the corridor running between Pomerania and East Prussia. Danzig, an entirely German city, was made a free city, governed by the League. The city of

Memel, another German city, was taken from Germany and given by the Allies to Lithuania. The area called Upper Silesia, partly Polish and mostly German in inclination, was split, with Poland taking most of the non-Germanic population, and the Germans given the option of leaving the Polish territory for Germany if they wished.

In all these transactions, the state of Germany lost twenty-five thousand square miles of territory, an area about the size of West Virginia, and about six million people, and many natural resources, particularly those used in steel manufacture.

Germany lost her whole empire. In Africa, The Cameroons and Togoland were divided between Britain and France. German Southwest Africa was given to the Union of South Africa. German East Africa was split between Britain and Belgium. In the Pacific, Germany gave up the Marshall Islands to Japan, New Guinea to Australia, Nauru to Britain, and Samoa to New Zealand. In China, the beautiful and prestigious colony of Kiaochow in Shandong Province went to Japan, and eventually back to China. As important as the territorial concessions were, treaty and trade rights in the Far East and Middle East and all of these concessions, extremely valuable to German business, were suddenly lost.

The whole German military machine was abolished overnight. The army was reduced to a force of one hundred thousand men, this country which had eleven million men under arms during the war. There would be no air force at all. The navy was cut to six battleships, six cruisers, twelve destroyers, and twelve torpedo boats, with no submarines at all. New ships would be limited to ten thousand tons, or about a third the size of a British battleship. The navy would be limited to fifteen thousand men, and all forts within fifty kilometers of the coast were to be destroyed. The fortress at Helgoland was to be dismantled.

The Allies said that Kaiser Wilhelm was a war criminal and should be tried, but the Dutch refused to turn him out of his refuge in Holland and the matter was dropped, as was the "punishment" of about a hundred other German leaders accused of "war crimes," including Field Marshal Paul Von Hindenburg, who was later elected president of the German Republic.

But the most deadly and most controversial aspect of the treaty was the section that dealt with war reparations. The Allies flung upon the Germans full responsibility for the war and everything that happened in the war years, and decided to bleed Germany white in revenge. It can be called nothing else. France and Belgium were particularly venal in their approach to the problem, and this attitude was immediately apparent to the people of Germany.

It had been expected that the United States, which had suffered virtually no physical damage in the war, would serve as a sort of buffer against the French and Belgians in the reparations commission, but when the United States Senate refused to ratify the Versailles Treaty, and the Americans did not participate in the League of Nations, the reparations problem became a football, the French and Belgians outvoting the British, and every country trying to get the most for itself. The German war debt was put at thirty-three billion dollars, which was more than twice the capacity of the German people to pay, by American estimate.

When the treaty was published, it aroused a storm of protest all over Germany. The main contention of the Germans was that the treaty violated the agreement the Germans thought they had with the Allies, accepting Wilson's Fourteen Points as the basis for peace. And this, of course, was true, because of the harsh provisions for reparations, which put the finishing touch on the shattered German economy and brought about a massive inflation that destroyed property rights everywhere.

In the discussions before the treaty, President Wilson had spoken loftily of "impartial justice" to rule this new world. But the Germans saw quite a different picture, with no justice at all for them in it. Germany was to be deprived of its national character and to be used as sort of an economic slave state by the victorious Allies. The

Germans claimed that the demands of the treaty would wreck German life, drive down the standard of living, and prevent a German economic recovery.

The Allied viewpoints were quite different, ranging from the American policy of isolationism to the French application of force, which led them to occupy the Ruhr in 1923 in retaliation for Germany's failure to meet some reparations payments. And once peace was established, the Allies were allies no longer, each going its own way; Britain concerned with her empire and economic problems, France deeply concerned with Germany, Italy concerned with building a new empire, and Japan busy with her own empire, building in Asia. Since there was no uniformity of belief, the Treaty of Versailles was never fully implemented. It served as a catalyst to reviving German nationalism in the early 1930s, and as a whipping boy for Hitler in his drive for power. The Treaty of Versailles brought neither peace, nor order, nor prosperity to the world, and fifteen years after it was drawn, it was in shards.

Germany entered the League of Nations in 1926 but withdrew in 1933, as Hitler was bent on the destruction that all Versailles stood for. Japan withdrew also in 1933, for her own reasons, criticism in the world forum for her seizure of Manchuria and its conversion into the puppet state of Manchukuo. The League of Nations' failure and the failure of Britain and America to stop Japanese expansionism was a root cause of the Pacific war. By 1935 the League was in shambles; Mussolini was embarking on his adventures in Africa, and would withdraw from the League in 1937 after conquering Ethiopia. The Soviet Union, which had joined the League in 1934, was expelled in 1939 as a result of its invasion of Finland.

By this time, Hitler had marched into the Rhineland, in defiance of the careful demilitarization policies, and had secured a (rigged) plebiscite in the Saarland wherein the people voted to return to Germany. Hitler had also engineered a hysterical plebiscite in Austria, which made it a German colony, and had bluffed and bulldozed Britain and France to destroy Czechoslovakia and add it to the growing German Empire. The German generals had first nurtured and then revived their army, the German navy was building, and the most modern submarines were in the design stage in defiance of Versailles. The sores caused by the arbitrary territorial changes of Versailles had festered and created grist for Hitler's war machine. The fact was that the Versailles Treaty never did work, because of nonparticipation of the Americans, who in that sense had to accept their share of the blame for what happened in Europe in 1939.

CHAPTER 2

The War Machine

In the aftermath of World War I, the German army was torn to shreds, by the victorious Allies and by the revolution that gripped Germany in 1918 and produced for a few months a radical regime. "Soldiers' councils" were set up, the Soviet system was imposed, and the whole army changed. In December the First Soviet Congress of Germany assembled in the Prussian Diet with the intention of dissolving the German officer corps. The demands grew riotous, and General Kurt von Schleicher at general staff headquarters gave orders to General von Lequis to march on the rebels and put them down. General Wilhelm Groener had assured the civil government of the army's support. That was enough to quell the soldiers' rebellion, and the officers remained in control of the army.

Under the Versailles Treaty, there was to be a German army of only one hundred thousand men, and most of the officer corps was to be put out to pasture. The General Staff was officially disbanded. The Allies wanted to kill off the German military memory.

But, in fact, in 1920 the *Reichswehr*—the army—overthrew the socialist government of Bavaria and installed a right-wing regime. Bavaria had become a center of military activity; General Ludendorff had settled there, and so had a number of other officers. All over Germany the army was deeply involved in the political scene. The army's leanings were far to the right, and here in Bavaria was born the alliance between the army and Adolf Hitler. The army gave him a job in the press and news bureau of the political department of the army's Bavaria command. The officer corps had been whittled down by the order of the Allies to a mere four thousand active-duty officers, and they were the cream of the crop. Others were waiting in the wings, of course, biding their time and expecting again to be militarily employed.

Colonel General Hans von Seeckt was the chief of staff of the army, and he was creating a military machine that was very much to the liking of Hitler, because left-wing officers were purged from the service, as were Jews. The army looked to the sons of the army, and looked askance at candidates from urban areas, who could be expected to be liberal in outlook.

In the fall of 1923 the army took over the government of Germany through the generals who commanded the country's seven military districts. They put down several rebellions, including one started by Adolf Hitler.

Hitler had seen in the person of General Ludendorff his instrument of power. Around Ludendorff he organized a political alliance which was so insurrectionary that General von Seeckt suppressed the newspaper *Volkischer Beobachter*. In Bavaria, however, the local commander of the army, General Otto von Lossow, refused to suppress the paper, which caused General von Seeckt to remove him from command of the army forces; Von Lossow was then appointed chief of the Bavaria military forces by the Bavarian state commissioner.

In this atmosphere Hitler staged his rebellion, and lost everything in the attempt, a march on the Munich government, which was suppressed by the police. Hitler was tried and sent to prison, and in the best tradition of political prisoners, he served his short term in a castle, a fortress at Landsberg on the Lech.

Hitler was released, his Nazi Party began to grow, and for a time, he and the Nazis were seen by the generals as a threat to the army. But Hitler made his peace with the generals at the 1930 trial of three young officers who had been proselyting for the Nazi Party. At their trial, Hitler declared that his party, known as the "revolutionary" party, was not that, and he did not anticipate any rebellion against authority. This statement quieted the fears of the generals and they began to look on Hitler benignly.

General Werner von Blomberg, who was chosen as minister of defense in 1933, was a Hitler man. When Hitler became chancellor of Germany, it was not long before he sacrificed his bullyboys of the *Sturmabteilung* to the army. He knew he would have to have the loyalty of the army generals to survive, and so Ernst Roehm, the leader of the SA, died by assassination, as did the most important of his followers. Soon the army had a new oath of allegiance:

"I swear by God this sacred oath, that I will render unconditional obedience to Adolf Hitler, the Führer of the German Reich and people, supreme commander of the armed forces, and will be ready as a brave soldier to risk my life at any time for this oath."

As soon as Hitler became dictator of Germany, after the death of President von Hindenburg, he set out to destroy the Versailles Treaty. The first step was the order to the army to treble its strength, from one hundred thousand to three hundred thousand men by October 1934. Hitler also told his generals that next year he would begin conscription and openly repudiate the military restrictions of the treaty. Publication of the list of officers was stopped so that the swelling number of officers would not be public knowledge, and Dr. Josef Goebbels, the propaganda minister, was warned that he must never allow the words *general staff* to be published. Army and navy leaders were warned to keep quiet about what was happening and to communicate orally rather than by writing. To the navy went a special admonition not to mention the new ships of twenty-six-thousand-ton displacement, another violation of the Versailles Treaty. U-boat construction was begun in total secrecy.

At the end of World War I, the Krupp arms firm had been specifically forbidden to manufacture arms, but the fact was that all the modern guns that would be used by the new German army were designed by Krupp in the 1920s. The I. G. Farben company set to work to make Germany self-sufficient in synthetic gasoline and synthetic rubber. In 1934 some 240,000 factories were mobilized to begin war production.

On March 16, 1934, Hitler proclaimed universal military service, and announced the planning of a peacetime army of five hundred thousand men. This was the official removal of the shackles of Versailles. Had the British and French resisted, Hitler was prepared to back down, but neither country said a word. Versailles was as dead as a dodo from that moment on. And after that moment, Hitler talked more and more of peace and disarmament, as he armed and made ready for war.

On May 2, 1935, General von Blomberg issued the directive to the armed forces to prepare for the reoccupation of the Rhineland, which had been demilitarized by the Treaty of Versailles. This was to be the acid test of the British and French will; if the Allies moved militarily, Hitler would beat a hasty retreat back across the Rhine. But the British and French did nothing, Hitler denounced the Locarno Peace Pact in a speech to the *Reichstag* and announced the marching of his troops into the Rhineland; the deputies to the *Reichstag* cheered hysterically.

But the generals did not cheer. General Blomberg was extremely nervous, and he had reason to be. The French government was eager to act to stop the German incursion, but the French general staff said no action could be taken without a general mobilization of troops. But when three battalions had crossed the Rhine, General Gamelin, chief of the general staff, sent thirteen divisions to reinforce the Maginot Line near the German frontier. This action was enough to make General Blomberg plead with Hitler to withdraw the three battalions that had crossed the line, but Hitler refused to budge.

The German action did precipitate a crisis in the French

government. The premier and the foreign minister felt it was important to stop the Germans at this point. The French foreign minister flew to London to plead with the British government to back strong French action, but he was told that the British would not risk war, even though at the time, everyone knew the Allied military forces were far stronger than the German. The French did no more and the British did nothing at all, and General Blomberg found that he had nothing to worry about. The major effect of the reoccupation of the Rhineland, then, was that it reinforced Hitler's growing contempt for his generals. Later he called Blomberg's behavior "nothing less than cowardice."

From the Western point of view, this time, March 1936, represented the last chance of the Western powers to put a stop to Hitler.

That autumn, Hitler predicted the future in a meeting with Count Ciano, the Italian foreign minister. "German and Italian rearmament is proceeding much more rapidly than rearmament in England." In three years, he said, Germany would be ready for war.

Soon General von Blomberg fell from Hitler's grace (over a woman) and was forcibly retired. Colonel General Werner von Fritsch then became commander in chief of the army. He too was disgraced, as part of Hitler's plan to take over personal command of the army and become dictator of Germany, which happened in 1938. The new commander of the army then became General Walther von Brauchitsch. General Wilhelm Keitel became the chief of the *Oberkommando Wehrmacht*—the German war machine—with Hitler at the apex, in personal command of the army, the air force, and the navy. This system would continue until the end of the Third Reich.

Hitler now "cleaned house," getting rid of several of the generals to whom he had developed particular animosity, such as General Beck and General Schwedler. In the political field he was taking over Austria and preparing to move against Czechoslovakia, and he wanted men who would do his bidding without argument. Soon

General Franz Halder replaced Beck as chief of the army general staff.

The natural follow-up to the march into the Rhineland would have been the fortification of Germany's western frontier, but this had been stalled by the army. In 1938 Hitler became furious over this matter, sent Hermann Goering to make an inspection tour, and turned over the building of fortifications to Major General Fritz Todt, the inspector general of road building. Todt developed a highly sophisticated organization, which was soon engaged in building what Hitler called his "West Wall." Within eighteen months, Hitler wanted ten thousand concrete structures built. That would bring him up to the last months of 1939.

Hitler's direction, heading to war, was now established, and he was molding the German armed forces to his will. In the beginning this was easy enough, for Hitler's desire for a militarily strong Germany coincided with that of the generals, who had never changed in their approach. As noted, the Versailles Treaty cut down the German army to one hundred thousand men and "eliminated" the general staff. In fact, it did no such thing, as the story of an obscure army captain named Heinz Guderian indicates. At the end of World War I, Guderian was chosen for general staff duty. In 1922 he went to Berlin to the transportation corps, to study motorization, and was soon deep in the works of Captain Liddell Hart, the principal British expert on armor.

In 1923 Captain Guderian was assigned to work for Lieutenant Colonel von Brauchitsch, on maneuvers testing the use of motorized troops and aircraft together. By 1928 he was teaching tank tactics, and dreaming of an armored force. By 1931 he was chief of staff to the inspector of armored troops, and was designing tanks. In 1932 he was on maneuvers with a new German armored car, a six-wheel truck covered with armor plate. In 1933 he met with Hitler and quickly convinced the chancellor of the value of tanks. "That's what I need," said Hitler. "That's what I want to have."

In 1933 Guderian was involved in the policy quarrel

between the modern advocates (Von Frisch) and the old-fashioned generals (Beck), a running battle that lasted for several years. In August he swore the new oath of fealty to Hitler himself. In the fall of 1935 three Panzer divisions were formed in the German army. By this time, Guderian had been promoted to colonel and he took command of the Second Panzer Division, was promoted to major general in 1936. When Hitler took over Austria, General Guderian commanded the armored troops that rolled into Austria. He soon commanded a corps; Hitler relied on him to show German power at his various confrontations, and in the winter of 1939 he was appointed general of Panzer troops and given control of panzer operations by Hitler's own orders.

After Czechoslovakia was taken over, Guderian incorporated the Czech armor into the German army, and on August 22, 1939, General Guderian was given command of the XIX Army Corps, and the plans for the German invasion of Poland, in which he was to play a major role.

CHAPTER 3

The Luftwaffe

According to the terms of the armistice signed on November 11, 1918, all air activity had to cease in Germany. The aircraft factories shut down, and the military aircraft were either destroyed or turned over to the Allies. Theoretically the German pilots were grounded forever.

Actually, many pilots left Germany to pursue their trade. Captain Hermann Goering, the last commander of the Von Richthofen Flying Circus, went to Sweden to fly a charter service. Some pilots joined the white Russian forces fighting the Bolsheviks in Russia. Others went to Colombia and organized an airline with Junkers planes, a line that remained in existence until bought out by Pan American World Airways in the 1930s. Some German airmen went to America, and some went to the Soviet Union.

When the Junkers factory closed down in Germany, the owners put up a new factory at Malmö in Sweden. There they assembled planes from parts still made in Germany—a legal operation under the terms of the treaty. The Versailles Treaty controlled everything; that was why the Junkers aircraft had three engines, all of moderate power, instead of two high-powered engines. Dr. Claude Dornier set up a factory at Altenhein, on the branch of the Rhine River that runs from the Bodensee, or Lake Constance. It was just a few miles from his old German factory in Friedrichshafen. There he built flying boats, even though the Germans were forbidden to build big airplanes.

To control the Germans, the Allies set up an Inter Allied Commission, which was to prevent the resurgence of arms manufacture in Germany. But by one means and another, many factories were saved, such as the zeppelin works near Friedrichshafen, which was preserved because the Americans wanted a zeppelin, and one had to be built for them. The order for this air machine came just in the nick of time, before the destruction started, and produced the dirigible *Los Angeles* for the Americans.

Forbidden to manufacture any aircraft that could conceivably be used for military purposes, the Germans turned to building airlines for other countries on order. In 1919 and 1920 many airplane clubs sprang up, and several newspapers devoted to aeronautical affairs began publication. The Germans also started airlines of their own, from Berlin to Hamburg, to Bremen, to the islands off Friesland, to Dortmund, Dresden, and Magdeburg; to Munich, and Stuttgart. The lines were efficient, and in spite of rough weather in northern Germany in the winter, they averaged more than 90 percent regular service. They carried mail, passengers, and freight. By 1920 the Junkers factory was in business again, producing a low-wing monoplane which had a remarkable resemblance to the JU 52, the medium bomber of World War II. The Germans were also building sports planes. In 1923 Dr. Ernst Heinkel set up in business for himself.

But most of the air activity in Germany involved gliders, because there was no restraint by the Allies on unpowered aircraft, and a pilot could learn as much or more about aeronautics in a glider.

In 1923 Ernst Udet, who had been a fighter pilot in World War I, was building single-seater aircraft with thirty-horsepower engines.

By 1924 the dozen German airlines began to merge, and came down to two lines, the Deutsche Aero Lloyd group and the Junkers group. That year under the new German constitution, the legislature established the Ministry of Transport, which began to give advice and some support to air industries. That year, too, a new agreement for regulation of the German aviation industry was signed with the Allies, providing for a little more latitude to the airlines. Military aircraft were still forbidden, but airliners could be built.

The provisions against military flying were still harsh. Only thirty-six members of the *Reichswehr* (army) were allowed to take part in "sporting flying" at their own expense, and Germany's quota of fully trained pilots was limited to thirty-six. This regulation was evaded by officers "resigning" their commissions, so that others could take their places in the quota. Also, fifty policemen were allowed to become pilots.

The big step in the development of the new German aviation came in June 1926, when the Ministry of Transport presided over the merger of all the German airlines into one, Lufthansa. That airline soon extended its network over Europe, to Turkey, to Russia and to England, then farther afield, to Afghanistan and Persia, then to Africa and Brazil; and finally, just before the war, it was flying also to New York.

Secretly, the airline was becoming a training ground for the pilots of what would be the new Luftwaffe. By 1927 a school was operating at Stettin; soon there were five more, each training one hundred pilots a year for Lufthansa. But these pilots wore neat blue uniforms and they saluted and clicked their heels and marched with precision. And secretly the Nazi Party, to which Hermann Goering now belonged as a trusted associate of Hitler, was giving the secret air force financial support.

Also by 1927 the glider clubs were giving way to flying sports clubs, particularly after the abolition of the "nine rules" that governed German aviation under the Versailles Treaty. New names were appearing: Dr. Focke and Engineer Wulf, Arado, Messerschmidtt, and Heinkel. Soon enough, these would be the manufacturers of military aircraft.

By 1930 the separate sports clubs amalgamated into the Deutscher Luftfahrt Verband, the Wissenschaftliche Gewsellschaft fuer Luftfahrt, and the Deutsche Versuchs-Anstalt fuer Luftfahrt. The DLV educated and trained the pilots. The WGL brought new ideas into the field, and the DLV conducted research, all this under the watchful eye of the German army.

Goering had become minister of transport in the Hitler government formed in 1933, and then air minister. In 1935 one day in March, Hermann Goering made a trip to a secret air station at Schleissheim to visit the pilots there and inform them that he was soon going to announce the formation of the Luftwaffe. Most of these pilots had been trained in Russia and Italy. One, Adolf Galland, was to become Germany's most famous fighter pilot of World War II, and a major air force commander. He gave a speech about the accomplishments of building up the air force, and he brought along a model of the new Luftwaffe uniform, of light blue, that he had designed. Instead of the old German high-collared tunic, the air force officers would wear soft collars and neckties.

Soon the DLV suddenly blossomed forth with uniforms and badges decorated with the swastika. Already Germany had thirty first-class airfields, including Tempelhof in Berlin, which was a sort of wonder of the aviation world. By 1934 also the German aircraft industry was building single-seat trainers and advanced trainers. The Heinkel machines began to have the appearance of fighter planes. In 1935 the Luftwaffe was born, and the names of General Albert Kesselring, Colonel Ernst Udet, and Erhart Milch soon became well-known in air circles. These were the leaders of the fledgling Luftwaffe. Goering was air minister and a colonel general. But the organizational genius of the Luftwaffe was Erhart Milch, who had spent the earlier years putting together the Lufthansa airline. In 1935 he became chief of Department VI of the Air Ministry, which meant the Luftwaffe, and a *General der Flieger*.

The entire air force program was enveloped in propaganda. The British government put out a white paper in which they reported German air strength at twenty-five hundred aircraft, but that was a wild overstatement. The German air force might have been able to put two thousand planes into the air, but many of them were old-fashioned biplanes.

However, Colonel Udet was working on one sort of aircraft that would truly amaze the world. It was the Stuka dive bomber, modeled after the American Hell-diver, but improved by Udet, who was a genius at aircraft design. Its most effective feature was the tremendous screeching noise of the aircraft as it made its dive and pulled out after dropping its bombs. The psychological effect was enormous.

In 1935, when the Germans were constructing the Air Ministry building in Berlin, the correspondent of a London newspaper jeered when Dr. Goebbels said that the ministry was to have one thousand rooms, and asked what in the world they would do with them. Three years later a visitor learned that the ministry actually had fifteen hundred rooms, and General Goering complained these were not enough. Major General Christiansen had been brought in as training director, and Ernst Udet had taken over the technical department, and that year the Luftwaffe sprang into being, full-blown. The senior officers came from the army and the navy.

By 1938 Goering had become a field marshal, and General Milch had become commander in chief of the Luftwaffe. General Kesselring had moved out of administration and into command of Air Fleet I, the prize combat unit of the Luftwaffe. Most of the aircraft with which the Germans would start the war, the Me-109, the He-112 with a speed of 480 miles per hour, the Focke Wulf fighter, and the JU 52, were already in production. Actually about half the German air force consisted of Stuka dive bombers and JU 52s, because the Luftwaffe mission in the beginning was support of the front line army troops and particularly the panzers.

In the middle 1930s, as the German air force was building, General Goering made of it an enormously effective instrument of propaganda. For many months he wooed French and British military men, brought them to Berlin and showed them his Luftwaffe establishments. He took them to airplane factories, to airfields, and to visit Luftwaffe units. He built up a picture of a modern German air force of enormous strength. During the Spanish Civil War, General Wolfram von Richthofen took pilots and planes to assist Franco, and Dr. Goebbels made certain that the world was aware of the performance of the German aircraft. When the American air hero Charles A. Lindbergh visited Germany, he was wined and dined by Goering, and given a tour of the air installations, carefully guided and amassed in power for the occasion. He went home to America to praise the Germans and particularly their powerful air force.

In 1938 the commander in chief of the French air force, General Joseph Vuillemin, and members of his staff made an official visit to Germany and was taken to the Messerschmitt factory at Augsburg to see the production line of Me-109s and Me-110s, and then to the Luftwaffe tactical experimental center at Barthe. Large numbers of aircraft were displayed for them, and they were shown bombing raids by medium bombers and by Stuka dive bombers, which dove down and smashed vehicles on the ground very effectively. When the general went back to Paris, he was thoroughly convinced that the Germans had the most powerful air force in the world. What he had seen, really, was a carefully prepared show. Aircraft had been returned to the Messerschmitt works from the field, to give the impression of a much greater production than was actually being carried on. Aircraft had been assembled at Barthe from all over Germany to give the effect of an enormous air fleet. Soon the political leaders of France were aware of this great power. They had already been frightened half to death by their own airmen, who, with others in the world, stoutly held that air power alone would determine the fate of nations in a second world war. So they were primed to be frightened by German air might. Goering's biographer, Leonard Moseley, claims that Goering's performance had an enormous effect on the Allied leaders who came to negotiate over the fate of Czechoslovakia at Munich, and that their fear of German power (which did not exist) was a major factor in their surrender of Czechoslovakia to the German headsman. When in the fall of 1938 Czech President Hacha gave signs of standing up to the Germans (with a very powerful army that gave the German generals pause), Goering hurried back from an Italian vacation to bully Hacha with threats of the destruction of Prague by his bombers, giving the impression that if the Czech president did not yield to Hitler, the German bombers would be over their cities within hours. The fact was that the German air force was absolutely incapable at that time of a major operation, and the flying weather was too bad if they had not been. But the threat worked.

CHAPTER 4

The Navy

The idea of the victorious Allies at the end of World War I was to reduce the German navy to a coastal defense force with no new ships to be built larger than ten thousand tons, with eleven-inch guns, and only six of those. Cruisers were to be only six thousand tons, with six-inch guns, and destroyers were to be eight hundred tons. All of these ship dimensions were far smaller than those of the other navies of the world.

In fact, the military restrictions on the navy were hardly necessary at the beginning of the peace, for the depression and then the inflation in Germany made it impossible to build even that much. As matters eased a bit, the navy began quietly to expand. Fifteen thousand officers and men were permitted in the service, but the navy evaded the spirit of Versailles by assigning civilians to technical and research work, so that the largest possible number of officers could be saved for the expansion of the navy. And as for the budget, by creating "black funds" for which there was no accounting, the navy managed to put aside money (with the connivance of the government) to plan and build prototypes of new weapons, naval aircraft, and radio systems.

Since the Versailles Treaty forbade the building of submarines by the Germans, the navy had to take a very careful approach to that matter. In July 1922, the German navy acquired an interest in a Dutch design company in the Hague that employed the best German submarine designers from the World War I days. Quite legally, they designed and built submarines for other countries, working out the problems and creating what would be the Type VII and Type IX oceangoing U-boats.

Meanwhile the navy took advantage of the latitude allowed it and built two groups of eight-hundred ton torpedo boats and the light cruiser *Emden*, six thousand tons, which sailed around the world showing the German flag.

In the 1920s the Germans began to rethink their naval strategy. Vice Admiral Wolfgang Wegener suggested that the German navy should acquire bases on the French west coast and movement of the German fleet there, to challenge Britain on the North Atlantic and Gibraltar trade routes. In 1928 Admiral Hans Zenker presided over the navy and a debate over the building of capital ships under the terms of the Versailles Treaty. Out of this came the construction of the *Deutschland*, the first of the "pocket battleships." Everything was done to save weight, she was built with an all-welded hull, but she still displaced 11,700 tons—1,700 tons over the Versailles limit. She had a top speed of twenty-eight knots, eleven-inch guns, and an all-diesel drive system, which gave her a range of 21,500 miles. Her design was definitely for a purpose; she was built to be a high seas raider. In the event of war, her presence on the sea would force the enemy to use much of their fleet as escorts for merchant shipping. So from the beginning, the new German navy was built for aggressive action, quite in defiance of the principles of Versailles.

The *Deutschland* gave the German navy control of the Baltic Sea, and gave the French such a fright that they built the *Dunkerque* class of cruisers as an answer. The Germans came back with two more, the *Admiral Scheer* and the *Admiral Graf Spee*. And to support these ships in time of war, the Germans set out in the 1930s to reorganize their old system of supply and bases in neutral countries. At the beginning of World War I the old Germany had a very effective fifth column that operated in South America and the Far East, and made it possible for raiders to work successfully for many months. The suppliers were members of steamship companies living abroad, and their responsibility in time of war was to arrange for the loading of German merchant ships with supplies for the raiders, and to schedule meetings between the supply vessels and the raiders. The system was secretly restored with money from the Germany navy. In 1928 Admiral Erich Raeder was appointed commander in chief of the German navy. He set about building the small force into an efficient one. He rejected the Wegener thesis, because he did not believe the Germans would again fight England. By tight discipline and personal attention, he was able to keep the German navy free of Nazi influence (until almost the end of World War II, when the Nazis put political officers aboard the ships).

The Nazi assumption of power in 1933 was accompanied by the change that made General von Blomberg minister of defense and commander in chief of all the armed forces—head of *Oberkommando Wehrmacht*. The idea was perfectly sound: a unified defense system coordinating the efforts of all defense agencies. But this system was swiftly upset when Hermann Goering, who was essentially the number two Nazi, assumed the post of minister of aviation, and began secretly to build the Luftwaffe, in the process attempting to take over the secret naval aviation group and the secret army aviation group. The navy fought, saying it needed a special air arm for sea operations. The struggle began with Goering claiming suzerainty over all but float plane operations, and the navy resisting, and demanding an air arm capable of cooperating with the submarine service.

In 1934 Admiral Raeder began planning larger ships than the *Deutschland* class. So work began on ships that were to be more than twice as large as the *Deutschland*, the *Bismarck*, and the *Tirpitz*.

In Holland, the German designers were building submarines for the Turks and the Finns, and sharpening their skills to build for Germany. The Finnish submarine, built in 1934, was used by the Germans for trials, before being turned over to the Finnish navy. This was the prototype of the 250-ton ''canoes'' or coastal submarines, developed by the Germans. The Turkish submarine was of the Type VII series, and became the prototype for the 500-ton boats.

In 1935, when Hitler broke out of the bonds of the Versailles Treaty, he announced the establishment of the Luftwaffe—forbidden by the treaty. That year the navy reluctantly accepted an agreement with the Luftwaffe, giving Goering control of the naval air force, which would be staffed by naval officers, but subject to Luftwaffe jurisdiction. In exchange, Goering promised to supply sixty-two naval squadrons with seven hundred aircraft and to maintain its support system.

In 1935 the Germans and the British drew up a naval treaty, which gave the Germans the right to increase the size of their battleships. The treaty had a special submarine protocol, which established new rules for U-boats, providing for the safety of merchant ship passengers and crew in time of war.

Eleven days after signing of the Anglo-German treaty, the submarine *U-1* was commissioned at Kiel, and a number of mysterious sheds that had been under heavy guard for two years were opened to reveal eleven small submarines, the first of the German U-boat fleet. The first German submarine flotilla of three 250-ton U-boats was given to the command of Captain Karl Doenitz in September 1935. Within the year, Germany had twenty-four submarines. But as Doenitz already knew, they were not the right sort of submarines for the war he wanted to wage. As a submarine commander in World War I, Doenitz had become alive to the possibilities of the weapon as yet untried. He wanted to use submarines in the North Atlantic theater, in concerted attacks on convoys to destroy commerce. He was working with radiomen to improve the communications system necessary to control submarine activity from Wilhelmshaven, the main submarine base of Germany. Practice in this sort of operation was begun in 1935, and in 1936 the U-boat force suffered its first casualty; *U-18* was rammed and sunk in exercises as she tried to break through the ring of escorts to attack a convoy at close quarters.

The Germans were building large destroyers in 1935, and the cruisers *Scharnhorst* and *Gneisenau*, and the battleships *Bismarck* and *Tirpitz*, the latter two with eight 15-inch guns, displacing around forty-two thousand tons. They were also building submarines rapidly, and torpedoes and submarine engines. Doenitz wanted to concentrate on submarines, anticipating war with England, but Admiral Raeder, taking his cue from Hitler, said England did not want to fight.

At the end of May 1938, Hitler told Admiral Raeder that he could expect that England would be one of Germany's enemies in the future. He wanted work speeded on the battleships. A plan to build 129 submarines by 1943 was drawn up. Doenitz protested that it was not enough, but he was overruled by Raeder, who wanted a balanced fleet.

In September 1938 the German navy established a committee to recommend changes in the shipbuilding program. This resulted in the Z plan, which Hitler gave precedence in January 1939. Under this plan, Germany would have large battleships within six years and would be able to challenge England on the seas, the Germans thought. The fleet would consist of the four big ships under construction and six superbattleships of fifty-six thousand tons, mounting eight 16-inch guns, plus twelve pocket battleships of twenty thousand tons, four aircraft carriers from ten thousand to twenty-seven thousand tons, the three *Deutschland*-class ships, five heavy cruisers, forty-four light cruisers, sixty-eight destroyers, ninety torpedo boats, and two hundred forty-nine submarines. Completion was expected by 1948.

The new German naval war strategy for this fleet was:

1. Begin commerce warfare by minelaying by destroyers and submarine attacks around the British Isles and the *Deutschland*-class raiders out in the far oceans.

2. Establish a fleet of old battleships, to tie down the British Home Fleet in the North Sea.

3. When the British overextended themselves by scattering their forces to protect convoys, the German fleet would go out in sections to search and destroy. Each section would consist of three superbattleships, one carrier, several light cruisers, and several destroyers.

The Z plan presupposed that German activity would have no effect on British naval plans, and it persisted. In 1939 the Z plan was slightly modified, but in essence, it remained. Commodore Doenitz had no use for the concept, for he believed that the British would not remain quiescent for long. The only vessels he saw as suitable were his submarines and the commerce raiders.

In July 1939 Admiral Raeder approved Doenitz's plea for three hundred submarines, the seven-hundred ton large Atlantic boat, and the eleven-hundred ton long-range fleet Type IX. But because of the emphasis on building, several research projects for radical new designs and systems had to be put on low priority.

In 1939 the Luftwaffe assumed almost full responsibility for naval air forces. It took over minelaying, aerial attack on enemy ships at sea, aerial reconnaissance over water, and the provision of naval aircraft. The air force was to provide nine reconnaissance squadrons, eighteen multipurpose squadrons, twelve carrier squadrons, and two shipboard squadrons of catapult aircraft. It would use thirteen bomber wings to do the naval bidding.

But to Admiral Raeder, who had been promised that he would have at least until 1943 or 1944 to prepare for a war at sea, all this was not very meaningful until September 1, 1939, when suddenly the navy was catapulted by Hitler into a war for which it was in no way ready.

CHAPTER 5

The Man Who Wanted War

One can argue interminably about the origins of the Second World War, whether the seeds were laid in the Versailles conference's treatment of Japan and China, for example. One can even argue that Mussolini was a major villain in the piece with his ambitions for a new Roman Empire in Africa. But one cannot argue as to who started the European general war and why. It was begun by Adolf Hitler, who never had any other intention, and its purpose was to restore the glory of Germany, more, to create the greatest empire in the world.

The Germany that Hitler inherited in 1933 was definitely the creation of Versailles and the blind hatred of the French, who seemed really to believe that they could trample their old enemy Germany into the dust and keep her there. Perhaps, had Britain been not so yielding to French insistences, had the people of the United States not been so at odds with their own government and so insistent of retreating into the cocoon of their isolation from Europe, affairs might have turned out differently. But in the 1930s, when all the events began to take place, the Western democracies lacked the prescience to see what was happening, east and west, and the energy to stop the drives for conquest. The democracies failed, and the only national energy that seemed to be abroad in the world was that of the totalitarian states. In this, Adolf Hitler's Germany led all the rest.

Hitler laid it all out in his "autobiography," *Mein Kampf*. After he took over the little National Socialist Party, Hitler set out first to conquer Germany and then to lead Germany in the conquest of his world. As the conquests succeeded, his world expanded until, just before the turning point of the war, the Nazis could speak of expansion into the Western hemisphere, and a linkage with the Japanese in the Middle East.

Hitler knew very well that he risked war. In fact, in the beginning, he expected war and he was ready for it long before his generals were. From the inception of Nazi power, every act that affected the outside world and Germany's relations with that world created a new risk of war.

Shortly after Hitler came to power in 1933, he told his generals that if France possessed any statesmen, that country would declare a preventive war against Germany immediately. But, of course, the Third Republic was already in disarray, shredded by corruption and weakness of will, and France did not declare war. The strong souls that had decreed the march into the Ruhr in 1923 were no longer there. And each vacillation in the face of German aggressive action only served to strengthen Hitler's growing resolve and his growing contempt for the Western democracies.

From before the days of Hitler, the German army general staff, too, had been planning for military resurgence. Deprived by the Versailles Treaty of an air force, never to have such a weapon again, said the Allies, the general staff had secretly maintained a planning agency ready to create a new air force. This consisted of 180 officers with experience in air warfare in World War I. German airlines flew greater distances with more passengers than any other in Europe. Germany was not allowed to build military aircraft or to enlist flying personnel, but the army secretly backed the formation and development of glider associations, in which thousands of young men learned the principles of aerodynamics and the practical lessons of flight, albeit flight without engines.

In 1934 Hitler moved to increase the ground forces from one hundred thousand to three hundred thousand men by the end of the year. Here was another cause for Allied military action, and what happened? Nothing.

Concurrently with secretly building up the army, the air force, and the navy, secretly building submarines, secretly building twenty-five-thousand-ton "pocket battleships" masked as ten-thousand-ton vessels, Hitler set up production of synthetic petroleum fuels and synthetic rubber, all for the same reason, creation of a war machine. By mid-1934, 250,000 factories in Germany were manufacturing war materials, most of them illegal under the Versailles Treaty. Europe's political leaders knew, but they did nothing. Winston Churchill, a back-bench member of the British Parliament, cried for action, but Parliament was not listening.

Hitler took his first international political step, the annexation of Austria, to begin the process of building the new German Empire. Local Nazis assassinated Austrian Chancellor Dollfuss, and began the drive for union with Germany. In a plebiscite that was rigged, the voters of the Saar industrial basin voted to rejoin Germany. Again the Western democracies might have marched, and they did not.

On March 16, 1935, Hitler ordered universal military training for Germans. The army was to be increased to five hundred thousand men. On April 11, the Western democracies met to condemn Germany's violation of the Versailles Treaty. The next day the Council of the League of Nations condemned Germany. So what? Condemnations were cheap, but nothing happened, except that the USSR signed a new defense treaty with France and one with Czechoslovakia. Those worried Hitler. He already regarded Stalin as his greatest threat.

Hitler secretly reorganized the armed forces, made Hermann Goering commander of the Luftwaffe, and on that same day, made a "peace" speech in the *Reichstag*. "War is senseless," he shouted as he prepared for war.

On March 7, 1935, Hitler took his first openly aggressive action outside Germany; the German army marched into the Rhineland, reoccupying that long-disputed territory which had been given to France as booty from World War I. Clearly this was open violation of the terms of the Versailles Treaty, and nobody could ignore the Hitler attitude any longer. The German generals were as nervous as cats at a dog show, and urged Hitler not to do it, and when he had done it, to immediately withdraw. They saw a deluge of French and British troops descending on Germany. Actually, despite the big noise, the whole operation was tentative. As noted, only three battalions of troops actually crossed the border, although the propaganda and the newsreel pictures made it seem like many more. They entered Aix-la-Chapelle, which would be rechristened Aachen, Kaiserslautern, and Saarbrücken. The generals were panicked. Here is General Wilhelm Keitel's recollection:

"The second battalion of the Seventeenth Infantry Regiment had entered Saarbrücken and was drilling on the market square while French guns were actually trained on the town. Hitler rejected any idea of withdrawing the battalions. If the enemy attacked, they were to fight and not to give way an inch. Orders to that effect were then issued . . ."

To his generals, Hitler seemed totally determined to stand at the Rhineland. But it was not true; he simply knew better than his generals that orders that are issued can be withdrawn and that a bluff might work. He was prepared to back down if anyone moved.

He called the march into the Rhineland "my greatest gamble so far."

"We had no army worth mentioning. At that time it would not even have had the fighting strength to maintain itself against the Poles. If the French had taken any action, we would have been easily defeated; our resistance would have been over in a few days. And what air force we had then was ridiculous. A few Junkers 52s from

Lufthansa, and not even enough bombs for them.''

And what happened? Britain and France consulted.
They talked and they fumbled. So the gamble paid off.
A collateral result of the move into the Rhineland was
to have far-reaching effects on the war. When the generals showed so much hesitation, Hitler was furious with
them and he lost all respect for their military prescience.
In the future, he would make the decisions. Thus was
forecast the nature of the European War, and its ending
in ignominious defeat for Germany.

In the summer of 1936, Hitler began his campaign for
empire by planning the annexation of Austria. Typically,
he began this action with a new treaty of noninterference
with Austria, lulling the people in Vienna even as he
planned to make them part of his great Third Reich.

In November Hitler called his three military commanders to a meeting in the chancellery, and there he
indicated his plans for the future. It was like a chapter
out of *Mein Kampf*:

''The aim of German policy is to make secure and to
preserve the racial community and enlarge it. It is a
question of space. Lebensraum. The German people have
a right to a greater living space than other peoples. Germany's future is therefore wholly conditioned upon the
solving of the need for space.''

Hitler spoke for four hours, and at the end, General
von Fritsch, commander of the army, Admiral Raeder,
commander of the navy, General Goering, commander
of the Luftwaffe, and Foreign Minister von Neurath, who
was also in attendance, knew that Germany was going
to war with France and Britain and that the real *Lebensraum* would come when Germany moved east, to take
over Czechoslovakia and Poland, after first taking Austria
in tow. The war should come by 1938.

By 1938 Hitler was right on schedule. He had not been
favorably impressed by the Von Fritsch reaction to his
plans, so he assumed the position of minister of war
himself, which gave him absolute control of the army.
His plan for annexation of Austria had been announced
to intimates in 1937. In January 1938 the Austrian Nazis,

who tended to jump the gun, planned a coup to overthrow the Austrian government. This scandal shocked Austria but did not solve the problem. On the urging of Franz Von Papen, the German ambassador to Vienna, Chancellor von Schuschnigg went to Berchtesgaden, Hitler's house in Bavaria, to discuss the problem of Austria's future. There Schuschnigg learned that only as a part of the Third Reich did Austria have a future. He and his government submitted, a plebiscite was arranged and rigged so that the Austrian people voted to become a tail to the German dog, and the first step of empire was taken.

The Hitlerian concept of a greater Germany demanded the incorporation of all German-speaking people into the Third Reich, and next were elements in Czechoslovakia and Poland. Hitler then set about taking over these territories.

What Hitler really wanted next was war with Czechoslovakia so he could exhibit his new military muscle. The German generals shuddered. They might well be beaten by the Czechoslovak army, which was well trained and well armed. And Czechoslovakia had treaties with France and the USSR. If Hitler struck and these countries went to war, Hitler most certainly would lose, the generals were sure, but Hitler could not see that and he prepared inexorably for a war that made the generals worry. The war would begin on October 1, 1938, and nothing else would do:

"It is my unshakable resolve to smash Czechoslovakia by means of a military operation," he said.

Once again, Europe had a chance to save itself and destroy Hitler. If he had gone to war, the Czechs would have resisted stoutly, and had France lived up to its obligations, Hitler could have been crushed very quickly, and that, the generals knew. In weaponry, for example, the Germans were very short. They had new weapons on order, but they had not been delivered, and their big guns would not be delivered until late autumn.

All that summer of 1938, Hitler kept Europe off balance, staging maneuvers endlessly. He welcomed a war because he was certain that his potential enemies would not fight. Shrewdly he assessed them:

Russia: Too backward in weaponry
France: Morally decadent; militarily obsolete
Britain: Will avoid confrontation as long as the Germans show no weakness.

In August, Hitler visited the West Wall, where the Germans were building fortifications, and the generals lamented that the work was going slowly. They hoped Hitler would call off his plans to attack Czechoslovakia, but he would not. In desperation the generals formed a conspiracy, agreeing that Hitler was mad and that he must be stopped. But the key to all was intervention by the British and French in the dismemberment of Czechoslovakia. The generals sent an envoy to Britain seeking assurances that the British would intervene. But they got nowhere. Official Britain would not commit itself. So the generals' plan had to be shelved for lack of support from the outside. It had been one of the many lost opportunities to prevent Hitler's plunge into war, and like the others, it had failed for lack of men of resolution and prescience in the West.

The Sudeten Germans of Czechoslovakia had established a militant stance, demanding special "rights" for the German-speaking people who had been drawn into this artificial new nation when it was carved out of the corpse of the Austro-Hungarian Empire. To avoid the confrontation Hitler wanted, the Czech government suddenly announced it would meet all the demands of the Sudeten Germans. Hitler almost panicked; this would make his move impossible. He sent secret orders to the Sudeten Germans to break off negotiations with the Czech government, charging harassment that did not exist. The Sudetens followed the orders. In London and Paris, the governments sought any method of avoiding war, and after consultation, Prime Minister Neville Chamberlain went to Munich to make peace at any price. The price was the dismemberment of Czechoslovakia, and the British and French paid it with scarcely a whimper.

On September 29, with the German army already in motion to move against Czechoslovakia, and the Czechs mobilized and ready to fight, Czechoslovakia was sold down the river by Britain and France, and President Beneš surrendered without a fight.

The consequences of the Western powers' surrender at Munich were enormous. The Allies of France and Britain could no longer believe in the alliances, and Poland, Yugoslavia, Hungary, and Rumania all began their own negotiations to make the most they could of this new German power that frightened Britain and France.

Poland made a deal, and took 650 square miles of Czech territory around the city of Teschen. Hungary got 7,500 square miles. The Germans took 11,000 square miles, which included the Czech military defenses. She also got two-thirds of the country's coal fields, 86 percent of its chemical plants, and about three-quarters of all its electric power and other industrial attributes. Hitler had done a good job of starting his new empire.

But it was only a start, as Hitler made clear to his generals on October 21, 1938:

The Wehrmacht, he said, must now be prepared to protect the frontiers of Germany, to liquidate the rest of what had been Czechoslovakia, and to occupy more territory. His aim at the moment was the Memel district, a Baltic port lost at Versaille to Lithuania.

The generals had known that the Czech army would have been a very difficult nut to crack, and had the Wehrmacht attacked and had the French honored their commitment to come to the defense of Czechoslovakia, then without even the participation of Britain, Germany probably would have been defeated in short order. But after seeing how Prime Minister Chamberlain seemed almost eager to be humiliated, Hitler began to believe in German power, and when he returned to Berlin after Munich, he complained about how easy it had been:

"That fellow Chamberlain," he said, "has spoiled my entry into Prague." Since that entry into Prague, at least partly to terrorize Britain and France, one would have thought that Hitler would have been pleased with the turn of events, but still stinging, always stinging, with the pain of the humiliation of Versailles, Hitler wanted blood, and he was determined to get it.

Hitler's next step was to detach Slovakia from Czechoslovakia and guarantee its "independence." This came about on March 14, 1939, along with Ruthenia, another area that could be considered no more than a principality, which went to Hungary, so all that was left of Czechoslovakia was Bohemia and Moravia, and they were taken over as German colonies. British Prime Minister Chamberlain then used the "independence" of Slovakia as an excuse to say that Britain's commitments to Czechoslovakia no longer existed because of the nature of the change in the territory.

But the British public reacted so violently to the dismemberment of Czechoslovakia, and the beginning of Hitler's drive to the east to gain territory for his empire, that Chamberlain had to reconsider and announce that the rights of Poland were going to be maintained. It was a warning to Hitler that Britain would fight, a warning that Hitler did not believe, although the German ambassador to London warned of a fundamental hardening of the British attitude toward Germany.

And so matters stood at the end of March 1939. The world was waiting for Hitler's next move.

CHAPTER 6

Advancing on Poland

At six o'clock on the morning of March 15, 1939, German troops crossed the border into Bohemia and Moravia without resistance, and Adolf Hitler made his triumphant entry into Prague, thus putting the lie to his previous claim that he wanted no empire, but only the reunification of German-speaking peoples. The Czech-speaking people of Prague did not qualify, and this was apparent to the world. As Hitler told the German people, "Czechoslovakia has ceased to exist."

Hitler's next step was to create a "protectorate," which was nothing but a colonial administration, and a very harsh one, with all power residing in the hands of the German governor, who was called "Reich Protector." To try to fool the world, Hitler appointed Baron von Neurath, the former foreign minister, to the post, but this moderate would not last long. The resources of Bohemia and Moravia from this point on would be totally at the service of Germany. Heinrich Himmler would soon be running the show here, and his stooge, the Sudeten German Karl Hermann Frank, would be the chief of police and principal oppressor of the Czechs.

On March 16 Hitler destroyed the new "independence" of Slovakia by faking a telegram from its prime minister, which called on Germany for protection from riotous elements, and German troops marched into Slovakia. It, too, would be at the service of the Third Reich in the future.

Ruthenia, at the tip of the old Czechoslovakia, had also been given "independence," and now it was to be invaded by Hungary as part of a deal between Hitler and Miklós Horthy, the dictator of Hungary, who was just then manufacturing a border incident to justify sending troops.

Britain's Prime Minister Chamberlain made a trip to Rome to try to improve British-Italian relations, which had been worsening since Mussolini took power and invaded Ethiopia in his search for glory and empire. But nothing came of the trip; for Il Duce had already cast his lot with Hitler in what would be the Rome-Berlin-Tokyo alliance. So in the spring of 1939, the war clouds darkened.

Mussolini confirmed Hitler's belief that they could do almost anything except actually invade the British Empire and the British would bluster and back down.

In the fall of 1938, Polish relations with Germany seemed to be flourishing. The Poles had connived in the destruction of Czechoslovakia and, with German approval, had seized a strip of that little country. But Germany already had her plans made, plans announced by Hitler in *Mein Kampf*. Just a month after the Munich showdown on Czechoslovakia, German Foreign Minister Joachim von Ribbentrop unveiled the demands Hitler was making on Poland: the return of the port of Danzig to Germany. It had been a part of the Versailles punishment of Germany, as was the Polish corridor set up to separate East Prussia from Germany. That too had to be dealt with, said Ribbentrop; the Germans must be permitted to build a motorway and a railroad across the corridor and have control of the property rights. There were several other matters, including the hitching of Poland's foreign policy to the German star, but in return, the Poles would get a twenty-year extension on the German-Polish treaty of nonaggression.

The Poles refused, and said that any attempt by the

Germans to take over Danzig would mean war. Hitler was quite willing to have a war, and he told his military leaders to get ready to occupy Danzig.

Hitler was not the first to say that the Versailles Treaty had made the liquidation of Poland a primary German objective. General Hans von Seeckt, the chief of the German army in the 1920s, had put the case about as strongly as it could be made:

"Poland's existence is intolerable and incompatible with the essential conditions of Germany's life. Poland must go and will go—as a result of her own internal weaknesses and of action by Russia—with our aid. The obliteration of Poland must be one of the fundamental drives of German policy . . ."

In the winter of 1939, Colonel Jozeph Beck, the Polish foreign minister, visited Berlin, and Hitler suggested that same plan that had been mentioned before, involving Danzig and the Polish corridor. Seeing that the Germans were unyielding in their demands, Beck decided he had best get to London and Paris and see what could be done about setting up alliances for Polish protection from Germany. His feeling was intensified by the German occupation of Bohemia and Moravia in March, when he suddenly realized that Poland was now flanked in north and south by the German army.

Hitler had the wheels in motion to take over the old disputed territories, but not in Poland alone. He also wanted Memel, another port; this one had been given to Lithuania in the Versailles handouts, but it was one to which the Germans really had a claim on historical grounds. Hitler went aboard the pocket battleship *Deutschland* on March 22, and at the same time told von Ribbentrop to negotiate a surrender from the Lithuanians, or the sailors would attack. It took a long time in the Hitler scheme of things, about twenty-four hours, but Ribbentrop did get his surrender, and the German naval troops victoriously occupied their new possession. At two-thirty on the afternoon of March 23, Hitler went to the Stadttheatre in Memel and there addressed a screaming, shouting mob of Memel Germans who had been carefully organized for months for this event.

It all seemed so easy. Hitler would make threats, and mobilize his forces, and the West would back down every time.

The news of the takeover was a clear warning to the Poles that the turn of events made new moves necessary. Just at that time, Britain's Chamberlain offered to give all assistance to Poland if she was attacked by Germany and resisted.

This was certainly a new British attitude. It shocked the Germans and surprised many other people, who were so used to seeing Chamberlain back down to Hitler that they really could not understand what was happening. And what was happening, of course, was that the British, having been gulled by Hitler time and time again, had had all they would stand of it.

When Hitler learned what Chamberlain had done, his first reaction was to go into one of his furies. He was with Admiral Canaris, his chief of intelligence, at the time, and he stamped around the room, pounding his fists on the table, and threatening the British in a voice choked with rage. The next day he had still not recovered, and in a speech at the launching for the battleship *Tirpitz* at Wilhelmshaven, he threatened Britain and France with war. He spoke of peace again and told the world how peaceful were Germany's intentions, and meanwhile he prepared for war with Poland, issuing a top secret directive to only five of his most trusted lieutenants.

September 1, 1939, was the date.

All spring and summer, the world speculated as to what would really happen. Most people found it hard to believe that the Western powers would really stand up to the German dictator. They expected the Poles to cave in. But some reporters who went to Poland to see for themselves came back with a different story. The Poles would not give in, they said. They would fight, and they would lose, because their air force was obsolete, they had cavalry to face German tanks, and they were surrounded by Germany on three sides now that Czechoslovaia had fallen to Hitler.

And what about the assistance promised by Britain and France?

That would be difficult, said the observers, because Germany was rapidly building the western defense wall against attack from the West.

Here is General Keitel's recollection:

"The summer of 1939 passed with feverish activity in the army general staff. The construction of the West Wall proceeded at an accelerated rate; in addition to construction firms and the Todt Organization, virtually all of the Reich Labor Service and several army divisions were employed in the building, the latter two concentrating on earthworks, barbed wire entanglements and the final fitting out of the rough concrete fortifications for the defense of Germany."

On a lower level, the German government was trying to avoid war for the moment, largely because various elements agreed that it was too early, not that they wanted to avoid war in the future. This was also true of Mussolini's Italy, Germany's new ally. Mussolini was worried lest Hitler start war over Poland that would drag in the whole world. Since the Germans wanted to protect their flank with Italian help, they agreed that war was unthinkable at the moment, and Foreign Minister von Ribbentrop and Italian Foreign Minister Count Ciano concluded a military alliance (suggested by Mussolini to further his own ends). Almost on a whim, it seemed, Mussolini committed himself to follow the Reich, of course, believing that there would be no war for three years at least, as Ribbentrop had indicated. So on May 22, 1939, the alliance was signed and the world went that further step toward war that no one said he wanted, but that Hitler was making inevitable, even to the time-table that he had snatched out of the air: September 1, 1939.

On May 23, 1939, Hitler called together the top leadership of the armed forces and their major assistants to hear that Germany was definitely going to war that summer, and why.

The real reason had nothing to do with Danzig or any

other trumped-up matter that Hitler was making so much noise about. The real reason for war was conquest, to restore a German empire, this one to be contiguous to Germany and not far-flung like the old empire that had reached around the world, but was made up of the leavings of the French and British. This new empire would be carved out of the Eastern countries, beginning with Poland and extending into what was now the USSR, including the Ukraine and the oil-rich Caucasus. Ultimately that path would lead to war with the Soviet Union, so much was clear.

Hitler spoke long, and in what some of his listeners believed to be a confused manner. But there was no gainsaying what he meant. Germany was about to embark on Hitler's war of conquest to avenge Versailles and bring the Third Reich to a position of world domination.

A few hours later, one of the generals in charge of armaments summed up the accomplishments of the armed forces that spring of 1939. In four years, the army had been jumped from seven to fifty-one divisions, including nine armored divisions. The navy had built two battleships, two heavy cruisers, seventeen destroyers, and forty-seven submarines. The Luftwaffe, starting from nothing, had built up a force of 260,000 men and twenty-one fighting squadrons. Germany was making more war materials than any other country. But the generals knew one thing: The war must be limited and must be controlled by Germany. She could not afford to fight in the West and in the East at the same time; World War I had taught the generals that lesson. Russia must be kept out of the war against Poland.

In June, Hitler was busily preparing his strike against Poland. By June 15, he had General Brauchitsch's master plan for the army's attack. They would strike with five armies, three in the South and two in the North. Everything would be ready by August 20.

This war Hitler was about to start was to be total war. All the resources of Germany were to be mobilized. Seven million men would be drafted. Prisoners of war and inmates of jails and concentration camps would be put to work. Hundreds of thousands of slave Czech laborers would be brought in.

By August 7, Hitler was busy moving people into Danzig, setting the great day of "liberation" as he had done earlier in the Sudetenland and Memel. His diplomats were trying to reach an accommodation with Russia that would prevent Stalin from acting in behalf of Poland when Hitler moved in.

Everything was moving rapidly, as Count Ciano learned when he visited von Ribbentrop at his estate near Salzburg.

"What do you want?" Ciano asked the German. "Danzig or the corridor?"

"Not that anymore," said Ribbentrop. "We want war."

Count Ciano and Mussolini were not ready for war, and the count said that if Germany attacked Poland very soon, they would have a world war on their hands. Ribbentrop scoffed and said the British and French would not fight.

A few hours later, Ciano was in Obersalzburg visiting Hitler, who also said the British and French would not fight.

"I, personally," said Hitler, "am absolutely convinced that the Western democracies will, in the last resort, recoil from unleashing a general war."

All this while, Hitler was urging speed on his generals, and Foreign Minister von Ribbentrop was working to negotiate a pact with the Soviets that would guarantee their nonintervention in the Polish situation, and at the same time rigging up an incident that would give him an excuse to attack Poland.

One of Reinhard Heydrich's young toughs of the *Sicherheitsdienst* was Alfred Naujocks, who had joined the SS in 1931 and moved over to the SD when it was formed in 1934. Heydrich called him in to his Berlin office on August 10, just twenty-one days before the deadline for the Polish war, and instructed him in special duties on the Polish border. He was to simulate an attack on the German radio station near Gleiwitz on the border, and to pretend that he and his men were Poles, for as Heydrich said, "Practical proof is needed for these attacks of the Poles for the foreign press as well as German propaganda." Another incident was planned, using thirteen condemned criminals who would be given poison injections and then shot afterwards to produce bullet wounds. They would be dressed in Polish uniforms, and the claim would be made that they were Polish soldiers attacking German troops.

The German navy was also getting ready to go into action against England if the war really developed. On August 19 orders were given to sail. Twenty-one submarines were sent out to positions around the British Isles. The pocket battleship *Graf Spee* left for the Brazilian coast to raid British shipping if war came. The pocket battleship *Deutschland* was to lurk off the British Isles and do the same.

Time—Hitler's timetable was growing shorter now. On August 23 the Germans and Russians concluded a nonaggression pact—for nonaggression one against the other. The victim was to be Poland, which would be partitioned into Soviet and German zones, and the Eastern Baltic states, which Hitler willed to Stalin. Those were the prices Hitler was to pay for Stalin's inactivity as the Germans swallowed Poland.

On August 25 Hitler heard that the British were on the point of ratifying their new treaty of alliance with Poland. He called in General Keitel, the OKW chief of staff, and asked if he could stop the movement of troops that he had already set in motion. He had bad news: he expected Mussolini to declare war if the British and French marched, and Mussolini had just told him he was not going to do it. So Hitler was frantically setting up his ducks in line, and thinking now again about a diplomatic coup of the Munich sort, even though he had said that such would be impossible in the case of Poland. Keitel brought the timetable, Hitler postponed D day until further notice, and called his senior generals to stop everything in motion.

Hitler worried all that night. On the afternoon of August 26 Hitler learned that the treaty between Britain and Poland had been signed the previous day. Hitler was frantic: "All troop movements are to be stopped at once. I need time to negotiate."

The chancellery was a beehive of activity; D day was postponed to August 31. Final orders were to be issued on the afternoon of August 30. British Ambassador Nevile Henderson called on Hitler that day and was given Hitler's demands about Poland:

1. Return of Danzig to Germany.
2. The rail and motor road across the Polish corridor.
3. The cession by Poland to Germany of all territories taken away at Versailles with 75 percent ethnic German population.
4. A plebiscite in the Polish corner to determine whether it would be returned to Germany.

Three of these were the old demands; the fourth was a new one, and everyone knew an election would be rigged, as had the Austrian election.

The demands were thoroughly unacceptable to Poland—as they had been all along. Hitler had hoped that if Mussolini would call up his troops, the British would be frightened into giving him another Munich. But Mussolini had now said that he did not have the raw materials necessary to conduct a war, and he gave Hitler a shopping list. When the list was examined, the generals found it outrageous, and could see that Mussolini had asked for the moon, knowing it would not be delivered, and that thus he had gotten out of living up to the mutual aid pact with Germany.

CHAPTER 7

The Last Crisis

The result of all the confusion regarding Mussolini's backdown was to delay the start of German military operations against Poland until September 1, but that, said Hitler, was the absolute end of it, and barring Polish capitulation to the demands, the war would begin.

All day long on August 26 in Berlin, the Germans waited. Rumor had it that the British were considering one proposal that Hitler had made, to guarantee the preservation of the British Empire if Britain would give Hitler a free hand in Europe. The idea, of course, was never under consideration in London, but the Germans around Hitler were grasping at straws. They saw equivocation in London and equivocation in France when there was none. The days of equivocation in both those countries had passed with the realization that the West had been duped at Munich; Hitler had spent all his currency of goodwill, wasted it in lying propaganda, and now the Western democracies did not believe anything he said.

But now that he did not have Mussolini's military support, Hitler was thinking again of the big bluff, and how he might drive a wedge between Poland and Britain. He assumed that Prime Minister Chamberlain would like to get out of his pledge to Poland. Also, others were trying to get into the act, notably Hermann Goering. All this was made possible by Hitler's sudden self doubts. General Franz Halder, chief of staff of the army, had noted at the time that Hitler was "considerably shaken" by Mussolini's refusal to go to war with him. His calculations on Poland had estimated that with Russia neutralized by the secret deal over Poland, and Mussolini on his side, the British and French would back down and defeating Poland would be easy. But suddenly he was faced with a real war, and he knew that his generals had told him the army was not ready. For this reason, when Goering and others offered suggestions, Hitler did not fall into one of his usual rages and put them down.

Hermann Goering had maintained friendships with a number of Swedes from the days when he was a barnstorming pilot hero of World War I, making his living in aviation. One of these friends was Birger Dahlerus, now a successful Swedish businessman with many connections in London. Dahlerus had offered to help in negotiations, and Goering had sent him to London with a message to Lord Halifax, the British foreign secretary. Halifax told him that he was in touch with the German government through Ambassador Henderson, and there was no need for private diplomacy. Goering had in mind another deal like Munich, buttressed by more German promises to London. Dahlerus finally persuaded Halifax that Goering somehow might influence Hitler in favor of peace, and so Halifax wrote a letter to Goering talking about peace and "a few days time" to achieve a settlement.

This letter reached Goering in the middle of the night of August 26–27, and Goering rushed Dahlerus to the chancellery to wake up Hitler and give him the message. They went, and then Dahlerus had to listen to a long, windy, circuitous lecture about Hitler's early life and struggles. Finally the Swede got a word in edgewise.

Sunday morning, August 27. Four days before Poland Invasion Day. Businessman Dahlerus was flown from Berlin to London in Hermann Goering's airplane, with the new proposals from Hitler engraved in his memory. He was not allowed to take any aide-mémoire. At the airfield he was met by foreign office and security men and taken by a roundabout road to a meeting with Prime Minister Chamberlain, Lord Halifax, and other British officials. They were prepared to take him quite seriously now, and realized that only some eleventh-hour magic could prevent war.

But Prime Minister Chamberlain saw immediately that these proposals would be unacceptable to the Poles. ''I see no prospect of a settlement on these terms; the Poles might concede Danzig, but they would fight rather than surrender the corridor,'' he told Dahlerus.

It was agreed that Dahlerus would leave for Berlin again that night with word that the British government was preparing some sort of message that could be regarded as a possibility for negotiations.

Dahlerus did go back to Berlin and spoke that night with Goering, who was disappointed in the standoffishness of the British, but so desperate not to be left out on a limb that he put the best face on the matter to Hitler, who, in turn, was concerned enough about the position he found himself in that he was grasping at straws to avoid the war he saw coming with Britain and France— the war he had really not expected because he had laid his plans to intimidate the British with Mussolini.

Dahlerus was urging the British to urge the Poles to negotiate immediately with the German government. They did just that, and the Poles accepted. Ambassador Henderson called on Hitler on the evening of August 28 and handed him a note from London. He also elaborated. Britain wanted amity with Germany, he said, and it wanted peace, but if Hitler attacked Poland, Britain would fight.

Henderson asked Hitler if he would negotiate with the Poles and if he was willing to discuss the question of an exchange of populations. He indicated that he was willing on both counts, but he did not mean a word of it. He was set to go to war with Poland on September 1— determined to do so—and all this folderol was for the single purpose of persuading the British to abandon Poland and stay out of it.

The optimistic Goering told Dahlerus early on the morning of August 29 that he thought the threat of war was past and there was every prospect of negotiation. Dahlerus passed the word on to the British Foreign Office, but the British had at last learned from their negotiations with Hitler, and the story was not believed.

At seven-fifteen on the night of August 29, Ambassador Henderson called on Chancellor Hitler again, and this time Hitler showed his angry side. He ended up demanding that the British produce in Berlin a Polish spokesman who could negotiate a peace. The ploy was the same that Hitler had earlier used, to bring a high official to Germany and there present him with an ultimatum. It had worked twice in the past in Austria and Czechoslovakia. If it did not work this time, Hitler reasoned, it might persuade the British that the Poles were being recalcitrant, and give the British a chance to get off the war hook. What Hitler still did not want to see was that the British were committed to Poland and determined to honor the commitment because they did not trust anything that Hitler said.

On August 30 messages flew thick and fast between London and Berlin, Hitler still hoping to achieve a new Munich, the British determined not to be fooled again, and the Poles wondering what all the shouting was about because they had not the slightest intention of giving in to Hitler's territorial demands.

At a final meeting at midnight on August 30, Ambassador Henderson was roundly abused and threatened by German Foreign Minister Ribbentrop, and no agreement was even indicated. The fact was that this last bit of the play had been put on for the German people, and Dr. Goebbels's propaganda machine was blaring the "facts" that Hitler had made every effort to peaceful settlement but was blocked by the unreasonable, warlike Poles. The offer made public (which had never been made to Poland) was so reasonable that in his book *The Rise and Fall of the Third Reich*, William L. Shirer suggested that if it had been really made in earnest, there would have been no war over Poland.

But there was no way these reasonable demands, for free elections and cooling-off periods and concessions to Poland, would have been really made, because Hitler did not mean a bit of it. It was all part of the German internal propaganda plan.

As Hitler put it:

"I needed an alibi, especially with the German people, to show them that I had done everything to maintain peace. This explains my generous offer about the settlement of the Danzig and corridor questions."

But Goering and his friend Dahlerus kept pressing, and eventually, on the morning of August 31, the Polish ambassador to Germany was shown the new "negotiating points" and asked by the British ambassador to consider them. So on the morning of the last possible day, distrusting Hitler every inch of the way, the British Foreign Office still hoped against hope for a negotiated peace that would stop the march of the Germans across the Polish border. (Hitler had no thought of entertaining such an idea, but he was still working to keep the British and French out of the war.)

On the night of August 30, Lord Halifax sent a message to Warsaw suggesting that the Poles lose no time in starting negotiations with the Germans, but reiterating the British decision to stand by its commitment to go to the assistance of Poland if that country was attacked by Germany. Foreign Minister Beck replied that he was ready to negotiate with the Germans but that he would not go to Berlin or send any powerful person; he recalled clearly what had happened to the Austrians and the Czechs, who had been mistreated and bullied into submission. Polish Ambassador Lipski tried to deliver a message to the German foreign minister all that afternoon and was not received until after 6:00 P.M. and then was abruptly dismissed when he said he had no full powers of negotiation. Thereupon Lipski returned to the Polish Embassy to find that the Germans had cut his telephone wires and he could not communicate with Warsaw.

That wire cutting was a symbol of what was really happening that last day of peace in Europe. Just after noon on that fateful day of August 31, 1939, Hitler had issued his final premarching orders to his high command.

DIRECTIVE NO. 1
FOR THE CONDUCT OF THE WAR

1. Now that all the political possibilities of disposing by peaceful means of a situation on the eastern frontier which is intolerable for Germany are exhausted, I have determined on a solution by force.

[This was nonsense. Hitler had decided months ago to attack Poland no matter what. All that had gone on since was window dressing to try to keep Britain and France out of the war. Hitler's desire for war had gone back to the first days after Versailles. He had never altered on this point, he had wanted to attack Czechoslovakia, and had been disappointed when he achieved his ends without war. If for some reason the Polish question had been settled, Hitler would within a few months have found an excuse for war with someone. What he wanted was a weak country; he did not want a war he could lose, and that meant war against Britain and France.]

2. The attack on Poland is to be carried out in accordance with the preparations made for Case White, with the alterations which result, where the army is concerned, from the fact that it has in the meantime almost completed its dispositions.

[Case White had been prepared months earlier. Everything was as ready as the professional soldiers could make it. There would be no delay. Three days earlier, Hitler had told British Ambassador Henderson, "My soldiers are asking me, yes or no? They had already lost a week and they could not afford to lose another, lest the rainy season in Poland be added to their enemies.''']

Allotment of tasks and the operational target remain unchanged.

Date of attack: September 1, 1939

Time of attack: 4:45 A.M. [This was inserted in red pencil.]

This timing also applies to the operation at Gdynia, Bay of Danzig, and the Dirschau Bridge.

3. In the West it is important that the responsibility for the opening of hostilities should rest squarely on England and France. For the time being, insignificant frontier violations should be met by purely local action. The neutrality of Holland, Belgium, Luxembourg, and Switzerland, to which we have given assurances, must be scrupulously observed.

[Hitler had no scruples about violating the neutrality of these countries, as will be seen, but he did not want to give any reason to the Western powers to enter the war at this stage.]

On land, the German western frontier is not to be crossed without my express permission. The same for all warlike actions or actions which could be regarded as such. Thus Atlantic forces will for the time being remain in waiting position.

4. If Britain and France open hostilities against Germany, it is the task of the Wehrmacht formations operating in the West to conserve their forces as much as possible and thus maintain the conditions for a victorious conclusion of the operations against Poland. Within these limits enemy forces and their military-economic resources are to be damaged as much as possible. Orders to go over to the attack, I reserve in any case to myself.

The army will hold the West Wall and make preparations to prevent its being outflanked in the North through violation of Belgian or Dutch territory by the Western powers.

The navy will carry on warfare against merchant shipping, directed mainly at England. The air force is, in the first place, to prevent the French and British air forces from attacking the German army and the German Lebensraum.

In conducting the war against England, preparations are to be made for the use of the Luftwaffe in disrupting British supplies by sea, the armaments industry, and the transport of troops to France. A favorable opportunity is to be taken for an effective attack on massed British naval units, especially against battleships and aircraft carriers. Attacks against London are reserved for my decision.

Preparations are to be made for attacks against the British mainland bearing in mind that partial success with insufficient forces is in all circumstances to be avoided.

Adolf Hitler

By August 31 the British had made it eminently clear that they intended to honor their commitment to the Poles, but Hitler still hoped Britain and France were so concerned about a major conflict that they would somehow back down. General Halder had indicated that he felt the Western powers would make a show at helping Poland but do nothing drastic.

Hermann Goering did all he could to that end on the last afternoon of peace. After a long and liquid lunch with his Swedish friend Dahlerus, he met with British Ambassador Henderson and spoke for two hours about the difficulties with the Poles and Germany's good intentions. Of course, at that time he knew that there was no chance of stopping the war, and that the next day his aircraft would be attacking Britain somehow. But still Goering hoped to keep Britain out of the war, and for some reason he felt that he had a special relationship with the British that should help persuade them to make peace with Germany. Goering warned Henderson that it would be "most imprudent" of Britain to declare war on Germany.

The meeting ended, Henderson told London that there was no further hope of accommodation and that all that was left was the necessity of meeting German force with force. So night fell on Berlin, and the border regions, and a million and a half German troops took their positions along the Polish borders, waiting for morning and the hour of 4:45, when the war Hitler had anticipated for so many months would begin.

In Berlin, people waited too, most of them dead set against war. But a week earlier, Hitler had prepared to counter that antiwar feeling, and had promised his generals that he would give a propaganda reason for starting the war. No one need worry about the truth of it. He intended to win, and no one ever asked a war's victor any questions.

At nine o'clock that night of August 31, all German radio stations broadcast Hitler's Polish peace proposals— the last ones that had never been discussed, but that fact was glossed over, and a long statement was made about the enormous effort the German government had made to achieve peace against the bloodthirstiness of the Poles. And very conveniently just then came an incident to prove the bloodthirstiness of the Poles.

The SA's Alfred Naujocks had been waiting at Gleiwitz on the Polish border for six days, to carry out his simulated "Polish" attack on the radio station there. SS men in Polish uniforms would do the shooting, and drugged concentration camp inmates would be shot, left dead and dying on the field, apparently casualties of the murderous Poles.

At noon on August 31, Naujocks had the code word about Canned Goods from Heidrich, and at 8:00 P.M., as Goering was telling his stories of the Polish atrocities, Naujocks received a concentration camp inmate near the radio station. The man was so heavily drugged that he could not move. He already had the gunshot wounds and was covered with blood. Naujocks put the body down outside the radio station, then attacked the station, broadcast a three-minute speech identifying himself as a Pole, fired some shots from a pistol, and left.

In Berlin, Hitler was calm, almost jolly. He was asked whether or not they should evacuate civilians along the West Wall, and he decided against it. He did not really expect the British and the French to prosecute a war even if they declared war.

CHAPTER 8

Hitler Starts His War

Daybreak, September 1, 1939
Place: Poland

Just as Hitler had said he would do when he set the course of his war in that spring of 1939, he sent his armies plunging across the Polish border from the north, west, and south, converging on Warsaw.

First came the fighter and bomber planes, to strike the Polish airfields, and find most of the aircraft on the ground, easy picking for the Stuka dive bombers, the Heinkels, and the Me–109s. Other aircraft hit Polish troop columns and ammunition dumps, bridges, railroads, and some towns and cities. But most of the aircraft were consigned to troop support this first morning, and from the outset, the Luftwaffe had control of the skies.

This in itself was surprising, because the Poles claimed to be a "great power." On paper they could muster thirty first-line divisions, ten reserve divisions, and eleven cavalry brigades. They had aircraft, and antiaircraft artillery.

But if one looked below the surface, their aircraft were too few and too old, their antiaircraft guns dated from the First World War, and their divisions were comparable in real strength to German regiments. And the Polish cavalry—horse-mounted—was absolutely no match for the panzer divisions of the Germans, tanks and half-tracks and armored cars. At one point a cavalry brigade attacked the panzers, pennants trailing from lances, sabers drawn, and the results were as expected: the German machine guns mowed the cavalry down, and the sabers clanged hollowly on the sides of the tanks. The cavalry was decimated.

The attacking German force consisted of forty-four divisions and two thousand airplanes. Virtually nothing was left at the West Wall, which was still being built. Hitler was counting on a quick victory in the East, and either no action in the West, or a delay in the mobilization of French forces and a delay in the movement of British forces across the English Channel.

Army Group North consisted of the Third and Fourth armies, the Third in East Prussia, while the Fourth was on the edge of the Polish corridor, prepared to split it and then join the Third Army on a drive to Warsaw.

Army Group South consisted of the Eighth, Tenth, and Fourteenth armies, all camped in Silesia and Slovakia. They were to advance to Warsaw from the south, thus creating a pincers movement to trap the Polish forces in Poznan and the territory west of the Vistula.

Altogether the German forces massed against Poland consisted of six panzer divisions and four light divisions. Each panzer brigade consisted of two regiments with 125 tanks each, and the rifle brigade had two rifle regiments and a motorcycle battalion. The light divisions consisted of two rifle regiments, each of three battalions, and a tank regiment.

To the world, the German power seemed enormous. Only the German generals knew where the holes were: The newsreels showed the powerful Mark IV tank, but only a few of these had come off the assembly line, and their armament was a low-velocity 75-mm gun. Next best was the Mark III, but it had only a 37-mm gun, and most of the tanks were Mark IIs, with only a heavy machine gun for armament.

Actually, the panzer units were very much in a formative stage. The panzer genius, General Heinz Guderian, had a great deal of experience in building and managing maneuvers, but this campaign would prove the real worth of the armored forces to the world.

Troop units had been waiting along the Polish borders for three days. Precisely at 4:45, as ordered, they swarmed across the borders. The key to the attack was the Fourth Army's move against the Polish corridor, and this was led by General Heinz Guderian's XIX Army Corps. That morning Guderian's force headed for the River Brahe, between Zempolno and Konitz, and then were to drive to the Vistula, cutting off the Polish forces in the Polish corridor. On his left, General Kaupisch's frontier defense forces were to move to Danzig. The Polish forces in the corridor numbered three infantry divisions and the Pomorska Cavalry Brigade, horse-mounted. They had some Fiat-Ansaldo tanks, but these were already outmoded and far inferior to the German armor. But the Polish side of the border was fortified.

History has painted the Polish campaign as a walkaway, with the superior German forces certain of their every move. But the opposite was the case, as witness the testimony of Colonel F. W. von Mellenthin, then intelligence officer of III Corps. The German forces were untried and nervous:

"The operations were of considerable value in blooding our troops and teaching them the difference between real war with live ammunition and peace time maneuvers. Very early in the campaign I learned how jumpy even a well-trained unit can be under war conditions. A low-flying aircraft circled over corps headquarters and everyone let fly with whatever he could grab. An air liaison officer ran about trying to stop the fusillade and shouting to the excited soldiery that this was a German command plane—one of the good old Fieseler Stoerche. Soon afterwards the aircraft landed, and out stepped the Luftwaffe general responsible for our close air support. He failed to appreciate the joke."

As the troops moved out that morning of September

1, General Guderian accompanied the Third Panzer Brigade, riding in a half-track. He was the first corps commander ever to accompany tanks into the field. He knew what was going on all the time, because his command half-track was equipped with radio and he was in constant touch with corps headquarters and also the command posts of the division headquarters.

A thick ground mist at first prevented the Luftwaffe from giving air support to the troops of this unit. Guderian went with them as far as Zempelburg, where they first encountered substantial units of the enemy. And the Germans made some real bloopers. The heavy artillery of the Third Panzer Division opened fire in the mist without knowing what it was shooting at. So the first shell came in, and landed fifty yards ahead of Guderian's command vehicle. A second bracketed him fifty yards behind. He figured the next shell would smash the vehicle and he ordered the driver to turn the half-track around and get out of there. But the driver was unaccustomed to the real noises of war, and he got rattled and ran the half-track into the ditch alongside the road at full speed, bending an axle and putting the steering out of commission.

Guderian got out of the half-track, hitched a ride to the corps command post, and then got a new vehicle. He stopped by Third Division artillery for a few words with the eager artillerymen. When Guderian's troops reached Zempelburg, the field was still enveloped in the low mist, but soon it began to lift in the warming of the sun. The leading tanks found themselves almost atop the Polish defensive positions at Gross-Klonia, an estate that had belonged to Guderian's family in the days before the Versailles Treaty, when it was part of Germany.

The Polish antitank guns were well manned and they scored several hits, putting some vehicles out of commission and killing one officer, one cadet, and eight enlisted men.

By the time Guderian returned to the Third Panzer Division in his new half-track, the forward element had reached the Brahe River, but he noticed that the troops had slowed down and seemed about to quit the fighting for the day. Guderian looked for the divisional commander, but he had been called up to the headquarters of General von Bock, commander of Army Group North, so he was not available for consultation. Guderian tracked down the senior officers of the Sixth Panzer Regiment and asked them to describe the situation on the Brahe. Nobody knew. The regimental commander did not believe they could cross the river that day, and he was not eager to find out. He would rather have the rest for his troops. Guderian was shocked to see that the regiment had forgotten the corps order he had issued the day before, that the Brahe was to be crossed on the first day. Furious, he walked away rather than lose his control, and thought about what to do next.

A young lieutenant came up to him. He had removed his tunic, and his shirt sleeves were rolled up. His arms were black with gunpowder. He looked like a real soldier.

"Herr General," said the lieutenant to his corps commander. "I've just come from the Brahe. The enemy forces on the far bank are weak. The Poles set fire to the bridge at Hammermuehle, but I put the fire out from my tank. The bridge is usable. The advance has stopped because there is no one to lead it. You must go there, sir."

So General Guderian got into the half-track and went to the bank of the Brahe, driving through a confusion of German vehicles and wrecked or stopped Polish vehicles. Before five o'clock he was at Hammermuehle, and there he found a group of staff officers behind a stout oak tree a hundred yards from the water's edge.

He heard shooting, and went up to investigate. The Third Rifle Regiment and the Sixth Panzer Regiment were firing rapidly. At what? Nobody knew; the enemy was concealed on the far bank of the river. The Germans were just wasting ammunition.

General Guderian got the firing stopped, and sent the motorcycle battalion across the river in rubber boats. Then he sent tanks across the bridge. In a short time the Polish positions were taken with few casualties. The area was very lightly defended by a Polish bicycle company.

The lesson was clear: The Sixth Panzer Regiment's senior officers had not wanted to move across the Brahe that day, believing it to be too difficult. But had they waited, the Poles might have organized much more serious resistance and they could have been days in crossing.

Having settled that difficulty, General Guderian then set his men to work building up a bridgehead on the far side of the Brahe, and sent a speedy armored reconnaissance battalion to drive ahead as far as the Vistula to find the main Polish forces and their reserves. Then he made sure the Third Panzer Division reached its first-day objective, Sviekatovo, which they did in the middle of the night.

He returned to corps headquarters at Zahn, and there found his own staff victims of first-day hysteria. When he came up, they were all wearing steel helmets, setting up an antitank gun on the road.

And what was this all about? asked the general.

The Polish cavalry was advancing toward the headquarters, and would be upon them at any moment.

Oh, said the general, then why didn't they wait to panic until the cavalry showed up?

That panic was a sign of the reputation of the Polish cavalry, certainly merited insofar as the employment of mounted troops was concerned. But mounted troops in 1939 were a total anachronism. There was no way a horse could stand up against armor, and the combination of machine gun and mortar and heavy artillery had made the beautiful cavalry obsolete.

But that was not to say the Poles were not stout fighters. That night the Second Infantry Division of Guderian's Corps was bogged down, unable to get through the Polish wire entanglements in their sector of the front. All three infantry regiments had made a frontal attack and failed. The reserves had all been committed and the division had no more men. So that night Guderian withdrew it from the front, and moved it to the right flank, where it was to advance next day behind the Third Panzer Division, and cut off Tuchel.

But that night the Second reported that they were being compelled to withdraw by Polish cavalry. Guderian told them harshly to hold, and they said they would hold. But he did not like the situation, so next morning at five, he showed up at the division command post, took personal command of the regiment that had withdrawn during the night, and led the troops to the north side of Gross-Klonia, and then sent it off to Tuchel.

Meanwhile that first day, the Twentieth Motorized Division took Konitz with difficulty but had not advanced much farther. He ordered it to continue on the attack during the second day.

The armored reconnaissance battalion had reached the Vistula by morning, but near Schwetz had sustained serious casualties in leadership by some carelessness. The main body of the Third Panzer Division was split by the Brahe, and cannily the Poles had attacked the troops on the east bank. It was noon before a counterattack could be launched and the division could be reorganized and move on.

The Twenty-third Division followed the Third Panzer Division, but only by means of forced marches. They made progress on September 2, a progress assisted mightily by the confusion and incompetence in the highest ranks of the Polish defenses. Colonel von Mellenthin, who later became a general and one of the most successful panzer commanders, called the Polish problems "an intellectual weakness of the Polish military leaders. They organized their army of 1939 along the lines of an army of 1918, with no appreciation of the new weapons and firepower." Their strategy was still that of the cavalry army. Colonel Mellenthin gave them credit for perhaps counting on France and the British Royal Air Force to supply power and divert the Germans (which they did not do). But the Polish military plans were totally unrealistic. They should have tried to gain time and help from their allies by strategic withdrawals. That way, Britain and France could have helped them. But the high command insisted on holding Poznan and the Polish corridor in great strength, and deploying their forces along a front of eight hundred miles, from Lithuania to the Carpathian Mountains, and even planning a counter-assault into East Prussia. Thus the Polish high command had dissipated its considerable resources, and dispersed them so that they could be picked off piece by piece.

September 2. The British and French were more concerned about their commitment to a world war than to their obligations to Poland under the defense alliance, obviously. On the afternoon of September 1, the German forces had advanced deeply into Polish territory. How could they not, coming on from three sides? And yet the British and French were still discussing the "possibility" of that war that was very much in evidence.

In Berlin, Hitler spoke to the *Reichstag,* and after delivering a patriotic, lying speech about the causes of the war, he named Goering as his successor, and Rudolph Hess as second successor. Certainly that was an indication of Hitler's feeling that the world was now at war. But the British and French dillied and dallied for more hours. The French were most reluctant to face the war situation, and the Chamberlain government was almost as reluctant, but the British people and the Parliament were much more with the spirit of the times. Messages from London to Paris to Berlin flittered like swallows across the airwaves. Mussolini got into the situation again talking about ways to achieve peace. And meanwhile many Poles died, as the Nazis talked but swept through Poland.

Talk. Talk. Talk. It continued all day on September 2 as the fighting went on, and into the night, and all the talk produced nothing but a state of suspended animation in the Western countries. In no way did it stop the German war effort.

The British had informed the Germans in the early hours of September 2 that unless the Germans withdrew their troops from Poland, there would be war. Then they lapsed into semantics. Was it an ultimatum? Hitler asked, stalling for time. No, it was not an ultimatum, the British lied, for it was certainly an ultimatum, and only the false hopes of the politicians could put any other interpretation on it. If the Germans did not stop the war and withdraw, then Britain would go to war with Germany. It was really very simple, but the politicians made a serious effort to confuse the issue, hoping to make silk purses out of sows' ears.

The British had sent their message to Berlin on September 1, but they had not acted. The French ambassador in London had said that Hitler was delaying everything to seize as much Polish territory as possible and then negotiate. But it was not really true; Hitler was simply trying to keep the British and French out of the war. The British were reluctant to declare it a world war, and the French were twice as reluctant.

Parliament pushed Prime Minister Chamberlain for action, and the French finally decided to do something, even though they were fearful that if the two countries declared war on Germany, the French would have to fight the Germans long before the British could arrive to help.

Finally the issue of war was joined, after all the shilly-shallying, by a telegram from Lord Halifax to the British ambassador in Berlin. Speaking of the statement that Britain would support Poland if the Germans did not withdraw, the telegram said:

"Although this communication was made more than 24 hours ago, no reply has been received but German attacks on Poland have been continued and intensified. I have therefore the honor to inform you that unless not later than 11 A.M. British summer time, today, September 3, satisfactory assurances to the above effect have been given by the German government and have reached His Majesty's government in London, a state of war will exist between the two countries as from that hour . . ."

So there it was at last. The Germans had the message at the foreign office at 9.00 A.M., and it was rushed to Hitler at the chancellery. Goering was there, the message was read, and Hitler looked around as if to blame someone for the whole problem. Goering turned to a foreign office professional:

"If we lose this war, then God have mercy on us!"

That mood dominated the chancellery that morning. Hitler had come to the end of his string of deceit and lies. Now he would have to fight.

CHAPTER 9

Raeder, Doenitz, and the Sea War

On the first day of the war, Admiral Raeder, head of the German navy, called his staff together to discuss revision of the German battle plans. The Z plan could not now be carried out; there was no time for long-term planning. The war was upon them, and they must fight it with what they had and what they could build quickly and efficiently. So the elaborate plans for a naval air force of four carriers had to be scuttled. One carrier was building, and that would continue for a time at least.

Two of the *Deutschland*-class ships, the *Deutschland* (whose name would soon be changed by Hitler because Goebbels said they could not face the prospect of a ship named *Deutschland* being sunk) and the *Admiral Graf Spee*, were at sea. Their captains already had instructions, and these were not to be changed. The Luftwaffe was now to lay a minefield in the German Bight, to discourage the British from trying to enter the German waters and the Skagerrak trade routes. Raeder expected to send some ships into the Norway-Shetlands area and the Iceland area, to keep British forces spread out.

The surface forces would play a limited role in this war. Raeder did not expect them to win control of the sea, as the admirals had hoped in 1914, egged on by Kaiser Wilhelm, who fancied himself as a naval strategist. But the surface forces could provide a positive impact by disrupting British communications all over the world, and tying up large elements of the British fleet, which would make the U-boat war more effective. The German ships were to operate singly or in small groups; they were to avoid open battle if at all possible, and concentrate on destroying commerce.

Already Raeder saw a major problem with the big battleships. The key areas of the British Isles to the west and southwest called the Western Approaches were the problem; it was a two-thousand mile voyage for a German war ship, north through the Shetlands narrows, and then south through the narrows around Iceland. If the battleships were to operate in that area, which was the most productive, they would have to have a fleet of tankers. And where would those tankers be based? That was the rub. Germany had no access to the Atlantic, as such, and she could not count on operating out of "neutral" countries, such as Spain and Argentina, no matter how friendly the governments might be to the Third Reich. Nor could she count on Italy, as Hitler already knew since Mussolini had refused to join in the war against Poland, thus throwing a monkey wrench into Hitler's plans. So the battleships were to be laid aside for the moment, until opportunity to employ them profitably could be found.

But the two *Deutschland*-class vessels could serve a very useful purpose from the beginning, by moving into their raiding zones. That would force the British to employ battleships and cruisers to escort their convoys; that in turn would require more destroyers; and that in its turn would mean a destroyer shortage, which would make convoys grow larger, and make the turnaround time for them much longer. In other words, the raiders would slow up the British more than a little, and this was what was wanted. More ships would move unescorted and then be prey to the submarines and aircraft attacks.

It was understood that the submarine would be the

essential naval weapon. But on this first day of the war, Commodore Doenitz offered little hope for immediate success. "With twenty-two boats and a prospective increase of one or two boats a month, I am incapable of undertaking efficacious measures against England," he said. He was referring to the twenty-two Atlantic-type boats, which he saw as the wave of the future. The first effort, then, must be in minelaying, and it would have to be a cooperative venture between the small 250-ton submarines, the Luftwaffe, and the surface navy. It would be two years, Doenitz said, before he would have submarines and trained crews to do the job he wanted to do. But that could only be true if the submarine construction campaign was accelerated to produce twenty to thirty U-boats per month.

Materials for the three hundred submarines Doenitz wanted were available, but the program simply could not work much faster than it was.

The first day, Admiral Raeder also surveyed his air situation. The naval Aviation Branch consisted of fourteen long-range squadrons, plus one shipboard catapult squadron. Six air force bomber wings were available for use by the navy, but the grid system codes and wavelengths of the air force and the navy were different, and this had to be adjusted swiftly. And Raeder discovered that in a major retooling of the aircraft industry for war, Goering had somehow left out any provision for new naval aircraft types. Here was a major problem; the navy wanted aerial emphasis on mines and torpedoes, and Goering said bombs were best. Something would have to be done about that.

On August 25, a week before the beginning of hostilities against Poland, the German ships abroad had all been instructed to run for home. Nearly a hundred ships, totalling five hundred thousand tons, reached Germany. A few were intercepted. Three hundred German ships remained in neutral harbors.

As expected, the British imposed a blockade of Germany immediately. The Germans responded in kind, because it was clear to them that the way Britain would be defeated was to cut her lifeline to the outside. As a small island mass, Britain could not be self-sufficient even in time of peace, and in time of war, she must have the raw materials and food from abroad if she was to survive. Anything that would prevent or delay the delivery of goods to Britain would serve the German blockade, as Admiral Raeder knew very well.

In World War I the Germans had developed the submarine and the strategy and tactics of undersea warfare more thoroughly than any other nation. Perhaps that was because the German navy always did have a tradition of commerce raiding, or what the French call *guerre du course*. From the days of development of the German colonies, most of them in Africa and the Pacific, they had recognized the superiority of the British fleet and had devised a defensive system employing cruisers, which in time of peace showed the flag and were big enough to put down a native uprising, and in time of war would roam the sea, destroying the enemy's ships at sea.

The first and most famous of these World War I surface raiders was the cruiser *Emden*, which worked the Pacific and the Indian Ocean in the first days of the war. She struck terror into the hearts of the British colonials, taking ships, and even bombarding ports, until she was brought up short in the Cocos-Keeling Islands by the Australian cruiser *Sydney*, which left her wrecked on a reef. In the early months of that war, the Germans lost the cruisers *Koenigsberg, Karlshruhe*, and several others which had gone a-raiding, and also the German East Asia Cruiser Squadron, commanded by Admiral Graf von Spee, whose heavy cruisers *Scharnhorst* and *Gneisenau* were sunk in the Battle of the Falkland Islands. Thereafter, the Germans relied largely on merchant cruisers as raiders, such ships as the *Wolf* and the *Moewe* and Count von Luckner's *Seeadler*. But the raiders were expensive in terms of men and material, and by the middle of the war, they had really been replaced by the submarine as the principal commerce destroyer. In the old gentlemanly scheme of things, where a raider announced itself with a shot across the bow and a demand to stop and be searched, the submarine was at a disadvantage. Only when the Germans began unrestricted submarine warfare in 1915 did the U-boat come into its own. It was the ideal weapon for stealthy attack.

Unrestricted submarine warfare was regarded by the rest of the world as barbarous: It was a major reason for the Americans to enter the war very late on the side of the Western Allies; and when the war ended, various nations tried to arrange for limitations on naval armaments and submarine operations. Thus came the Washington Naval Conference of 1920, which was succeeded by several other naval meetings, trying to maintain control of warship building.

The Germans, who had been defeated in the war and were limited to very small defense forces by the Treaty of Versailles, were not party to these initial conferences, but after 1935, when Hitler repudiated the Treaty of Versailles and its restrictions, they had to be brought into the counsels. Thus in 1936, to keep Germany from unrestricted building of warships, the British worked out the Anglo-German Naval Agreement. London knew very well that the Germans were already building submarines, or having them built in Dutch shipyards. So the British, in their pragmatic way, sought to control the building of German warships by giving half a loaf.

The Versailles Treaty had given the Germans the right to build and keep only those four battleships of ten thousand tons each, besides six ten-thousand-ton cruisers. These ships would be about half the size of a British battle cruiser, and even smaller in comparison to a battleship.

But in 1935 British intelligence discovered that the battleships the Germans had just completed, the *Scharnhorst* and the *Gneisenau*, were twenty-six-thousand-ton ships, equal in size and superior in armament to any but the most modern British battleship.

Again, in the 1930s, the Germans had plans to build a navy that would support Hitler's international political ambitions. Grand Admiral Raeder proposed a fleet of surface ships that would be capable of challenging the

British under certain conditions. So a few battleships were started, but also "pocket battleships," heavy cruisers, and destroyers. Almost all of these ships were bigger and more heavily armed than their British counterparts.

The British purpose of the Anglo-German Naval Agreement was to limit the German fleet to one-third the size of the British. The Germans accepted that restriction because they knew they could not outbuild the British fleet, but they cleverly secured a codicil that gave them the right to build as big an undersea fleet as the British had.

In this connection a very important part of the Anglo-German Naval Agreement of 1936 was a codicil known as the London Submarine Agreement, which set down new rules for the operation of submarines in wartime. The key to that agreement was one paragraph that was aimed to deny the submarine the right of secret approach and secret firing of its weapons. A submarine approaching a merchant ship must surface, and by wireless or other signal, make its demand for the other vessel to stop and be searched. If it was a neutral vessel, it should be immune to attack, unless it was shown to be carrying implements of war or supplies to an enemy nation. Neutral or enemy, the ship's crew and or passengers must first be guaranteed safety. In this sense, ship's lifeboats were not considered to be a safe place. If there was not another ship about capable of taking the personnel aboard, then the submarine would have to take them aboard, or escort the ship to a safe place where they could debark, and only then could the submarine sink the ship. Since the peacetime crew of a submarine of any nation averaged about thirty-five men, obviously a passenger vessel in particular could not be molested.

As the Germans said so loudly at the meetings, their U-boats would never again be used against ships. In fact, the British would have liked to outlaw the submarine altogether, and had been restrained at the naval conferences of 1930 and 1934 only by Japanese and American insistence that the submarine had a basic value as "the eyes of the fleet," a concept that ruled both those navies between the wars. So the British admirals were eager to ignore the submarine and concentrate on keeping down the size and number of German surface vessels.

In fact, the Germans were embarked on a major naval building program that they hoped would give them naval equality with the British by 1944 when the German navy expected to go to war with Britain. They started construction of the *Bismarck* and *Tirpitz*. The largest British battleship was thirty-five thousand tons. These two ships each displaced more than forty-five thousand tons.

So that was the London Submarine Agreement, which was supposed to control the activities of the submarines of a future war. Such students of sea warfare as Winston Churchill, then an obscure member of the British Parliament, who had served as First Lord of the Admiralty briefly in World War I until his policy at the Dardanelles caused his downfall, snorted in disbelief. He did not trust the Germans, and fully expected that they would adopt a policy of unrestricted submarine warfare as soon as trouble broke out, for World War I had proved that the submarine was most effective as an instrument of surprise.

As an independent member of Parliament, for many years now Churchill had been one of the most voluble critics of British policy toward Germany. In Hitler's circles, Churchill was regarded as one of the most implacable enemies of the Third Reich.

The Germans were very clever to keep to themselves their feelings about the submarine, and indeed, Admiral Raeder regarded the submarine as of very little use. But within the German naval organization were a number of dedicated men, holdovers from the First World War, who had served in U-boats. Leader of these in the 1930s was Captain Karl Doenitz, who was chosen to head the German submarine arm. So little was thought of the job that when he did get a promotion, it was only to commodore, not admiral, as the chief of a division ought to have been. In 1935, after the signing of the naval agreement with Britain, he got his first three new U-boats. After that, he was busy teaching a whole new corps of men how to manage a U-boat. Although on paper he had fifty-seven U-boats as of the end of August 1939, actually only twenty-two were fit for sea just then. And from experience he knew that once operations began, two-thirds of his fleet would be laid up for repair or maintenance at all times, and only one-third would be operational.

On September 1, 1939, the day that the Germans marched into Poland, Commodore Doenitz had sent an urgent message to Admiral Raeder, pointing out once again the weakness of the German submarine arm, and the great opportunity afforded if only they would hear his pleas for strengthening the U-boat corps to the three hundred boats with which he could win a war against Britain. Two days later, at noon, he was standing in the chart room of his headquarters at Wilhelmshaven looking mournfully at a chart that showed the disposition of his boats at sea. Now only eighteen boats remained at sea, although two days ago, there had been twenty-two. The door opened and a staff officer entered, bearing a telegram.

It was an urgent message from Raeder, announcing that Britain had declared war on Germany. That afternoon, meeting in council, the staff of OKM, the supreme command of the German navy, decided that the construction of U-boats must be increased to provide twenty to thirty new boats per month for operations. As everyone knew, this had to mean the curtailment of the surface building program, but that program could not possibly bring about decision in this war, and there was at least a chance that a big U-boat force could do so.

That day, Commodore Doenitz sent out his own urgent order to all the U-boats at sea: "Commence hostilities against Britain forthwith."

This was followed by a much more detailed message emphasizing the difficult rules under which the U-boat arm had so far pledged itself to operate.

"Battle instructions for the U-boat arm of the navy are now in force. Troopships and merchant ships carrying military equipment to be attacked in accordance with prize regulations of the Hague convention. Enemy convoys to be attacked without warning only on condition that all passenger liners carrying passengers are allowed to proceed in safety. These vessels are immune to attack even in convoy.''

Those instructions were as clear as they could be. But they did not represent all of Commodore Doenitz's thinking on the subject of submarine attack. In conferences with his captains in the past few months, Doenitz had often expressed his concern about the possible tactics of an enemy, particularly a British enemy. His own experience told him that the British armed merchant cruisers, manned by naval personnel, with guns capable of sinking a U-boat, were a great danger under the London Submarine Agreement. The U-boat would have to surface and stop near the ship. To be sure, the gun crew would be manning the deck gun, but it was still a very perilous position. And if the ship happened to be a Q-ship, an apparently innocent passenger or merchant ship with concealed guns, the U-boat could be in great danger. He had emphasized this factor more and more to his captains as it became apparent that the British seemed to be preparing to live up to their obligations to Poland. Be careful, be careful, be careful, he had told them.

CHAPTER 10

A Minor War Becomes Major

September 3, 1939

France had mobilized her reserve troops on August 24, and presented a belligerent front to the Germans for the negotiations in those last days, except that it was undermined by the French diplomats, who swung this way and that. Three hundred and sixty thousand reservists reported for duty, and Paris officials said on August 31 that France would firmly fulfill her obligations to Poland. But two days later, the French military were dragging their heels on the promises.

And what had France promised Poland? Unlike Britain, which had issued only a general promise to go to war if Poland was attacked by Hitler, the French had a kind of timetable. General Mobilization was proclaimed September 1, so three days later, France should be ready to launch an offensive, depending on what the Germans did. They told the Poles they would have thirty-five to thirty-eight divisions for that purpose.

But by the time of mobilization, the French general

staff was singing a different tune, and General Gamelin said it would be two years before the French could launch an offensive, and then only if they had the support of the British and American weapons.

General Keitel, chief of staff of OKW, and the army high command, fretted, because they did not like to see their west flank so open to attack, but Hitler ignored their fears. Keitel said:

> We were fobbed off with the assertion that the ultimatum and declaration of war by Britain and France had been unjustifiable meddling in our eastern affairs, which were issues for Germany and Poland to thrash out between ourselves, and of no economic or like consequence for either Britain or France as none of their European interests was being compromised in any way. We soldiers would see, he told us, how groundless were our fears for the western front: of course, Britain had to make some clear and unambiguous gesture in the spirit of her newly signed treaty with Poland, but she was in no position to intervene with force either at sea or—indeed far less—on land, and France was hardly likely to be dragged into a war for which she was quite unprepared just because of Britain's obligations to Poland. The whole thing was a rattling of sabers for the benefit of the rest of the world, certainly nothing worth taking too seriously.

He had no intention of being taken in by methods such as these. That was the tenor of Hitler's daily incantation both to the war office and to us during our journeys to the front.

Despite our grave doubts, it did seem almost as though even now Hitler's intuition was to prove right again, for the daily reports from the West brought only news of some minor skirmishing with outlying French units in the zone between the Maginot Line and our West Wall. They were suffering bloody reverses at the hands of our weak defending garrison. In no place had heavy fighting broken out.

The generals lamented the precipitous start of the war, nonetheless, but not nearly so much as did Admiral Erich Raeder and Captain Karl Doenitz, his submarine commander. Raeder was still operating under the Z plan, which called for Germany to build a fleet that could challenge the British. But not yet. He was four or five years away from that strength.

"Today," wrote Raeder in his diary, "the war against France and England broke out, the war which, according to the führer's previous assertions, we had no need to expect before 1944. The führer believed up to the last minute that it could be avoided, even if this meant postponing a final settlement of the Polish question . . .

"The navy is in no way adequately equipped for the great struggle with Great Britain, and the submarine arm is much too weak to have any decisive effect on the war. The surface forces moreover are so inferior in number and strength to those of the British fleet that, even at full strength, they can do no more than show that they know how to die gallantly."

And as for Captain Doenitz, much earlier he had written that if the high command would give him three hundred U-Boats with which to start a war, he could bring England to her knees in six months. But instead of three hundred boats, Doenitz's fleet numbered fifty-six, and of these, only twenty-two were ocean going modern boats; the other twenty-six were small submarines suitable only for coastal work or use in the shallow North Sea.

Still, to the surprise of the world, it was the German navy that made it clear the world was really at war, and would not be the same again. The agent of the change was Oberleutnant Fritz Lemp, commander of the *U-30,* one of Doenitz's Atlantic-class U-Boats.

During the period between the wars, the major powers had discussed naval warfare and had come up with some rules for the conduct of submarines in war. The submarine was constrained by international agreement (particularly the British-German submarine agreement) to surface and call upon its quarry to stop for search. If the ship was a neutral, and not carrying contraband to the enemy, it was to be let go unharmed. If it did not thus qualify or if it was owned by an enemy, the crew was to be taken off, guaranteed safe conduct, and then the ship might be sunk. Only an enemy warship was to be attacked without notice.

But on the first day of the war, within hours of receiving the message from Wilhelmshaven that the British had declared war, Lieutenant Lemp found the British passenger liner *Athenia*, two hundred miles west of the Hebrides Islands, and torpedoed this ship without warning. Rescue vessels began to come from afar, but the *Athenia* sank with the loss of 112 civilian lives, 28 of them Americans. The British immediately claimed that the ship had been sunk by a U-boat, and ships' officers so testified. The German government denied all knowledge. (They had no knowledge because Lemp had not reported the sinking by wireless, and they did not learn the actual facts until he returned to Germany.) Grimly Winston Churchill, the First Lord of the British Admiralty, immediately ordered the arming of merchant ships with deck guns, which was another violation of the rules of war at sea, but Churchill took the position that you could not trust a German. The German propaganda ministry charged that the *Athenia* had been sabotaged by the orders of Churchill, and managed for almost a year to keep the issue alive, although most people in the world realized that the U-boat war was on.

The affair was a major embarrassment to Hitler from the beginning. He made haste to order his navy not to sink any French vessels at all, and a few days later ordered the total stoppage of sinking passenger ships.

The failure of the French to take any action in the early hours of their commitment to the war, kept the pressure totally on the Poles. On September 3 General Guderian inserted his Twenty-third Infantry Division between the Third Panzer Division, which had pushed to the Vistula, and the Twentieth Division, and by this maneuver, managed to encircle the Poles in the wooded country north of the Schwetz River. This was the point at which the

Pomorska cavalry brigade charged into the teeth of German armor, with such disastrous results. The problem continued to be valor against armor. A horse-drawn artillery regiment was decimated by armor, and an infantry regiment marching up the road was smashed by Stukas and tanks. The Polish air force had been destroyed in the first two days of operations, with almost all of its five hundred planes wrecked, most of them on the ground in the first surprise attacks. Because the French did not move, the Luftwaffe could concentrate all its efforts on Poland, and did.

By September 4 whole elements of the Polish army were in disarray. General Guderian was supervising the elimination of the enemy remnants in the pocket of the Polish corridor. And at the end of the day, the *corridor* was no longer a meaningful word.

On the morning of September 5, General Halder met General von Brauchitsch and General von Bock of Army Group North, and they agreed that the Poles were about finished five days after the beginning of the campaign. The Germans moved very fast, thirty and forty miles per day. The Polish general staff had completely miscalculated its defenses, and thus there were no defenses, but a mass of troops being cut to ribbons by slashing air attack and panzer strikes. Could Poland have been saved? It seems unlikely, given the obvious decadence of the Polish general staff and the vast weapons superiority of the Germans, but General Guderian writes of so much incompetence and error in the operations of the German troops that, had they been attacked from the West by the French and had the British Royal Air Force come in to assault the panzers, the Germans might have had some second thoughts. But as it was, the Poles were absolutely alone and absolutely inferior in every way to the enemy, except in spirit. Time and again Guderian mentions the bravery and sacrifice of the Polish troops in the field.

But the Germans, as it was, rolled up the Polish line with razzle-dazzle tactics that astonished the world and immediately became known as the ''Blitzkrieg''—Lightning War. On September 5, Hitler came up to the line to see how his people were making out, and Guderian took him for a motor ride along the path of his victory.

"We passed the destroyed Polish artillery, went through Schwetz, and then, following closely behind our encircling troops, drove to Graudenz, where he stopped and gazed for some time at the blown bridges over the Vistula. At the sight of the smashed artillery, Hitler had asked me: 'Our bombers did that?' When I replied, 'No, our panzers,' he was plainly astonished."

Meanwhile the Russians, who did not trust the Germans, had been invited to join the assault on Poland, but their political leadership looked for some hidden catch in the invitation, and Foreign Minister Molotov said vaguely that the Soviets would attack "at the suitable time."

So General Gunderian continued to drive to the east, to get around to the east of Warsaw and encircle the Polish capital. On September 6 his XIX Corps staff crossed the Vistula and set up headquarters in the Finckenstein castle, which Napoleon had once used in his drive against Russia. By September 8, all of Guderian's divisions had crossed the Vistula.

The high command's next thought was to attach Guderian's panzer corps to the Third Army and move toward the eastern side of Warsaw. But Guderian saw himself being bogged down by the infantry, when the value of the panzers was their ability to move fast. So he argued, and won, that he should move fast, and head along the Bug River to Brest-Litovsk, to prevent the Poles from reorganizing and setting up a new defense line on the Bug. On September 9 he had his orders and began moving. But again, the Tenth Panzer Division disappointed him with its slow movement and were avoiding an attack on a fortified Polish position. Guderian came up and led the attack himself. Then came a comedy of errors with the infantry. Guderian reached Vizna and ordered bridges built over the Narev River. But by orders from the Twentieth Motorized Infantry commander, the bridges, which had been built, were dismantled before his troops got there, and taken farther south to be erected for the Twentieth's use. So Guderian had to wait a full day for more bridges.

On September 10 Guderian's troops were engaged in heavy fighting, near Zambrov, which was still a long way from Brest-Litovsk. But Guderian crossed the Narev River that day, and then next day had to fight Polish forces that had cut across the German path south of Zambrov. The thrust was turned.

On September 12 German troops of the Twentieth Motorized Division and the Tenth Panzer Division surrounded a large body of Polish troops, and the corps headquarters moved to Bielsk.

The panzers moved so fast that they sometimes ran into trouble. On the morning of September 13 the division commander of the Second Motorized Infantry got out ahead of his troops and was surrounded between Bransk and Bielsk. Guderian sent an armored force that brought him out safely.

The campaign proceeded, with the panzers moving fast. By September 17 they captured the citadel of Brest-Litovsk, and General Guderian transferred his headquarters to that city.

But now the Russians were beginning to get nervous, because the Germans had virtually finished the campaign in Poland, and the Soviets were concerned about the deal they had made to split the territory, so they moved on September 17 to cross the Soviet border into Poland. Like the rest of the world, the Russians were surprised by the speed of the German advance, but unlike the rest of the world, the Russians had a territorial stake, and now they found that the Germans had captured and were occupying territory that they were supposed to have. Seeing what had happened, Stalin decided to give the Germans a bigger share of Poland, and in exchange to take untrammeled possession of the Baltic states. So Hitler gave up Latvia, Esthonia, and Lithuania, for two Polish provinces. That meant the Germans took over the vast mass of Polish population, but one part of the Polish territory the Russians were to have was Brest-Litovsk, and on September 22 General Guderian moved his forces out of that city and the Russians took it over. General Guderian then headed for Berlin expecting to be employed again very quickly in the campaign in the West, which had to be prosecuted if the war was to be carried on.

The war in the West that autumn was next to nothing at all, for the French had ensconced themselves behind their Maginot Line, and sat there, waiting for developments. Hitler had instructed his senior military officers to do nothing to upset the situation in the West if the French did not attack, and the French had no intention of attacking, at least until the British Expeditionary Force would cross the English Channel, and that time was weeks away.

Hitler saw in Poland how swiftly his new army could move. He visited the front several times, the last with General Keitel when they flew in and then drove over the Vistula north of Warsaw to the command post of the Second Army Corps artillery. Here he had learned of the death of Colonel General von Fritsch, who had been the army chief of staff before he was forced aside, and he watched the artillery bombardment of Warsaw in these last days of the lightning campaign.

But Hitler had to cut his visit to Poland short because von Fritsch was to be given a hero's funeral in Berlin, as a part of Propaganda Minister Goebbels's campaign to build up the reputation of the German army. Already that army was regarded as "invincible," although it was not nearly so mechanized or motorized as the propaganda pictures, and even the results against the disorganized Polish forces, had indicated.

The war in Poland ended with a military parade through the streets of Warsaw and an enormous banquet given in Hitler's honor by the generals, who had taken over a hangar at the Warsaw airfield for the event. Hitler refused to participate in the festivities—to do so would seem to reinstate the generals in his eyes, and he rushed back to Berlin.

Very soon the divisions began to follow him west, headed for the western front that really did not exist. The first troops went to Aachen, on Hitler's express orders, because he said the forces fronting on Holland and Belgium were far too weak.

But the general atmosphere in Berlin was that the war was really over. On September 20 General Keitel was shown an order by the army that called for partial demobilization of the army. Alarmed because he knew Hitler, General Keitel telephone General Halder, the army chief, and warned him that it could not be sent because Hitler had not authorized it, so the order was quietly withdrawn. But Halder's view was unaltered. He and the other generals of the old school had the same faith in the power of the Maginot Line that the French had when they built it. The line was a magnificent structure of blockhouses, fortifications, concealed weapons, that could house whole armies as in a city, with electric lighting and all the facilities of a barracks, all this underground. It was the result of World War I and the trench warfare of the time. The German generals' view was stated by Keitel, who referred to "the formidable Maginot Line against which there were then virtually no weapons of destruction."

The generals said that now that the Polish campaign was over, the army must have time to regroup, remobilize, and complete training of the men under arms, and to reequip, particularly the motorized and armored divisions. The military high command, with the exception of such junior generals as Guderian, were still wedded to the ways of the past. General Keitel put their case:

"Particularly doubts were expressed about winter warfare, with the fog, and rain, the short days and long nights, which made mobile warfare virtually impossible. In addition, the fact that the French had not exploited either the good weather or the weakness of our western defenses earlier could only lead us to conclude that they did not really want to fight, and that any attack we might launch would only foul up the process of peace talks—probably making them impossible. It was clear to us that the Maginot Line would oblige us to press our attack through Northern France, Luxembourg, and Belgium, and possibly even through Holland, with all the consequences we had suffered in the 1914–1918 war.''

Nor were the German generals the only ones talking peace. The French really did not believe in this war. Sisley Huddleston, longtime resident and student of France, put it this way:

The declaration of war in 1939 did not come simultaneously from Britain and from France. There was a difference of only a few hours but it was sufficient to give many Frenchmen the impression that France's hand was forced. Such errors or psychology are of no little importance . . . nor must we overlook the strong pacifist propaganda, perfectly respectable in its sentiment, which had been propagated in France for years . . . Virtually all the literature inspired by the war of 1914–18 insisted on the horrors of the carnage and predicted still more terrible sufferings not only for the combatants but for the civilians . . .

The successive governments were to blame for the material unpreparedness of the French. Demagogy had been triumphant. Political parties no longer urged the people to work but on the contrary to play. The forty-hour week, paid holidays, fetes and commemorations and manifestations, strikes, notably of the sit down kind in which the workers virtually took possession of the factories, were the order of the day and abundance of leisure was accorded to all . . .

Worse still, perhaps was the propagation of fear by the governments . . . Instead of staying where ever we might be . . . we were encouraged to desert even before the invader arrived . . . We were told too that poison gas would be let loose, we were all furnished with gas masks, and shelters were hastily dug. . . . In England Mr. Chamberlain had declared that war would mean the end of civilization and his cry was repeated in France . . .

These and many other forebodings came to me in my study. There was with me a middle aged Frenchman, a relative of mine, from Paris. He burst into tears. " 'Tis the end of everything," he cried, and to console him I could only assure him that things were never as bad as they seemed to be—and as they had been painted by government spokesmen—and that perhaps the war would never start in real earnest . . .

And in Germany as well as France, the people were talking peace as the war in Poland ended. "Tonight the press talks openly of peace," noted newspaper correspondent William L. Shirer wrote in his diary on September 20. "All the Germans I've talked to today are dead sure we shall have peace within a month. They are in high spirits."

Small wonder, then, that Hitler, too, began to talk of peace just then. In a hall in Danzig he made his first overture. "I have no war aims against Britain and France," he said. "My sympathies are with the French *poilu* (soldier). What he is fighting for, he does not know."

Six days later, September 26, the day after the fall of Warsaw virtually ended the Polish war, the German propaganda machine opened full blast in a drive for peace. Why should Britain and France fight?—there was nothing to fight about, was the German propaganda line, and it was very appealing to some. Soon the Russians, who had those secret agreements with the Germans cutting up and destroying Poland as a country, also added their propaganda for peace. Their cynical declaration was issued on September 28 and roundly endorsed by the Germans by even more cynical statements. Together, the two dictatorships announced, they would now pursue the struggle for world peace. As Dr. Goebbels said: "Should, however, the efforts of the two governments remain fruitless, this would demonstrate the fact that England and France are responsible for the continuation of the war . . ."

On September 26 Hitler was still talking to Hermann Goering's friend, the Swedish businessman Dahlerus, who seemed to have such good access to London. Dahlerus indicated that his sources in London wanted peace, but they needed a face-saving gesture of some sort from Hitler.

"If the British really want peace," Hitler said, "they can have it within two weeks without losing face."

If they would accept the fate of Poland, which could not be changed, then he was prepared to guarantee the security of France, Britain, and the low countries. He then began talking grandly about the method by which the talks would be handled, and Goering and Dahlerus joined in with suggestions.

But as Hitler was talking peace to the direction of Britain, he was planning his war against the West with his generals. On September 25, the day before he had spoken so grandly to Dahlerus, they had spoken to General Halder about the plan for the attack. The day after the Dahlerus meeting, Hitler met with his chiefs of the Wehrmacht and informed them of his decision to attack the West as soon as possible before they could get ready to fight. November 12 was the date he set at that meeting.

So what was the truth of the matter? Did Hitler want peace or war? Count Ciano, the Italian foreign minister, probably had it right when he suggested that Hitler wanted peace as long as he did not have to make the smallest sacrifice. Perhaps. More likely, Hitler would offer peace and lull the British and French, and perhaps separate them and eat them separately. For by this time it must be clear to anyone looking at the scene dispassionately that Hitler was obsessed with the desire to recreate the German Empire and would stop at nothing to do it. Peace gestures, saber rattling, they were all the same to him. The Western powers would pay for Versailles. They would pay and pay and pay.

On October 6 Hitler took his machinations to the *Reichstag* again. At noon he began a long speech dedicated to "peace." He spoke for an hour about Germany's accomplishments and then began to get to the point.

As to France:

"My chief endeavor has been to rid our relations with France of all trace of ill will and render them tolerable for both nations . . . Germany has no further claims

against France; I have always expressed to France my
desire to bury forever our ancient enmity and bring together these two nations, both of which have such glorious pasts . . .''

As for Britain, Hitler said:

"I have devoted no less effort to the achievement of
an Anglo-German understanding, nay, more than that,
to an Anglo-German friendship. And at no time, in no
place, have I ever acted contrary to British interests. I
believe even today that there can be real peace in Europe
and throughout the world if Germany and England come
to an understanding.''

CHAPTER 11

U-Boat Attack

"The war at sea . . . began from the first hour with full intensity and the Admiralty therefore became the active center of events."

Winston Churchill

German Propaganda Minister Goebbels made a serious strategic error almost on the outbreak of war with England in trying to cover up the sinking of the British liner *Athenia* by charging that Winston Churchill had personally ordered the liner sabotaged. The charge was so ridiculous that none but American Anglophobes could take it seriously. And as far as the British were concerned, it brought immediate, and violent, reaction.

The first British reaction was to institute the convoy system on the Atlantic immediately. The second was to arm the merchant marine, thus effectively putting an end to the London Submarine Agreement before any chance was given for it to work.

On their part, the British honored the agreement punctiliously. The German liner *Bremen* had first sheltered in the Soviet port of Murmansk, and then started a run for home. She was discovered by the British submarine

Salmon just as the *Athenia* was found by the *U-30*, but British submarine captain Bickford did not sink her.

In fact, of course, it was much easier for the British to honor the agreement than for the Germans, because the Germans had relatively little shipping afloat, whereas the sea had always been the lifeline of England.

The decisions about convoys and arming of ships were made at the first British Admiralty conference on the night of September 4. Within the week the convoys were being organized, even though there was some problem in finding enough protection for them. The Red Sea was closed to all but military traffic, and the decision was taken for the time being at least to route shipping from Australia and Asia south around the Cape of Good Hope instead of through the Mediterranean.

The two British problems involved the incursion of U-boats into British harbors to lay mines, and the air attacks of the Luftwaffe. The first menace was much easier to combat than the second, because it involved harbor booms, which could be devised, and blockships. The second menace was more difficult to combat, because the British were very short of antiaircraft gun factories. For the moment the best that could be done was to devote the guns to the fleet, and as many aircraft as possible to the fleet and the merchant fleet's offshore protection.

On September 4 Commodore Doenitz had a strong feeling that Lemp had sunk the *Athenia*, although there had been no report yet and would not be until the end of Lemp's war patrol. But the sinking had definitely been inside *U-30*'s patrol area. That day Doenitz reiterated his orders to the U-boat corps. He told his suspicions to General Keitel at OKW, and soon Hitler knew. He was furious: the case was almost a parallel to that of the *Lusitania*, the British passenger ship sunk by the Germans during World War I, which had ultimately brought the United States into the war against Germany.

Hitler issued a new order.

"By order of the führer, passenger ships until further notice will not be attacked even if in convoy."

But the fact was that at this point of the war, except

for Lieutenant Lemp's blunder, the German U-boat command was comporting itself in a most respectable manner.

Two days after the sinking of the *Athenia*, the *U-48*, a Type VII Atlantic U-boat, overhauled the British steamer *Royal Sceptre*, which was on its way from Buenos Airies to Belfast. The ship was steaming off the Spanish coast when the submarine came up. The U-boat surfaced five hundred yards behind the ship off the port side. When the officer of the watch saw the U-boat, he immediately changed course and began to run away from her. At that point, commander Herbert Schultze ordered his gun crew to open fire on the merchant ship. This was within the rules of submarine warfare, because the ship was trying to escape. The fire straddled the *Royal Sceptre* and then one shot carried away the radio aerial. The captain came on deck and ordered the ship abandoned. Still she did not stop. The Germans continued to fire, and one shell hit the captain's boat as it was being lowered into the water, and killed the captain and wounded several men.

The men got into the two boats, except two men who were stranded on board. In the panic of escape they had inadvertently been left behind. Captain Schultze came up in the *U-48* and told the first mate to go back and rescue those two men. The submarine had ceased fire.

The submarine captain also made sure that the men in the boats had food and water, and he told them he would send assistance, for he knew of another ship not far away. The boats moved, and the U-boat then sank the *Royal Sceptre* with a torpedo. The survivors drifted, but that afternoon, as promised, a steamer did come and rescue them. They were landed by the rescuing ship at a port in Brazil, and worked their way back to England.

The *U-48* continued her patrol, Commander Schultze conforming to the laws of war and the London Submarine Agreement. He also sank the British ships *Winkleigh* and *Firby*, but there was no cruelty, and no breach of the rules.

But as the days went on, the war became more intense.

Churchill's answer to the sinking of the *Athenia* was to arm the steamers. Undoubtedly he would have done so anyhow, since he had no confidence that the Germans would abide by the rules of war any more than they had three decades earlier. But one excess begets another, and on September 6, when the *U-38* stopped, surfaced, and called on the seventy-two-hundred-ton British steamer *Manaar* to surrender, her captain chose to fight. He had something to fight with, a big deck gun mounted aft and a crew trained to use it. His men manned the gun, and began shooting at the *U-38*. They very nearly hit her. The *U-38* finally sank the *Manaar*, but the Germans claimed "foul" and began propaganda against the British "breach" of the London Submarine Agreement.

But just now the Germans continued to behave very properly. Lieutenant Otto Kretschmer in the *U-23* complained that these restrictions kept him from sinking several ships that should have been sunk because they were carrying materials to England. Perhaps timber was not a war material, but this timber was bound for the Welsh coal mines, to help provide coal, which the British would use to make steel for tanks and ships and guns.

On September 6 came a new restriction imposed by Hitler. He knew that the French enthusiasm for the war was much more limited than the British, and he hoped if he could not persuade the British to declare peace, that at least he could separate the French from them. So orders were issued that all French ships were to be let alone:

"Our actions, including action against merchant vessels, will be confined solely to those necessitated by self-defense. Vessels which have been identified as French will not be stopped. Any incident with France will be rigorously avoided."

Doenitz's captains returned to Wilhelmshaven to complain that steamers were using their radio as soon as they sighted a U-boat. Often British aircraft or warships would appear then, forcing the U-boat to submerge and abandon its operations against that steamer. The Germans noted that British distress calls now said SSS SSS SSS instead of the old SOS distress call of times past. It was true the

SSS call was an Admiralty addition, to indicate "under attack by submarine."

On September 6 the *U-38* was fired upon by a merchant ship as soon as she surfaced near the ship.

On September 14 the British destroyers sank their first U-boat. She was the *U-39*, which was trapped by three destroyers. Next, on September 20, was the *U-27*, which was unfortunate enough to meet seven destroyers on an antisubmarine patrol. The *U-27* was the victim of a torpedo failure that was not then known to be serious; the submarine fired two torpedoes at her enemies, and both of them exploded prematurely. The destroyers then went after the U-boat with their asdic sounding devices. Depth charges came raining down on the submarine. She went deep—to 390 feet—but the depth charging continued, and in the middle of the night, the submarine blew her ballast tanks and surfaced. One of the destroyers prepared to ram her, but the U-boat was not fighting: the men who came to the deck jumped overboard rather than trying to man the deck gun. The fact was that the *U-27* was about to sink. The destroyer came up and took all the Germans off, and made them prisoners of war. And then the *U-27* sank, victim of the new antisubmarine campaign of Britain.

The British claimed several other sinkings in September, but the fact was that there were only the two. Still it was a fairly gentle sea war, with both sides taking prisoners. It would not remain that way for long. In October, as noted, Lieutenant Prien sank the British battleship *Royal Oak*, which won him an Iron Cross, and secured the promotion of Commodore Doenitz to rear admiral. It was the first indication of Hitler's recognition of the importance of the submarine arm, and a distinct contrast to Admiral Raeder's opinion at the outbreak of war about the future of the U-boat service. From the beginning, Winston Churchill recognized the special threat of U-boats to Britain's supply system, but at first he was hopeful that the British between-the-wars progress in sound systems had made the U-boat virtually obsolete. He would soon learn that the contrary was true, and the anti-U-boat war would be his first concern for the next three years.

Just now, in early October 1939, the submarines and the British were very much concerned with minelaying. Of the nearly sixty U-boats available to the Germans, more than half—thirty—were the old, small Type II—250-ton ''canoes'' which were too small to operate in the Atlantic. They could cruise in the North Sea, but their major effectiveness was as minelayers, so the initial impact of the U-boat war, despite the spectacular occasional sinking of a ship by torpedo, was in mining British waters.

Each of the 250-ton boats could carry six to eight mines instead of torpedoes. From the beginning of the war, the little U-boats went out with their mines, to the northern and southern passages between Britain and Ireland, the North Channel and St. George's Channel, into the Firth of Clyde, and the approaches to the English Channel and on the east along the shipping route in the North Sea, especially the estuaries of the Thames and Tyne rivers. Some daring skippers went into the harbor mouths.

As many as half these mines found targets. Lieutenant Schepke was the leading minelayer, and of six mines he laid on one voyage, three claimed ships. This was not a spectacular way to attack British shipping, but very effective and cheap in terms of losses.

Mines cost the Germans two more submarines in those few days, the *U-12* and the *U-40*, as noted. In the sinking of the *U-40* came a note that would soon be all too commonly sounded in Wilhelmshaven: sunk—no survivors. She had hit a mine and she went down like a log and never came up.

By October 1, 1939, because of Churchill's arming of the British merchant ships (he had armed 150 by that time), Doenitz warned his U-boat captains against engaging in surface gun battles with merchant ships. They should remain out of gun range, and accomplish their sinkings by torpedo. It was obvious at this early date that the kid gloves bestowed by the London Submarine Agreement would soon be lost forever. Too much was at stake for the U-boat captain to risk his boat by taking a chivalrous approach, and Doenitz's messages reflected the change.

"Do not take trouble about the steamer's boats. Weather conditions and distance from land are immaterial. Think only of your own boat. We must be hard in this war. The enemy started this war in order to destroy us, and it is that issue, nothing less, that is at stake."

Merchant ships sailed without lights, like warships. It was difficult at night to tell whether a ship was a warship or a merchantman. In order to tell, the U-boat had to close to a short range. It then would signal by lamp for the ship to stop, or use its searchlight. Either way, the position of the U-boat was shown exactly, and if it was a merchant cruiser or a Q-ship, the U-boat might be in trouble.

On September 30, 1939, the German restrictions on the sinking of neutral ships with cargoes bound for Britain were lifted. No longer would a U-boat surface, challenge the ship, and carry out a physical search for contraband. Most of these ships and cargoes were Norwegian or Swedish or Danish, and they were coming across the North Sea. There were too many British armed trawlers about and too many British aircraft to make this anything but a dangerous venture. So it was ended within one month of the beginning of war.

And the attrition of "gentlemanliness" continued.

Here is the assessment of German historian Harald Busch:

"As further indication of their belligerent role, British merchant ships were ordered to be blacked cut at night, to report immediately by wireless the position of any U-boat encountered, and finally, as Churchill announced on October 1, 1939, their captains were instructed to ram all U-boats on sight. Thereupon German U-boats were instructed that they might in future attack without warning any merchant ship that was definitely seen to be armed. On October 17 an amendment to this instruction was issued, substituting 'any enemy merchant ship' and omitting the qualification concerning armament.''

So, officially, it was good-bye chivalry forever. The concept of the gentlemanly war at sea had vanished in World War I, been reinvigorated in the early days of World War II, but six weeks after war began, it was abandoned forever by British and German governments. Some U-boat captains followed Doenitz's new instructions completely in their attacks on convoys.

Britain's immediate problem with the war at sea was the shortage of escort vessels for the convoys. Convoys? Many of these groupings of ships in the early days of 1939 were not convoys at all in the sense of World War I, but groupings of ships that clung together for comfort. Under such circumstances it was debatable whether they might not have been better off sailing alone. And for one convoy, the gentleman's war came to an end October 12, when a four-ship unescorted convoy was attacked by the *U-45* when bound from Jamaica to Liverpool. First the British *Lochavon* was torpedoed without warning, then the French ship *Bretagne*, which was also shelled until she sank, and no attention paid to survivors. The *Karamea* tried to ram the U-boat in accordance with Churchill's instructions, and failed. The *U-45* then flung a torpedo at the *Karamea*, which missed. The *Karamea* ran, and the U-boat followed, firing her deck gun. She shelled the *Karamea*—shot at her—for four hours and fired thirty shells, but only one even nearly missed the merchant ship. All the while the *Karamea* was sending a steady stream of messages on her wireless, which was another violation of the old gentlemen's rules. The U-boat followed them until the morning of October 14, and they were coming into the Western Approaches to Britain. Luckily for the *Karamea* and the fourth ship of the convoy, the French ship *Oregon*, a destroyer then came up to escort them into British home waters, and the *U-45* vanished into the sea. Two ships of the convoy were saved when the convoy came within the purview of the slender British destroyer force, but that force was so far extended that it had been a matter of sheer luck.

In the last months of 1939 the U-boat war became grimmer, although it had not reached the ferocity that it would soon. The U-boats were most effective still as minelayers. The mines that fall sank as many ships as the torpedoes, about 160,000 tons of ships. As the year drew to an end, Admiral Doenitz's building program was beginning to show, and he had thirty 500-ton U-boats, capable of going into the Atlantic, fifteen of the 750-ton boats, and one experimental 1,100-ton boat.

In November Winston Churchill grew a little complacent about the U-boat war, but that was soon to end, even though by the end of November, the British had sunk nine U-boats. But that month the U-boats sank another twenty-one ships, and there was a major change in German strategy: the neutrals were coming under the gun, and in December, thirty-nine ships were sunk, twenty-two of them neutrals. Since the emphasis was on minelaying because of the suspicions about the German torpedoes, Doentiz's losses were slight. In December only one U-boat was lost.

January brought a real difference, which was noted by the British Admiralty.

"At the end of six months of war, the German U-boat commander who pays any attention to International Law is the exception. Neutral ships as well as belligerents have, for some time in the past, been sunk without warning. There appear to be two objects in this policy, to frighten neutrals away from English ports, and to decrease the world tonnage, since this will work to the Allies' disadvantage."

In Germany, production of the 250-ton boats had been stopped entirely, and although production of the 500-ton boats was the matter at hand, Doenitz was looking forward to a fleet of 750-ton Atlantic-class boats that could make the voyage to America, operate there, and then return. When he had that, he would have the weapons for the deadly sea war of the future.

From the beginning of the war, until March 1, 1940, when the torpedo problem was recognized as serious, the German U-boats sank 199 ships with a tonnage of seven hundred thousand. In those first six months, the shape of the sea war was indicated. Doenitz was going to count on the Type VII U-boats, the 517-ton boats, which, he discovered, could operate at greater distances than he had expected.

As of October, the Luftwaffe had not yet combined forces with the U-boat arm. The reason for it was simple enough: The Luftwaffe was primarily an army instrument of power, dedicated at this point to support of panzer operations. The highly overblown Stuka dive bomber was the key element in the blitzkrieg. Only a bit later would the Stuka fall by the wayside as too slow and too vulnerable to Allied fighters. For the moment the almost deadly combination of air-sea attack was not considered by the Germans.

As for the British, their coastal air defenses were primitive in the extreme. The bomber people did not yet understand the best weapons to use against submarines, and the bombs the coastal planes dropped were far too small and far too weak to do the job of sinking a submarine except almost by accident. An example was the case of the *U-35* on patrol which was attacked by an aircraft 180 miles west of Scotland. The plane dropped three bombs, and they were so close that they knocked out light bulbs in the submarine. But they did not sink her, which they should have if they had been powerful enough for the job.

As noted, Admiral Doenitz was eager to use the wolf pack technique, but the time was not yet. The sea war still had a few vestiges of decency in October 1939. The *U-35* ran across the Greek ship *Diamantis* in the English Channel in early October. The submarine surfaced, fired a shell across the bow of the steamer. The crew panicked and got into the single lifeboat and cut the falls so she capsized. The U-boat crew spent an hour in very rough water, rescuing Greek sailors. Having rescued the crew, Commander Lott then sank their ship with three torpedoes, and then he landed the Greeks by rubber boat in British waters. It was a chivalrous and extremely dangerous action, because the U-boat had to lie just offshore, easy prey to a passing aircraft and easy to be trapped by destroyers. Earlier Commander Lott had seen the liner

Aquitania off Cherbourg, but he had ignored her in obedience to Admiral Doenitz's orders. He had come across the Belgian steamer *Suzon* and had fired on her; she had stopped, and since she was an enemy vessel, he had sunk her with a torpedo, but only after the crew had abandoned ship and was within sight of land in their boats.

CHAPTER 12

Navies

"A realistic policy would have given Germany a thousand boats in the beginning."

Admiral Doenitz

The reason Commodore Doenitz started World War II with only fifty-seven U-boats was very simply that Hitler had not prepared for war against Britain to begin until 1944 and had given very little thought to the German navy. He was concerned with the establishment of a land empire in Europe and would turn his attention to Britain only if she tried to interfere with his plans. The management of the navy was entrusted to Grand Admiral Erich Raeder, who was concerned about building a surface fleet primarily and who did not expect the submarine arm of the navy to play a major role in the war. Britain would be let alone if she let alone. The United States would be isolated, and such bases as Iceland seized by Germany, so that the U.S. would be intimidated into the inaction Hitler expected because of the general isolationist attitude of Americans.

The German navy's mission in World War II, said Admiral Raeder, was to defend German coastal waters and attack enemy shipping. So little was thought of the submarine by the German naval administration, that only three shipyards were devoted to construction of submarines, while a dozen were building capital ships. Battleships, pocket battleships, and cruisers would be used to raid Allied shipping, and the submarines were relegated to close coastal work. That is why by 1939 more than half the German U-boats were the Type II 250-ton coastal boats, suitable for minelaying and operations in the North Sea, but not in deep water.

Another disadvantage of the German navy at the outbreak of the war was the fact that it had no air arm of its own. The German aircraft developed by 1939 were more suitable for support of land operations than for attacks on shipping. The Stuka, the showpiece of the Luftwaffe, did not have the range or the capacity for war on shipping. It was only later, when the Germans discovered the suitabilty of two types of bombers for work with submarines, that the air arm began to develop.

The British began the war with a much more sound naval program. Their navy was about equal in strength to that of the United States in capital ships, and superior to the U.S. in cruisers. The big shortage of the navy was in destroyers and other craft that could conduct antisubmarine warfare, because, like the Germans, the British had concentrated on building capital ships in the period between the wars.

The Royal Navy began the war with a primitive air arm. To build up the Royal Air Force, it had been given total responsibility for air affairs in the post–World War I years, and the fleet had been sadly neglected. Britain's carrier fighters and torpedo bombers were relicts; the latter were still constructed of framework and cloth, with applications of ''dope'' to make the cloth airworthy and toughen it. It was not until the war was well begun that several of the RAF fighters and bombers were adapted for carrier use.

The RAF had planes, but they were not considered for antisubmarine use. Quickly the RAF set up Coastal Bomber Command, to which it assigned nineteen squadrons of aircraft. The Americans contributed naval aviation techniques, which they had been working on since World War I.

The Canadian navy would make an enormous contribution to Britain's war almost from the beginning. Canada had no navy until 1939, but it quickly began to develop just what was needed, escort vessels to guard the convoys on their roads across the Atlantic. The Canadians specialized in two types of ship, the corvette and the frigate. Several of these were produced for Canada by the United States where the corvettes were called gunboats. They were armed with a four-inch gun and machine guns and depth charges, and equipped with sound listening devices to combat submarines.

The frigates were to be a later development, based on experience with the corvettes, that showed that a large and more heavily armed vessel was more useful for deep sea work in the Atlantic. The great advantage of these two sorts of ship was the speed of construction, which was a vital element in the early days of the war, when Britain began with totally insufficient numbers of destroyers.

The United States began World War II with a large navy, but it was generally Pacific oriented, as the American defense plan indicated that the most likely enemy of the United States would be Japan. But in January 1939, recognizing the reality of European politics that was leading toward war, the United States Navy organized the Atlantic Squadron, which when war broke out was made up of four old battleships, four cruisers, a destroyer squadron, and two aircraft carriers.

When war came between Britain and Germany, the first American act was the organization of a Neutrality Patrol in the Western hemisphere, on orders from President Franklin D. Roosevelt. The order was issued two days after Britain declared war on Germany. The purpose was to discourage belligerent powers from sending naval forces into the Western hemisphere and the technique was for American naval forces to track any foreign naval forces that came into the waters off the United States or the West Indies. This plan was accepted by the other American states at a meeting later in September, and so the patrol was extended to include the Atlantic coasts of North and South America.

At first eight American warships covered offshore waters from Newfoundland to the Guianas. Soon the Coast Guard was enlisted and integrated into the U.S. Navy for the duration of the war.

When the war broke out, the Royal Canadian Navy immediately came to the side of the British, and within hours was working out plans for convoys to keep the lifeline open between Canada and Britain. The first convoy sailed from Halifax on September 16, and thereafter, convoys left Halifax about every eight days. Out of Halifax, the convoys were escorted by capital ships of the British Royal Navy and Canadian destroyers. At first the convoys were escorted partway, and then had to run the gauntlet of the open sea for the middle section of the journey, because of the shortage of escort vessels. Then on the last part of the trip, the ships were picked up by the Royal Navy and brought into Britain.

In the beginning, the central portion of the trip was usually uneventful, because the Germans were not operating their submarines in mid-Atlantic. It was too far from the German ports in the Baltic, and it would be only after the fall of France that the sea war would change remarkably.

At first the convoys were very small, and sometimes altogether unescorted, as indicated. But eventually they would grow to comprise forty to sixty merchant ships, steaming in as many as a dozen columns.

There were no losses from the Halifax convoys during 1939, because the Germans simply were not yet organized. The Royal Canadian Air Force furnished air protection for about five hundred miles off the coast, and air protection was picked up at the other end. The first convoy ship to be torpedoed was lost in February, and she was a straggler, which had lost contact with the convoy. After that, there were only a handful of losses until the fall of France changed the German situation completely, giving Doenitz bases in France that extended his field of operations to the western shore of the Atlantic.

In the first weeks of the new year 1940, however, Doenitz did send some of his Type VII boats into the Atlantic to challenge the convoys, even though he was not yet ready to take on the wolf pack technique because of the torpedo situation and the shortage of oceangoing U-boats. This reluctance to gang up added to Winston Churchill's feeling that Britain had a "handle" on the treatment of the U-boats. The British had by this time sunk nine U-boats, and the Admiralty reported they were losing more ships to mines than to the submarines. The change over the months in the battle of the Atlantic was apparent in the story of convoy OA 80G.

This convoy had been divided into three parts, one from Southend, one from Portsmouth, and the third part from Liverpool. They were to assemble in mid-Atlantic for the voyage south to Gibraltar. Because of the shortage of escort vessels, the Southend section had but a single sea escort, the sloop HMS *Fowey*. The rest of the protection would have to come from air cover, but the weather was so foul that planes were not flying, so rough that the Southend section missed the link point with the Portsmouth section on January 29 and had to go it alone to the next rendezvous point, where the Liverpool section was to join up on January 30. The weather was so bad that several of the ships were having trouble keeping in convoy formation by the time they were about one hundred miles southwest of Land's End.

Shortly after midnight on January 30, the *U-55* sighted this convoy. The submarine captain, Lieutenant Werner Heidel, was moving on the surface, charging the batteries of his electric engines with the diesels. The *U-55* was moving comfortably in the stormy weather, for this was her element. She was one of the newest of the Type VII boats, and Lieutenant Heidel had been given her command because of his remarkable performance in the old *U-7*, one of the 250-ton boats. Heidel had taken her out on a cruise and sunk three merchant ships in the North Sea.

Heidel had brought the *U-55* on a perilous journey already, out through the Kiel Canal behind an icebreaker in the third week of January. He then moved into the North Sea, which was always dangerous water, but was lucky enough to sink two merchant ships. And then Heidel had pleased Admiral Doenitz no end by sinking the British destroyer *Exmouth*. He had rounded the north of Scotland in the freezing weather and then come south to the hunting grounds.

It was no accident that Lieutenant Heidel encountered this part of the OA 80G convoy. The Germans had broken the British naval code, the one used for the routing of convoys, and Admiral Doenitz had a pretty good idea where the convoy would be found. By high-speed transmission, he had notified Lieutenant Heidel of the opportunity, and Heidel had moved into position to intercept. Immediately he dived.

Two ships of OA 80G had fallen behind the group, the tanker *Vaclite* and the steamer *Beaverbrae*. Lieutenant Heidel selected the tanker, and in about an hour after the sighting, moved up close and torpedoed her. The tanker put up two red rockets, but in the bad weather, nobody in the convoy saw them except the officers of the *Beaverbrae*. Soon the tanker went down. The *Beaverbrae* put on full steam and eventually caught up with the convoy and reported the rockets, although he did not then know that the *Vaclite* had actually sunk. The convoy commander counted ships and tried to raise the *Vaclite* on the wireless. No answer.

Meanwhile Lieutenant Heidel moved the *U-55* around to intercept the convoy head-on. When the convoy came to him, he shot down the throat, and because the ships were zigzagging, his torpedo struck the third in the starboard column, the Greek freighter *Karamiai*. Immediately the captain of the *Fowey* gave chase, spotted the periscope of the submarine, and attacked with depth charges. The charges were set to explode at five-hundred feet, and the *U-55* did not get down so far, so the depth charges did not sink her, although they exploded underneath her. But the depth charges did loosen the plates, and the submarine took on water inadvertently, which made her very sluggish in maneuver. Lieutenant Heidel moved away from the scene to what seemed to be safety and surfaced, to try to put things right with the submarine.

Now the *Fowey* radioed for help, and soon a Sunderland flying boat came up and, through a hole in the heavy cloud cover, saw the submarine lying on the surface. The Sunderland attacked and dropped a depth charge. The U-boat made no attempt to dive, because Lieutenant Heidel was not sure she would come up again if he did. So the U-boat remained on the surface. The Sunderland pilot then radioed the position of the U-boat, and soon the destroyers *Whitshed* and *Ardent* were on the scene. When the sounds of their propellers were heard, Lieutenant Heidel had no option but to take the U-boat down again. Soon the destroyers had sound contact and they began dropping depth charges. One blew the U-boat to the surface, and when she came up, the *Fowey* opened gunfire. The *Fowey* lost contact in the fog and did not do any damage to the U-boat, but the French destroyer *Valmy* came along, saw the U-boat, and began firing. The *U-57*'s deck gun chose that time to jam. Lieutenant Heidel then saw that fate had delivered him into the hands of his enemies, and he decided to scuttle the U-boat so it would not fall into British hands. He and two others went below and opened the sea cocks. The others came up, but Lieutenant Heidel, trained in the tradition of Doenitz, chose to go down with his ship and remained below. The submarine sank, the crewmen clung to rafts, and the Allied ships rescued them. Forty-one members of the crew were saved to become prisoners of war. There was still some vestige of the chivalry of the past, which led the British and French seamen to risk the storm to rescue their enemies. It would not last long.

Because of the torpedo failure, several of Doenitz's Type VII U-boats came around to the Western Approaches to Britain and laid mines, as at Liverpool harbor, Swansea, and Falmouth. These mines sank ships, although there was no glory in the job for the U-boat commanders, whose sights were now set on the sinking of one hundred thousand tons shipping and then joining the ''stars'' of the U-Boat fleet. While it was true that Hitler in particular honored the captain who sank a warship, Doenitz's eyes were on the greater advantage. He, almost alone among the German leadership, seemed to understand the great value of commerce raiding as opposed to spectacular sinkings.

In February Doenitz sent eight U-boats out to work the Western Approaches to Britain. The *U-41* attacked convoy OB 84, bound for America. She sank a ship, but then encountered the single escort, the destroyer *Antelope*, whose captain broke the rules and went after this submarine and sank her. The British problem in this period was that there were so few escorts that they often did not know which way to turn when a U-boat attacked.

The Type VII boats were sinking many ships, most of them vessels that were trying to avoid the convoy system and making runs to the West independently. At the end of January, seven U-boats were working in the Western Approaches, the largest number of the war so far. Winston Churchill, who had been sanguine about having defeated the U-boat menace a few weeks before, now suddenly saw it rising up again, worse than ever from the British point of view. So in February 1940 the war cabinet took an extremely long look at the anti-U-boat operations, and set about strengthening them.

CHAPTER 13

Readying for Battle

As Adolf Hitler spoke to the *Reichstag* and the world on October 6, 1939, he was at his most persuasive. Why should the British and French want to war with him? he asked. The issue was settled. The monster Poland, created at Versailles to punish the Germans by making a jigsaw puzzle of their territory, had been wiped out. Poland ''at its very birth was termed an abortion by all those not of Polish extraction,'' he said.

What other reason was there for Britain and France to fight? If it was to destroy the Third Reich, then the Western powers would have to be prepared to sacrifice millions of lives. (And the implication was clear that the West would not succeed.)

Rather than sacrifice the world, why did not the Western powers listen now to Hitler's plan for peace? He agreed that the world had many problems to solve. Formation of a Polish state was one of them. Solution and settlement of the Jewish problem was another. The establishment of colonies for Germany to replace those taken away at the end of World War I was another. Settlement of minority problems in Europe was another.

These were high on Hitler's agenda. In exchange for solutions to be worked out to these problems, Hitler said, he was willing to guarantee peace unconditionally, reduce armament, regulate air warfare (the great unknown quantity, which just then was regarded as more dangerous than any other sort of warfare), outlaw poison gas, control submarine warfare, and address any and all problems of nations. To achieve these ends, Hitler proposed a conference of leading European nations.

"It is impossible that such a conference, which is to determine the fate of this continent for many years to come, would carry on its deliberations while cannon are thundering or mobilized armies are bringing pressure to bear on it."

Hitler's proposal was seductive, as he intended it to be, and it was aimed primarily at the French, who had no stomach for the war, as Sisley Huddleston observed.

"I spent some months in Paris or my Normandy village and was more and more dismayed. Evidences of disorder were everywhere. Troops, as they marched, imitated the cries of sheep, humorously suggesting that they were being driven like lambs to the slaughter. Certain contingents that I saw were totally undisciplined, and the reserve officers could not control them. There were inconsiderable requisitions of automobiles, camions, and horses, left to rust or starve, respectively, in the field. From the factories which should have been working at full speed, specialists were sent to their regiments and the countryside was depleted of farm workers . . . There were five million Frenchmen under arms, but there was a serious lack of organization."

The German foreign office had been busy working for Hitler in these last few days, trying to ascertain from the Spanish and the Italians just what the French attitude really was at the highest levels. During September the French government was hoping that as soon as Poland was defeated, an accommodation could be reached with Germany. There was no stomach for the war, and therefore the French did not lift a hand to fulfill their commitments to Poland.

Now that Poland had been swallowed, there was a surge of reaction in France toward ending the war. Four days before Hitler's speech, the Italians had informed the Germans that the majority of the French cabinet were in favor of a general peace conference, but that France must have a means of saving face. Prime Minister Edouard Daladier replied the next day that the precondition for any discussions would have to be guarantees for a real peace and general security. Prime Minister Chamberlain of Britain did not reply at all immediately, so Hitler repeated his arguments in a speech on October 10.

Two days later, Chamberlain did reply in an address to the British House of Commons. He referred to the vague and uncertain nature of Hitler's proposals and put his finger on their frailty: they ignored the wrongs done to Czechoslovakia and Poland. Chamberlain had learned, and now he spoke of the false representations of Hitler. "No reliance can be put on the promises of the present German government," he said. "If Germany wants peace, acts—not words alone—must be forthcoming."

So finally Hitler knew that as far as Britain was concerned, he had bluffed his last bluff, and would not be believed again. It did not surprise him, he was already preparing to strike, even as he talked peace. On October 10, the day that he renewed his peace talk at the opening of the Winter Help program, Hitler called his military chiefs together and gave them Directive No. 6 for the conduct of the war. He was demanding an attack against the West as soon as possible.

The generals listened to Hitler and were appalled. They had already told him that Germany was in no position to launch an offensive. It would take several months to refit the tanks that had been used in Poland. There was ammunition for only about a third of the German divisions to last for only two weeks.

Hitler did not listen to them. He gave his orders. They would prepare for an attack through Luxembourg, Belgium, and Holland as quickly as possible. The purpose was to knock France out of the war and to gain as large a base as possible in France and the low countries for operations against Britain. Hitler's war aim was thus revealed:

"The German war aim is the final military dispatch of the West, that is, the destruction of the power and ability of the Western powers ever again to be able to oppose the state consolidation and further development of the German people in Europe."

That aim had to extend beyond the European borders to the Soviet Union, and on the West, across the Atlantic to include America. The only way that any of these potential enemies could avoid attack by Hitler was to surrender. Hitler would employ propaganda to gull the world, but his war aim was unchangeable: "It is and remains the destruction of our Western enemies."

The participation of the United States in World War I, and its presence at Versailles, automatically included that country in the list of enemies, although the Americans did not know it and would not have believed it if told.

On October 13 Hitler threw the whole responsibility for the continuation of the war on Britain's shoulders.

Having told his generals to get ready for war against the Western powers, Hitler was soon at them for a summation of their war plans. Generals Jodl, Halder, and Keitel were assembled for a discussion of the army proposals. Halder, the commander of the army, did the talking. Hitler asked for his maps, and Halder handed them over. Hitler sneered.

"This is just the old Schlieffen (World War I) plan, you know. You won't get away with an operation like that twice running. I have quite a different plan, and I'll let you know about it in a day or two . . ."

For since the march into the Rhineland, Hitler had not had much use for his generals, and particularly for their strategic planning, which was much too conservative for him. Just now he was listening to a junior general, Fritz Erich von Manstein, chief of staff to Field Marshal von Runstedt. Von Manstein liked the idea of breaking through the Allied lines at Sedan, below the Maginot Line, cutting across the low countries, striking for the channel coast at Abbeville, and then swinging around the rear of the Allied armies, which should be advancing in the traditional manner on the French-Belgian frontier. The Germans would move fast with the panzers, cut them off, and roll them up into a neat package for surrender.

True to his word, Hitler advanced this plan a few days later to the War Office, and the generals, as he expected, said it was quite impossible. But von Manstein spoke up in agreement, much to the annoyance of his peers and superiors. So Hitler was satisfied that his plan was best, and he ordered the army to prepare to attack through Luxembourg, Belgium, and Holland. Of course, this meant violating the neutrality of these nations, but that was a small matter to Hitler as long as his enemies did not do so, and they had been scrupulous in their inaction.

Having moved to the coast, and destroyed the French and British armies, Hitler would then have his submarine bases a thousand miles closer to the deep Atlantic, and his air bases, right across the channel from England. Meanwhile, what the French called the *drôle de guerre* and the Allies had begun calling the ''phony war'' and some called ''the war of nerves'' went on. The French sat behind their Maginot Line and fretted. For them it really was a phony war, the term that had been coined by U.S. Senator Borah of Idaho, an old-line Populist Republican and sincere isolationist, who had no use for Europeans and their ways. Borah was contemptuous of the war, and everything about it, and wanted simply to be sure that the United States stayed out. His characterization, however, was misleading. The fact was that when Britain declared war on Germany to live up to her new commitment to Poland, her leaders knew that they were totally unready for the struggle. Their aircraft industry was in a state of flux, trying to assimilate new models. The army was far below strength, and the craft needed to bring that army across to France were not ready. Only the Royal Navy had any semblance of readiness, and it was far under strength in the matter of ships to guard against and fight U-boats, for the new First Lord of the Admiralty, Winston Churchill, knew precisely what sort of war an intelligent German naval command would wage against London, a war to starve the country out of the struggle.

One of the people who saw clearly what was happening was Sumner Welles, U.S. under secretary of state and a brilliant observer of the European scene:

It was true that after the devastation of Poland the Germans had refrained from undertaking any air offensive against the western powers. Nor had the German armies yet made any move to invade the Low Countries or to break through the Maginot line. But to even the most casual observer familiar with the working of Hitler's mind it was obvious that Hitler was waiting for two developments. First, he hoped that Germany's overwhelming superiority in the air and in mechanized equipment, as evidenced in the invasion of Poland, would persuade Great Britain and France that a negotiated peace granting Germany, as a first step, hegemony over Europe would be preferable to the probability of annihilation and occupation. Second, should this hope fail, he knew that the winter months would give his propaganda and subversive agencies much valuable time in which to break down the morale of the French armies. In this manner he would improve his chances for a military pushover as soon as the approach of summer made weather conditions more propitious for an all-out offensive.

Why any considerable segment of public opinion in the United States should have regarded the war as a Phoney War, in view of constantly accumulating evidence of Hitler's military strength and in view of the ruin which Poland had already suffered must always remain a mystery . . .

The fact was that there was a real war on, at sea and in the air. From the evidence and the propaganda coming out of the Spanish Civil War, and the ease with which the Luftwaffe polished off the understrength and outmoded Polish air force, the world expected something special from the Luftwaffe, some sort of horrible surprise to be thrust on the Allies. But the fact was that Goering's air force was a very special instrument, largely equipped in 1939 for the support of the panzer armies but in no way suitable for heavy bombing of strategic targets, and only partly effective in the matter of thrust against Britain's sea lanes.

But as the war began, no one knew the facts about air power. In Britain the popular view held that the airplane was a superweapon, capable of winning a war all by itself, a view promulgated by the Air Ministry and the Royal Air Force. But what the British thought they could do, they thought the Germans could also do, and as war began, Britain was prepared for massive air raids, and had reserved 250,000 hospital beds for air raid casualties. Even as Prime Minister Chamberlain was telling the British they were at war, an air raid was announced by sirens, and people trouped underground for the first time. It was what they had expected: war in the air. This time it happened to be a false alarm.

By October, there in the air, however, and under the sea, is where the very real war was being waged, as Britain turned every effort to arm herself and prepare for the struggle on land and in the air as well.

As the British knew very well, the sea was their lifeline; from the sea came the food to feed her millions, and necessities for manufacture of the goods of war. From experience the British knew that Germany would have to concentrate on that lifeline and try to break it. Winston Churchill, who had served as First Lord of the Admiralty at the beginning of World War I, now returned to Chamberlain's war cabinet, and even before his appointment was official, had taken charge at the Admiralty, for, as he said, "the opening hours of war may be vital with navies."

The Royal Navy had begun its preparations for war in June with a call-up of the reserves, and by August was ready for operations at Scapa Flow, the fleet base in Scotland on the North Sea.

Churchill had assumed that the Germans would begin the war with the raiding of commerce, and the sinking of the SS *Athenia* less than half a day after the declaration of war proved his point.

The British merchant fleet in 1939 totaled 21 million tons, but a number of ships had to be reserved for defense purposes, so the actual useful tonnage was 15.5 million tons.

The great enemy of the merchant fleet was the German submarine, but at the outbreak of war, it was not recognized for the dangerous instrument it had become, because the experts of the Admiralty had made much of the development of the asdic underwater sounding system, which was supposed to be the answer to the U-boat.

Very quickly the British learned of the limitations, as the sinking of the *Athenia* was followed in the next few days by the sinking of the *Bosnia*, *Royal Sceptre*, and *Rio Claro*. Very quickly, too, Churchill learned that the Germans had sixty U-boats and would have more than a hundred early in 1940. Immediately the defense was being strengthened by the conversion of sixty trawlers to become antisubmarine vessels. Immediately the convoy system of ship movement was begun again. Immediately the shipbuilding program concentrated on the construction of destroyers and cruisers.

Churchill, for one, was grateful for the "twilight war," as Prime Minister Chamberlain had dubbed it. Within the first three months, he had equipped a thousand ships with deck guns for use against submarines. The greater immediate danger to shipping, as he soon discovered, was air attack, for few merchant ships had antiaircraft guns, and they were in short supply in Britain, and would be for a year.

Not only did the British begin operations against submarines and surface raiders on the first day of the war, but they also set up the blockade of Germany, and within a short time had captured fifteen German ships to add to their merchant shipping. This was expected by the Germans, who recognized that they would be blockaded. Their own hopes for empire in 1939 meant largely contiguous land masses.

By September 8 the British had organized a system of

convoys to the west and in the North Sea. All independent sailings were canceled, and shipping went on a total war basis.

The U-boat war was very real. More merchant ships were lost to U-boats. On September 14 the carrier *Ark Royal* was cruising west of the Hebrides as part of an antisubmarine patrol when she was attacked by the *U-39*. The torpedoes malfunctioned and the *Ark Royal* was not hurt; the escorting destroyers finished off the *U-39* and captured the crew. Three days later the *U-29* sank the carrier *Courageous* in the Bristol Channel. Obviously there was something wrong with the policy of putting capital ships at risk to chase submarines, and the policy was quickly revised. There was no question about the great value of an aircraft carrier in the war against the U-boats, but what were needed were small carriers, and this idea was put into motion. It took time, however, to convert a merchant ship with a carrier deck, and so some desperate measures were introduced, including the catapulting of wheeled aircraft from merchant ships, knowing that they would either have to find land or would go down in the sea at the end of their flight. A number of planes and pilots were lost in the next two years, but many submarine attacks were also frustrated by this method.

So was the rest of the war at sea real. From the beginning, Hitler had planned war with the West, no matter how often he denied that. On August 19, eleven days before the attack on Poland, Admiral Raeder had sent twenty-one submarines to sea, and the battleships *Deutschland* and *Graf Spee*, which were to raid British commerce. In the first month of the war, the submarines and commerce raiders sank 150,000 tons of British ships, and fifteen neutral or Allied ships. Churchill, while warning against overconfidence, was quite hopeful that by year's end the U-boat menace would be reduced to a minimum. The British naval construction program changed direction, and cut back on ships that would take two or three years to build, setting out to augment the destroyer fleet, for although First Lord of the Admiralty

Churchill was hopeful, he was also mindful that the Germans might build two or three hundred submarines in the next year or so. For that reason, naval construction must be maintained, and help sought everywhere it could be available. The naval force was augmented, too, in September, when three Polish destroyers and two submarines escaped from Polish waters and appeared in England.

Four divisions of British troops were formed into the British Expeditionary Force, and prepared to go to France and join the defense line, but there was no fighting on the land, and the British government, so as not to provoke the Germans into action, did not even allow the aerial bombing of military objectives inside Germany.

But even the expeditionary force was deficient in weaponry—not enough tanks and mortars and other infantry weapons.

In this sense, the war had its "phony" side, as British and Germans waited for the other shoe to drop. But that did not mean that Britain had any questions in mind about prosecuting this war. The problem was that Britain had not really thought about a general war almost until the day war was declared. Nothing like the German *Oberkommando Wehrmacht* existed, there was no supreme command. It was relatively easy for the Royal Navy to pull itself together, because it had always to be in a state of readiness anyhow. But as for the Royal Air Force and the Army, it was totally different, and as of the date of the war's opening, the men involved did not know quite where they were going or what they wanted. In the first month, the British government set up a committee to advise on the size and constitution of the British Imperial Army that would be created to fight Germany, and it was settled that fifty-five divisions would be manned, two-thirds of them to be ready in eighteen months. The Air Ministry fought against the proposal, making its own plans for an all-powerful, overwhelming air force that it wanted to create in two or three years, on the premise that air power would decide the war.

The outside world, the Germans, and particularly the

Americans wondered why the British did not bomb the Germans. The policy was deliberate, and it, again, related to Britain's needs. London and other cities were feverishly building bomb shelters and other defenses, of which there had been none prior to the outbreak of war. Winston Churchill put it this way:

"We should not take the initiative in bombing, except in the immediate zone in which the French armies are operating, where we must, of course, help. It is to our interest that the war should be conducted in accordance with the more humane conceptions of war, and that we should follow and not precede the Germans in the process, no doubt inevitable, of deepening severity and violence. Every day that passes gives more shelter to the population of London and the big cities."

Weapons were an enormous problem for a country that had stored away its war materials from the 1914–18 war. Big guns of 1918 were brought forth and refurbished and polished up, but they were still big guns of 1918 and not the guns of 1939. Small wonder that Britain was playing for time before the war became real and deadly; everything in her arsenal was in a state of flux. Germany, the aggressor nation which had planned for war, had an enormous advantage in these early months, and although the German generals did not know it, Hitler did.

CHAPTER 14

Hot War at Sea, Cold War in France

Only in the spring of 1938 had the British realized that the threat of war with Germany was real and that some planning had best be done. The War Office set up a special section then, but by September 1939, its plans were still far from complete. So wrapped up in thoughts of peace were the British that for several years there had been no war games at all: the regular army was short twenty thousand men, and five thousand of those were officers. In fact, as the four divisions of the British Expeditionary Force made ready to sail for France, it was not yet known where they would set up camp. It was finally decided that they would deploy south of Lille along the Belgian-French frontier.

The question of getting the British troops to France was another poser. The high command had developed an inordinate fear of air power, and expected the troop ships to be bombed if they came within range of German aircraft, so only the southern French harbors were used. This meant a long voyage and then a long trip of 250 miles back up from the South to the border area. The trek began in September with dispatch of an advance party and continued into October and November, so that ultimately five divisions reached France.

They were formed into two army groups, which went into a defense line not far from, but not in contact with, the enemy, and there began building pillboxes and other defenses. When the British troops arrived, they were assigned to a sector behind an antitank ditch, with a pillbox about every one thousand yards, which provided enfilade fire along the ditch. So the British organized what they called a sort of Siegfried Line here, with a continuous belt of barbed wire along the front. It seemed very formidable. By spring 1940, they had built four hundred pillboxes, but still there was no fighting. Five more divisions of British troops came over to France, and still they did nothing but sit and wait. In fact, the respite was invaluable, because the men trained and trained and trained. They needed every bit of it, for most of them had learned little but how to march and how to salute.

By May they had forty more miles of revetted antitank ditch and huge quantities of barbed wire spread in great coils along it. The British were coming to stay for a while. They built fifty airfields and established communications lines with buried cable reaching back to Nantes, and spreading along corps and army commands.

The British poured in supplies and ammunition, until they had ten days supply between the Seine and the Somme, and seven days more supply north of the River Somme. They found that they were not bombed, so gradually began to use other ports to the north of Le Havre, until they operated in thirteen French ports altogether.

The French had many more miles of Maginot Line, but only around Metz were they in contact with the Germans, and that contact, by mutual agreement, it seemed, was limited to patrol actions.

Meanwhile on the other side, the Germans were working hard to extend and strengthen their West Wall along the Siegfried Line. Western air power at this point was largely devoted to intelligence work, and aerial photos showed the Germans extending the Siegfried Line northward from the Moselle River.

Even as Hitler spoke about peace to the *Reichstag* in early October 1939, he had provisionally fixed the date for the attack on France at October 25. But when that date approached, his generals told him it was impossible: The tanks used in Poland were still being overhauled, and tank parts were in very short supply; some units were still waiting for them. The weather was very spotty and not at all suitable for armored operations. Hitler was willing to wait; he wanted several good days running of flying weather for Goering's Luftwaffe. So October passed with rain and mist.

At sea the hot war continued. At the end of September, Grand Admiral Raeder ordered the pocket battleships *Deutschland* and *Graf Spee* to go into action. They had been waiting, and Hitler had been hoping France, at least, would withdraw from the war. But it had not happened, so the war was to be brought to France, too, in order to put pressure on her government. A restriction on U-boats against sinking French vessels was removed, as well. The U-boats continued their sinkings. September ended with the sinking of 153,000 tons of shipping; October was about the same. But there was one coup for the Germans at sea in October, an event that shook the British navy from stem to stern.

Admiral Doenitz's submarine command staff at Wilhelmshaven had been following the movements of the British navy and came up with the idea that a U-boat might penetrate the British Home Fleet anchorage at Scapa Flow in the Orkney Islands of Scotland. This was tried twice during World War I, but both attempts failed and the U-boats were lost. In 1939, however, matters concerning U-boats had changed a great deal. The airplane had made it possible to examine and map the enemy's territory, and by studying photographs and charts, Admiral Doenitz had concluded that an approach to Scapa Flow through the narrow Kirk Sound might work. If a U-boat could sink a capital ship there, it would have a devastating effect on British morale, Doenitz thought. It would also give him an enormous boost with Hitler, who had so far not been much interested in Doenitz's pleas for three hundred U-boats with which to assault the British sea lanes. What was needed was an experienced U-boat skipper who was long on patience and navigation. He turned up in the person of Lieutenant Guenther Prien, commander of *U-47*. Doenitz called him in, swore him to secrecy, asked if Prien wanted to try the desperate mission, and gave him forty-eight hours to think it over. Prien studied the charts, decided that it was just possible to make that attack and survive, and said he wanted the job.

Prien was again sworn to secrecy and then left to ponder the charts and find his way. He, in turn, left port in secrecy, not even his officers knowing where he was bound, and he maintained a closed mouth until October 13, when he was almost in position near the Orkneys. Only then did he tell the crew what they were going to try to do, and he was half-afraid they might balk, because movement into the heart of the enemy fleet territory was about the most dangerous task a U-boat captain could ask of his crew.

But the crew responded with cheers, and so the dangerous mission began. Doenitz had set the date after consulting with his weathermen. It was the dark of the moon, a perfect night. But then as darkness became complete, the aurora borealis began to light up, and the sky threatened to betray the U-boat. To go on or not to go on, that was the question. Prien knew that if they did not make the attack this night, it would be several months before the tidal and moon conditions would be right again. So he decided to continue.

Kirk Sound was regarded by the British as impassable, because they had sunk several blockships there. In fact, Prien ran aground and fouled the cable of one of the blockships. But at about half past twelve that night, the *U-47* was through and into the main anchorage area. To the north, Prien saw two big warships and several smaller ones anchored there, one of them of the *Royal Oak* class, he thought, and the other of the *Repulse* class.

Cautiously Prien moved in, on the surface. If the British saw the *U-47*, they thought it was a British boat, for it seemed impossible to believe that the sanctuary of the Home Fleet could be penetrated by the enemy. He moved closer and closer. From four thousand yards he fired four torpedoes from the bow tubes. Three went true, but one misfired. One of the torpedoes struck the side of a ship, but it did little damage, so little that the captain thought the impact was from an internal explosion. Prien turned away, expecting to be attacked at any moment, but no one paid any attention to him.

When it was clear that the British were not in any way suspicious, even now, Prien had the men reload the bow torpedo tubes. He headed back toward the ship he had hit before, and fired another salvo at 1:16 A.M. This time a torpedo struck a magazine, and giant columns of water and smoke and fire shot into the air. Wreckage began shooting up and falling into the water around the U-boat. Thirteen minutes later, the ship sank.

Prien was confident that he had sunk a battleship, but he did not know then which one. It was, in fact, the *Royal Oak*, and she went down with 24 officers and 809 men, including the admiral in command.

Suddenly the British realized they had been attacked and searchlights began to probe the harbor, and ships got up steam. Prien ordered all power, and began running out of Kirk Sound as fast as he could go. He left a wake, and it was spotted by a British destroyer, which gave chase, but then turned away and began dropping depth charges on some object, perhaps thinking Prien's was a friendly craft. Prien clung to the cover of the coastline; he could see automobile lights flashing along the road by the shore, but nothing happened, and he got clean away, using the electric motors hooked up to the diesels for greater speed. They came to the narrows, threaded it again successfully, went out between the blockship and the wooden jetty, and finally were out in open sea and fairly safe.

So the mission had been a success. Had they waited,

it would not have been, because the British had brought up another blockship to go into Kirk Sound, and it was sunk there the next day. But all was well that ended well, for the Germans at least; the job was done. The British were told the truth; they admitted the sinking of a major battleship and identified it as the *Royal Oak*, and Lieutenant Prien had one of the great coups of World War II.

Three days later, the Luftwaffe staged its first air raid on the British fleet. A dozen bombers came over the Firth of Forth and bombed, damaging the cruisers *Southampton* and *Edinburgh* and the destroyer *Mohawk*. Twenty-five officers and men were killed, but the naval fighters shot down three bombers, and the antiaircraft guns brought down another. Next day the Germans were back, attacking Scapa Flow from the air, and sank a battleship. When they returned to base, they crowed, but the fact was that the ship was the old *Iron Duke*, outmoded even in World War I, and now good for nothing but work as depot ship. She sank to the bottom just a few feet below her keel and rested there for the remainder of the war, functioning as she had before. One more German aircraft was shot down in this raid.

By mid-October the *Deutschland* and the *Graf Spee* had sunk seven British ships and taken as a prize the American ship *City of Flint*, on the basis that she was carrying war materials for the British. But the war at sea was not all one-sided, as the British gained skill in combating the U-boats. Soon the number of U-boat sinkings would increase.

In spite of the hopes of the German navy, Hitler was not really paying attention to the war at sea, which was in reality his first line of offense against England. He was bemused with the coming attack on the Western powers in France. The generals were stalling, and one of them, General Wilhelm Ritter von Leeb, made so bold as to suggest that the planned attack through the lowlands was immoral, illegal as well as controversial from a military point of view. Von Leeb also suggested that the German people wanted peace.

But Hitler wanted war. He was tired of the stalling, and on October 14 he called in Generals Halder and Brauchitsch. Nothing was decided. Brauchitsch saw Hitler again on October 17, and this time the impatient Hitler demanded action not later than November 20. "The British will be ready to talk only after a beating," he said. "We must get at them as quickly as possible."

The arguments with Halder and Brauchitsch continued. The result was first a change in the manner of operations of the top German decision makers. Previously everything had been decided informally by verbal directives, with Hitler as supreme commander and Keitel as his personal chief of staff of *Oberkommando Wehrmacht*. But as Hitler continued to lose faith in his generals, and they in him, the verbal was supplanted by the written. OKW's staff wrote up the orders and elaborated to Hitler's ideas, and then they were issued over the signature of Hitler or of Keitel. Thus, because of the quarrels with Brauchitsch and Halder, the army lost its primary position and easy access to Hitler.

On October 27 Hitler laid down the law to his generals. He gave out a handful of medals, and then made a speech to the assembled generals about the coming attack on the West. The meeting ended in violent words and recrimination. A few days later, it was repeated. Hitler kept setting dates for the attack—November 7, November 9— and then postponed them when the army said it was patently impossible. But every postponement was accompanied by tirades against the army by Hitler. One day General Brauchitsch left the chancellery in a state of shock and did not remember how he got from there to the army headquarters in Zossen, eighteen miles away. He tried to resign, but Hitler would not let him. Finally he was reduced virtually to despair and stopped arguing with Hitler. And the debate went on, with fourteen postponements of the date of attack by the Germans.

On October 13 the British Admiralty announced the sinking of three U-boats in one day, a new record. But of course, the good news was immediately outbalanced by the sinking of the *Royal Oak* and all that implied. The British had to move their fleet from Scapa Flow until its defenses could be assured. What to do? Where to go? They could move to the River Clyde, but this would put the battle fleet far from the scene of activity and would mean a need for more destroyers, when destroyers were already in short supply. The other alternative, and it was chosen, was Rosyth, which was much nearer to London.

The move and the protection of the fleet occupied the Royal Navy's planning efforts for the next few weeks, but the war at sea continued. Submarine sinkings of vessels were about the same in October as September, but they fell off in November, largely because Doenitz was having troubles of his own with maintenance and shortages.

But the submarine was not Germany's only naval offensive weapon. The reconstitution of the German fleet in the 1930s had been partly an attempt to challenge the British fleet, but also to build big, fast ships that could raid the seas. The *Graf Spee* and the *Deutschland* were already out. A big threat now came from the reports that the *Scharnhorst* and the *Gneisenau*, two battle cruisers, again overbuilt according to the Versailles specifications, were going to go out and scour the seas. It was hard for the British to contain such activity if the big ships could break through the blockade, which meant running around the north of Britain and getting into the open sea of the Atlantic. Then they could work the North American sea lanes, or go south to hit South American traffic and the traffic coming up from Africa. For, of course, with the war and the uncertainty in the Mediterranean, sea traffic from India and the Pacific had been routed down around the Cape of Good Hope.

On the afternoon of November 23, the armed merchant cruiser *Rawalpindi* was patrolling the blockade area, between Iceland and the Faroe Islands, when her lookouts sighted a warship. Since Britain had a shortage of patrol vessels, she was employing big merchantmen, mostly passenger liners, which were given several guns and sent out to stop German merchant traffic and to check on neutrals in the war zone. They were not intended to take on major enemy warships, but before anyone knew, the *Rawalpindi* was hauling up on this other vessel. The *Rawalpindi* had four old six-inch guns, relics of World War I. The vessel she was approaching was actually the German battle cruiser *Scharnhorst*, although the captain of the *Rawalpindi* thought it was the pocket battleship *Deutschland*. Even so, it was an act of great bravery, for each was as deadly as the other to the merchant cruiser.

In half an hour the *Rawalpindi* was blazing from one end to the other and was dead in the water. She sank after darkness fell, with her captain, and 270 members of the crew. Only 38 survived. The Germans picked up 27 of them, and the other 11 men were rescued two days later by a British ship.

The Germans were not happy with the encounter. They had gone out of port two days before, in company with the *Gneisenau*, but instead of running the British blockade and getting to open sea, they had the misfortune of fighting one of the merchant cruisers. Now all the Royal Navy would be on the lookout for them, so the element of surprise had been destroyed. The captain of the *Scharnhorst* then decided that the game was not worth it, and he and the *Gneisenau* headed back into a German port, to wait and try again.

One reason for the decision was the speed with which the British reacted. The *Rawalpindi* was still afloat when the cruiser *Newcastle* came by, saw what was happening, and with the cruiser *Delhi*, began to pursue the Germans. It was much too uncomfortable for the Germans then, and they could expect to have the Home Fleet after them soon. The *Newcastle* almost came up close enough for battle, but when she approached the two ships, she saw in the gathering darkness, six-fifteen at night, that the weather was closing in. In the gloom, the *Newcastle* lost the Germans, and they escaped further trouble.

Indeed, the Royal Navy moved that night, and in two directions to anticipate German action. Several ships set off into the North Sea to intercept the Germans on their way home. But in case the two cruisers had decided to double back and run the blockade, sea and air patrol were hurried out to watch all exits from the North Sea, and a force of cruisers was sent along the coast of Norway. In the Atlantic the battleship *Warspite* searched in the Denmark Strait, a principal route of egress from the blockade area, and the *Hood*, the *Repulse*, the *Furious*, and the French battle cruiser *Dunquerque* searched, too, from Halifax to Iceland. By November 25, fourteen British cruisers were on the watch for the Germans, with destroyers, submarines, and air cover all cooperating.

On November 28 Radio Berlin boasted that Guenther Prien's *U-47* had just sunk another major British warship, and for several hours there was a great stir at Royal Navy headquarters. But the report proved untrue. What had happened was that the *U-47* had tracked the *Norfolk* as she was searching for the German warships, and Skipper Prien had fired torpedoes at her. One torpedo had exploded in her wake, and the upheaval of water had convinced Prien that he had a hit. He had dived deep, and when he came up, he saw no cruiser, so he hopefully assumed that he had sunk her.

Meanwhile, heading for the Baltic and safety, the two big German ships had approached the Norwegian coast on the morning of November 26. The weather was blockade runner's weather, thick fog and heavy overcast. The British cruiser line neither saw nor heard anything, and the Germans passed through to safety. For seven days the search continued, and then it was obvious that somehow the Germans had gotten through the net, and normal activity was resumed.

At this point, the sinking of the *Royal Oak*, and the escape of the two German battle cruisers after destroying the *Rawalpindi*, created a most unfavorable public impression of the Royal Navy. Partly to counter this, First Sea Lord Winston Churchill made a visit to France to coordinate British and French naval activity in the hope of more success.

Churchill was expecting an increase in German U-boat

activity as the winter came. He wanted the fullest co-operation of the French.

Britain was building warships as fast as possible. Six large destroyers had been started in 1936 and would be ready in 1940, but they were needed for ocean convoys. Fourteen small destroyers had been started in 1939 which should also be completed in 1940. Britain was also building eighteen minesweepers and sixteen submarine chasers. But he could not expect the new ships he was building to be ready before the end of 1940, and that was still a long way away. He arranged for the British to supply the French with the asdic antisubmarine system, and prepared to supply every French antisubmarine craft. He hoped the French would send at least fifty vessels to Portland, the asdic center.

Soon the British would be bringing elements of the Canadian and Australian armies to France to engage in the war, and they would need help. They intended to keep the blockade in the North from Greenland to Scotland, which would require twenty-five armed cruisers and four 8-inch gun cruisers, plus the battleships and others in case of a breakout by a major German vessel.

The French were most cooperative. They accepted the British offer of asdic, and promised to put the new *Richelieu* and *Jean Bart* at community service when they were completed in the summer and fall of 1940.

In this autumn of 1939 the Germans unleashed a new weapon that they hoped would help bring the British to surrender. It was the magnetic mine, a high-explosive underwater device that would be attracted by the vibration of ship's engines and metal contact. During September and October, a number of merchant ships had been sunk, particularly at the entrance to British harbors in the North Sea, and the Admiralty suspected the small coastal submarines and the magnetic mine. They were quite right. Minelaying at harbor entrances was a primary job of the smaller U-boats that fall. These boats, called by their crews "canoes," were so small that they could carry only a handful of torpedoes, and their range was very limited, but they were admirable as minelayers.

The Admiralty was quite at a loss as to how to combat this menace about which they knew so little. It had so far cost the British fifty-six thousand tons of shipping. But in November, all that changed one day. Admiral Pound came to see Churchill at his country house, to state that the day before, six ships had been sunk in the approaches to the Thames by mines. How the mines were arriving was not quite known, but the British suspected it was a combination of air drops and submarine laying.

Then one November day, the British had a break. On November 22 a German plane dropped a large object with a parachute into the sea near Shoeburyness. The pilot could not have chosen a better place, from the Admiralty's point of view. The tide varies a great deal and the bottom was mud, which meant the mine should be very safe to handle.

Specialists in underwater weapons were called, and that same night they found the mine five hundred yards below the high-water mark. They plotted its position, and the next time the tide dropped, they undertook to take the mine apart without blowing it up. It took the combined efforts for four experts to dismantle this mine, and there was another waiting for them a few yards off. The mines were taken to Plymouth for study by the antimine warfare people, and soon a defense was devised, involving mine sweeping and premature explosion of the mine fuses. But the most effective method of combating the mines was by the process of "degaussing" invented by the British. It involved the girdling of ships with electric cable which demagnetized their steel hulls and made these mines ineffectual.

But before degaussing could become standard procedure, several ships were hit. The cruiser *Belfast* was damaged, and the battleship *Nelson* was mined at Loch Ewe. Two destroyers were lost and two more damaged on the North Sea coast. In addition, although the German efforts at sea were hampered by bad weather in November, they did not stop, and the U-boat war continued. The score of ships sunk by U-boats in November was down to twenty-one with a total of fifty-two thousand tons, and in December it was only slightly higher, at eighty-one thousand tons. But more U-boats were starting to come to the fleet, and this indicated problems for the British in the months ahead.

CHAPTER 15

The Graf Spee

1. Your mission is to reach the Atlantic unobserved, and even there you are at first to avoid every ship that appears on the horizon. These instructions must be obeyed even after hostilities have broken out between Great Britain and Germany, until you receive a radio order to go into action.

2. Your mission is then to disrupt and strangle enemy shipping by every available means. You are as far as possible to avoid contact with enemy naval forces. Even inferior warships should only be engaged if such action is conducive to your main task of interfering with the enemy's supply lines.

3. Frequent change of location in the operational area will have the effect of bewildering the enemy and will at the same time obstruct shipping, even if no directly perceptible results are achieved. Evasive action from time to time in remote sea areas will likewise increase the enemy's perplexity.

Oberkommando Marin orders to Captain Lansdorff of the pocket battleship *Graf Spee*.

On August 15, 1939, Admiral Raeder reported to Hitler that the pocket battleships *Deutschland* and *Graf Spee* were ready to sail for their stations in the Atlantic Ocean. What did this mean? That no matter what Hitler said about his hopes that the Polish war would be sequestered and not lead to World War II, he had to be prepared for that eventuality. If it came, the twenty-one submarines available at the moment would be put to work, and above all these two big ships, in which Admiral Raeder placed so much hope.

On August 19 the *Graf Spee* moved out toward the Brazilian coast and the *Deutschland* moved to the British sea lanes in the North Atlantic. Again they waited.

During the first week of hostilities, the German U-boats sank eleven British ships. Then, suddenly, the sinking stopped. That change came about because Hitler conferred with Admiral Raeder and ordered the navy to go slow. Hitler was very pleased with his initial victories in Poland in the first week of September, and also with the failure of the French to attack on the ground, and the failure of the British to bomb German cities. Hitler had the feeling that the war could be stopped, and so he told Raeder to put his two big pocket battleships back in mothballs for the moment. "The general policy would be to exercise restraint until the political situation in the West has become clearer, which would take about a week," wrote Raeder in his diary.

Actually it took considerably more time, before Hitler was convinced that he could not have the easy peace he wanted.

The *Graf Spee* had disappeared on August 21, and nothing more was heard of her whereabouts, except that she was out somewhere in the Atlantic, until September 30. On that day the *Graf Spee* sank her first ship, the five-thousand-ton British liner *Clement*, off Pernambuco. Then in short order came news that three freighters, the *Ashlea*, the *Newton Beach*, and the *Huntsman*, had vanished off the west coast of Africa.

In London, the news that a raider was out in the South Atlantic brought the most serious concern. Here is Winston Churchill's recollection:

It was by no means clear to the Admiralty whether in fact one raider was on the prowl or two and exertions were made, both in the Indian and Atlantic oceans. We also thought that the *Spee* was her sister ship, the *Scheer*. This disproportion between the strength of the enemy and the countermeasures forced upon us was vexatious. It recalled to me the anxious weeks before the actions at Coronel and later at the Falkland Islands, in December 1914, when we had to be prepared at seven or eight different points in the Pacific and South Atlantic for the arrival of Admiral von Spee with the earlier edition of the *Scharnhorst* and *Gneisenau*. A quarter of a century had passed, but the puzzle was the same. It was with a definite sense of relief that we learnt that the *Spee* had appeared once more on the Cape-Freetown route, sinking two more ships on December 2 and one on the seventh . . .

But there were others sunk before, such as the *Trevanian* and the tanker *Africa Shell*, on November 15, whose captain, Patrick Dove, was taken prisoner aboard the *Graf Spee*, although his crew got away in the ship's boats. He claimed the ship was captured inside the territorial waters of the Portuguese colony of Mozambique, a charge that was ignored by the *Graf Spee*. Many of the crewmen of these ships were held captive, aboard the supply tanker *Altmark*.

The hunt off the South American coast was conducted by Commodore Henry Harwood-Harwood, with the eight-inch gun cruisers *Cumberland* and *Exeter* and the six-inch gun cruisers *Ajax* and *Achilles*. It was true that the pocket battleship outgunned them and outsped them, with twenty-eight knots and six 11-inch guns and eight 6-inch guns . . . but . . .

What was also clear as December came was that the German navy's estimate of the damage that could be done by a raider was precisely correct, and that unless the British could eliminate this one, their whole lifeline to South America and to Africa was in jeopardy.

CHAPTER 16

The Battle of the River Plate

Before the invasion of Poland, Hitler's directives to his Wehrmacht had included instructions to the German navy to go into action against the British if they declared war. The two pocket battleships *Graf Spee* and *Deutschland* were sent to get out into the Atlantic, before the British imposed a blockade around Scotland, and wait to see what happened. When war came on September 3, the two ships were ordered into action. The *Deutschland* did not accomplish much. In two and a half months, she sank only two small ships traveling alone, and captured the *City of Flint*, an American ship that was carrying war materials to Britain, but the *Graf Spee* headed off into the South Atlantic and was soon heard from. These ships, built generally within the ten-thousand-ton limitation imposed on the German navy by the Treaty of Versailles, each carried six 11-inch guns, larger than anything but a British battle cruiser, and were capable of making twenty-six knots, which was a fast speed in 1939. The combination made the *Graf Spee* a formidable warship, ideal for the task of commerce raiding, which was her reason for being.

The *Graf Spee* crossed the North Atlantic trade route

and headed south of the Azores Islands. She was accompanied by an auxiliary merchantman, which carried fuel and stores for her. Until September 30, that was all that was known about the *Graf Spee*, that she was out and that her job would be disruption of the British overseas trade. As noted, on that day she sank the British liner *Clement*, five thousand tons, off Pernambuco. Immediately the British Royal Navy swung into action. All the major resources of the fleet were turned out to hunt the two pocket battleships, including the five carriers and four battleships. In the next few weeks, nine hunting groups would be formed, comprising twenty-three ships. If any proof was needed as to how important Britain considered her sea lanes, that was it. The resources of the Home Fleet and the Mediterranean Fleet were considerably strained to provide this much coverage, but the raider could not be allowed to operate without chase.

In the next few weeks, the *Graf Spee* operated in the South African route, and sank three ships, but no one knew it, because those ships were all traveling alone, and it as only after they did not turn up in their designated ports of arrival after a reasonable time that it was presumed they were lost. In November the *Deutschland* moved back to Germany, but the *Graf Spee* stayed out in the Atlantic working off the Cape of Good Hope and as far as the Indian Ocean. The *Graf Spee* was successful because she followed a pattern laid down by the light cruiser *Emden* in World War I. She would make an appearance at some place, take a ship or two and then disappear, and reappear far from the last place. On November 15, at about the time the *Deutschland* was getting home, the *Graf Spee* sank a ship in the Mozambique Channel between Madagascar East Africa in the Indian Ocean. But then Captain Langsdorff doubled back and moved around the Cape into the South Atlantic. On December 2 she sank two ships near the Cape, and then another ship December 7. Several groups began looking for the *Graf Spee*, but she suddenly disappeared again. Commodore Henry Harwood-Harwood, the British officer in charge of defenses off Rio de Janeiro and the

River Plate, as noted, had a feeling that the *Graf Spee* was now coming his way.

After the December sinkings, Commodore Harwood-Harwood estimated that the *Graf Spee* would head for the River Plate and would arrive on the thirteenth, so he planned to be there too. One of his cruisers, the *Cumberland*, was laid up for supplies, but the three others were available. So on the night of December 12, the British ships were off the Plate, and sure enough, at 6:14 in the morning of December 13, the *Graf Spee* showed up.

Captain Langsdorff at first thought he saw one light cruiser and two destroyers, but soon realized that the ships were more powerful. He could have turned away and escaped at least temporarily, but he chose to fight, and came on so that the two forces were approaching each another at fifty miles per hour. The *Graf Spee* then trained her guns on the *Exeter*, the largest of the British cruisers. Soon they were in range and the *Exeter* was firing and hitting the *Graf Spee*. But the *Graf Spee* put an eleven-inch shell into the *Exeter*'s B turret, which destroyed the turret, and knocked out the ship's communications to the bridge. The *Exeter* was out of the action for the moment, until steering control could be regained. The *Graf Spee* then turned its attention to the light cruisers.

But soon she was receiving so much fire that she turned away into the River Plate, under a smoke screen. She again fired on the *Exeter*, which had one turret working for a time, but then the power failed and the *Exeter* was out of the fight. She had taken more than a hundred shells, one turret was smashed, and three guns were knocked out; sixty officers and men were killed, and another twenty wounded.

The *Ajax* and the *Achilles* continued to pursue the German ship. But soon the two after turrets of the *Ajax* had been wrecked by the German fire, and Commodore Harwood-Harwood turned away from the action, taking both light cruisers. The *Graf Spee* went into Montevideo, and began to land her wounded and take on stores from the supply ship that was waiting for her there.

That night the *Cumberland*, which had been in the Falklands, left port and hurried to the scene. She arrived on the fourteenth and took position outside the harbor.

Captain Langsdorff then asked Berlin for instructions. He was trying to lengthen his stay at Montevideo, but international law gave him only seventy hours. He had landed his wounded and taken supplies from the German supply ship. Now what should he do if he had to go out? Should he seek internment, or should he scuttle the ship? The British were bringing up battleships and aircraft carriers, so it seemed most unlikely he could escape.

When this news reached Berlin, Hitler was furious. He wanted the *Graf Spee* to go down fighting to the last man. He told Langsdorff to fight or scuttle, but not to take internment.

So on the afternoon of December 17, Captain Langsdorff moved most of the crew of the *Graf Spee*, with their bags and provisions, from the warship to the German auxiliary ship in the harbor, and shortly afterwards, the *Graf Spee* weighed anchor. At 6:15 that evening an enormous crowd of Uruguayans came down to the harbor to see the great ship sail, and she moved out toward the sea.

Outside the territorial waters of Uruguay, the British warships waited and their seaplanes circled, watching for the enemy ship to come in sight. But they were disappointed. At 8:54 that evening the sun went down, and shortly afterward the aircraft of the *Ajax* reported that the *Graf Spee* had "blown herself up." Captain Langsdorff had not wanted to see if his crew destroyed, fighting a hopeless battle, and he had not wanted to give up his ship, so he scuttled her. Hitler, of course, had wanted a gallant fight to the end that he could use for propaganda purposes, and he did not care about the fate of the crew. They got off, and took to boats, and soon made it to Buenos Aires and safety. There, two days later, Captain Langsdorff committed suicide. Although he had been given full permission to do as he felt best under the circumstances, Langsdorff must have learned in Buenos Aires the full extent of Hitler's displeasure.

* * *

What an affair it had been, and how costly to the British. They had stripped their Home and Mediterranean fleets to put four battleships and battle cruisers, fourteen cruisers, including four French ships, five carriers, and scores of destroyers into the chase of this single ship. They had searched from the Indian Ocean to the Cape of Good Hope, and from the Cape to Freetown in Northwest Africa, down the center of the South Atlantic and along the South American shore. At the end the battleship *Renown* and the carrier *Ark Royal*, which had been at Capetown, were heading toward the scene, as was the cruiser *Neptune* and three destroyers. Besides, four other forces were sweeping down on the single German vessel.

This enormous effort was an indication of the importance the British put on their ocean lifelines. On December 23 when the American republics, including the United States, protested that the action on the Plate was a violation of the American security zone, the British got a little testy, because they knew as well as anyone the amount of pro-German feeling in such places as Montevideo and Buenos Aires. They did not really apologize but instead stressed the importance of keeping the seas free of raiding, in the interests of all concerned.

As First Lord of the Admiralty Churchill put it at the end of the year:

"The presence of even a single raider in the North Atlantic called for the employment of half our battle fleet to give sure protection to the world's commerce. The unlimited laying of magnetic mines by the enemy was adding to the strain on our flotillas and small craft. If we should break under this strain, the South American Republics would soon have many worse worries than the sound of one day's distant seaward cannonade and in a short time the United States would also face more direct cares."

The French were still in the war, but Britain felt very much alone. As Churchill added in his assessment, the end of 1939 left the war still in its "sinister trance." No ally had appeared on the horizon, and the British found the Americans distinctly cool to their overtures. True, the British Empire was coming to the fore, troops from Canada and Australia were arriving to share the load, but the attitude of the Americans was a matter of serious concern in London. The Americans gave no sign of knowing what was at stake in this war, and that Hitler regarded them as one of his implacable enemies to be dealt with when the proper time came.

CHAPTER 17

The Fruits of Conspiracy

Until the 1990s, the world paid very little attention to what happened in the Baltic region in the fall of 1939 and the winter of 1940, so obscured was the fate of the nations involved by the greater tragedies of Poland and Western Europe. It was, as it turned out, all part of the same pattern of the expansion of totalitarianism and a continuation of the uneasy conspiracy between the Nazis and the Soviet Communists that was a prelude to the deadly struggle they engaged in later.

In the offer to partition Poland and wreck the Baltic states of Estonia, Lithuania, and Latvia, the Germans had opened the eyes of Stalin to the possibility of extending his empire to the west. He welcomed the opportunity. The Soviets marched into Poland on September 17, and armed with an agreement with Hitler that gave the Russians free movement in the Baltic, on September 24, the Estonian foreign minister was summoned arbitrarily to Moscow, and within the week, his government signed a pact of "mutual assistance" with the Russians, which gave Stalin the right to have bases in Estonia and garrison them. Within a month the Red Army had taken the bases and was building airfields. The same techniques were used on Latvia and Lithuania. So before November 1, 1939, the Russians controlled the road to Leningrad, by way of the Baltic states. The second route to Russia for Germany was across the Gulf of Finland, and this, too, was protected by the new bases against the German aggression the Russians expected at some time in the not distant future.

One area of approach from Germany remained, and this was through Finland, by way of Poland and the Scandinavian countries, which Stalin fully expected Hitler to occupy.

In October 1939, J. K. Paasikivi went to Moscow representing the Finnish government, to negotiate some demands of the USSR. The demands were enormous:

1. The Finnish frontier must be moved back more than twenty miles to protect Leningrad from hostile artillery fire.
2. Several islands in the Gulf of Finland must be ceded to Russia.
3. The Russians must have a lease on the Rybathy Peninsula and a port on the Arctic sea, Petsamo.
4. The port of Hango, which lies at the entrance to the Gulf of Finland, must be leased to the Russians as a naval and air base.

The Finns were ready to concede all but the last demand, and they refused that because it would destroy the national security of Finland. The Russians insisted. The Finns resisted. The negotiations lasted more than a month but then broke down on November 13, and the Finnish government began to mobilize its reserve army forces and strengthen the defenses on the Karelian Peninsula. On November 28 the Soviets announced that they would no longer honor the Russian-Finnish nonaggression alliance and on November 30 they crossed the frontier and attacked the Finns. Finnish defenses were most difficult because they shared a thousand-mile border with the Russians.

The strength of the Russian attack was against the defenses on the Karelian Peninsula, the part of Finland the Russians coveted, and the major onslaught came against the Mannerheim Line, a defensive system that extended back twenty miles from the border, running the width of the peninsula through forest country that already was deep in snow.

The unprovoked attack aroused indignation in Britain and France and in the United States, which had a fairly large Finnish population. The League of Nations expelled the Soviet Union for aggression. The British and French began to talk of war with the Soviet Union as well as Germany. One of the most provocative actions of the Soviets, before the Finnish attack, was an agreement with the Germans to purchase needed goods abroad and ship them to Germany, thus making the British blockade of Germany largely ineffective. But the French had a serious problem: their Communist Party, which followed the Moscow line, denounced the governments of Britain and France as capitalistic, while praising Germany, which, the line now held, had joined Russia in the anticapitalist camp.

The British were much more concerned with what happened in Scandinavia than the French seemed to be, because they knew that the German war industry of the Ruhr Valley was largely dependent on ore from Sweden, which reached Germany in the winter, transshipped from the port of Narvik on the west coast of Norway. The British navy wanted to mine the area, to prevent the Germans from shipping ores, but the foreign office objected to violations of neutrality, and so nothing was done that fall of 1939. For that reason, Winston Churchill as advocate of the navy, and some others, saw in the Russian attack on Finland an opportunity to help Finland resist the Russians, and at the same time solve the iron ore shipment problem.

The Finns resisted the Russian invasion stoutly and with surprising effectiveness. The Finnish army of two hundred thousand men fought very well, and the Russians got no place. The Russians from the first bombed Helsinki, the capital of Finland, and other cities, but if they expected to strike terror in the hearts of the Finnish people, they were disappointed. Their invasion was first carried out by troops of the Leningrad garrison who were not well trained, certainly not in the arts of winter fighting in snow country, while the Finns were expert skiers and forest fighters. The Russians penetrated about thirty miles in the peninsula region, but then were set upon by flankers, who attacked day and night. By the end of December, the Soviet plans were in shambles, and they had suffered heavy losses. It was divisions against battalions, but that made no difference; in almost every area, the Russians were turned back or stalled. Against the Mannerheim Line, the Russians threw twelve divisions, but they had the wrong equipment, light tanks and inadequate artillery, and they suffered heavy losses.

By the end of 1939 the Russians stopped to reconsider. Stalin could see that the conquest of Finland, instead of being easy, was going to be a real problem, demanding major military effort. This, in turn, took preparation, so at the end of the year the front became apparently as stagnant as was the western front of the Germans, and for the same basic reasons. The Russians had decided to launch their major effort against the Mannerheim Line, and they had to bring up equipment and reserves for a siege.

In Britain the emotional fires of enthusiasm for the Finnish cause were strengthened by the fact that to help the Finns, they would be using the same railroad that carried iron ore to Narvik. Admiralty First Lord Churchill saw that by helping the Finns with supplies and even volunteers, he could make a sort of base of Narvik that would keep the Germans from using that port and would seriously affect the German war effort. He presented this case to the cabinet, but again got no action, because the rest of the members of the cabinet were too much concerned about the violation of Norwegian and Swedish neutrality. All the Scandinavian countries were trying to stay out of World War II, and they thought they might be able to do so by remaining totally uncommitted, which showed how little they knew their Hitler.

In France, too, there was even talk of bombing the Russian oil fields in the Caucasus to help the Finns, and a plan was made to do so beginning March 15. Also a French expeditionary force was to be sent to Finland in March, 1940. But when the French and the British began negotiations with Sweden and Norway to send troops through their territory, the repercussions were immediate. In the end the plans had to be shelved and Finland really had to be left to her own fate. Despite the Soviet miscalculations, that fate had to be obvious for a small country on the border of a very large one.

One corollary result of the Finnish war was a Soviet backing of the German cause to undermine the resistance of the French. The communists denounced the "imperialist captialist" war and exercised a subversive influence within the French army.

The beginning of the New Year found the Finns still struggling gamely against their behemoth enemy, still alone because the British could not make up their minds to risk the violation of the neutrality of Sweden, Denmark, and Norway. The defense line in France remained static, with the Germans busily preparing for an offensive and the French and British working on defenses. In January the Finns resisted stoutly, and the Red Army made no progress. The Soviet air forces continued to bomb Helsinki and Viipuri. The Finns asked Britain and France for aircraft, and the French promised planes. The British sent about a hundred planes. Still the cabinet refused to agree to an occupation of any part of Norway. Meanwhile, the Germans, who had no such qualms about violating neutrality, were planning to take over Scandinavia.

Hitler continued to talk about "immediate" invasion of the low countries in the strike against Britain and France. It was postponed just after Christmas, and set on January 10 "absolutely" for January 17 at "fifteen minutes before sunrise." The Luftwaffe was to start bombing three days earlier, on January 14.

But on January 10—later in the day—something happened to throw all Hitler's plans awry. A Luftwaffe plane carrying Major Helmut Reinberger, a courier in a hurry to deliver some papers from Muenster to Cologne, got lost in bad weather over Belgium, and the plane landed at Mechelen sur Meuse. Major Reinberger was indeed carrying important material—the complete plan for the German attack on the West. Belgian soldiers surrounded the German aircraft, and the major headed for some bushes nearby and set fire there to the contents of his briefcase. The Belgian soldiers suspected that here was something important and put out the fire. They took the major and the papers to their military headquarters. When Reinberger got there, he was frantic, and he acted swiftly. He grabbed the papers as they were being handed over to an officer, and thrust them into a lighted stove. A Belgian officer snatched them out of the stove, and preserved many of them.

As soon as he could get to a phone, Major Reinberger reported to the German Embassy in Brussels that all was well because he had destroyed the papers. But there was something fishy about his story, and Luftwaffe headquarters did not believe, and General Jodl did not either. He told Hitler he had no conception of what the enemy might now know about the German plans. In the excitement that followed, the airwaves between Berlin and Brussels crackled with messages, but in two days the Germans decided the plans had been destroyed. But then the reaction set in. The Belgians began to change their troop dispositions.

Actually the French and British governments were also given copies of the German plans. The problem was— was it a plant? The Belgians thought it might be. The British were sure it was not. But no one knew, and so the Allies did nothing. Hitler meanwhile delayed the invasion again and made some changes in the plans.

The Allies were warned, but they did not really believe, at least not enough to change their own plans. Instead, they continued to wait. The British trained, and trained and trained some more. But the problem was that they were still behind the times, and did not have one single armored division among the ten divisions in France. What they did have was a tank brigade, seventeen light tanks and one hundred "infantry tanks," which were equipped basically with machine guns, and in the modern sense of 1939, were almost inoffensive.

The Germans swallowed the problem of the war plans, and on January 27, 1940, Field Marshal Keitel was given the responsibility for putting the new plans and the new schedules together.

The British and French were still talking about aid to Finland—talking, not doing. On February 5 Prime Minister Chamberlain and Winston Churchill went to Paris to talk about sending three or four divisions of troops to Finland and to persuade the Swedes and Norwegians to let them pass through their countries. The Swedes refused, so the whole plan went flying.

At this very late date the British-French supreme war council decided that Finland should be saved. Her minister had told the British that without about forty thousand trained soldiers from abroad, the Finns could not hold out much longer. Spring would bring long days and shorter nights, and the Russians would be able to make better use of their air and ground resources. Churchill wanted to send troops through Narvik to kill two birds with one stone, help the Finns and stop the iron ore from getting to Germany.

The sea war again speeded up that January. The Germans began attacking the convoys with new techniques, and the losses rose. Also the German auxiliary ship *Altmark* headed home after the end of the *Graf Spee*, and she was carrying about three hundred Allied prisoners from sunken ships. As noted earlier, a British ship went into the Norwegian fjord, and despite assurances from the Norwegians that the *Altmark* was clean, seized her and liberated 299 prisoners. This was very good propaganda in Britain, but it had its reverse twist. Hitler had already decided to invade the Scandinavian countries, but he had not set a timetable. After the capture of the *Altmark* in Norwegian territorial waters, he hurried the plans. On February 20 he selected his commander for the invasion of Norway, General Nikolaus von Falkenhorst. The attack was set for March. The invasion of the West would have to wait a little while; Hitler needed to prevent the British from occupying Norway, and to save their iron ore. The British had telegraphed their intentions, without doing anything. From the standpoint of Winston Churchill, who had been urging action on Norway since September, it was one of the big mistakes of the British government in the war.

The Luftwaffe, with nothing to do in France, began a campaign against British shipping at the first of the year. Most of the coastal trading vessels around England did not have antiaircraft guns, which were still in very short supply. The navy now turned to all sorts of weapons, machine guns being the most effective. Spare machine guns from the Home Fleet were distributed among the coastal vessels along with naval crews, who shifted with their weapons from ship to ship. Soon the Germans who came down to strafe the helpless craft found that they were not helpless anymore, and after some German planes had been shot down, the incidence of strafing attacks on coastal vessels decreased.

The change that came to the sea war was largely brought about by Winston Churchill's decision to arm the merchant fleet with deck guns capable of sinking a submarine. When the practice became general, the Germans abandoned all pretense of abiding by the London submarine warfare convention of 1930, and began sinking ships with torpedoes without notice. That aspect of the war was settled by the winter of 1940.

By the end of February, sixteen U-boats had been sunk, but nine new ones had been added to the U-boat fleet, and the boats were Atlantic boats, capable of crossing the ocean and returning, and carrying as many as eighteen torpedoes. Churchill was very upbeat these days, because as he pointed out in the first six months of the war, Britain had lost only two hundred thousand tons of shipping, and had gained more tonnage in ships captured from the Germans in these first months. All this was going to change, but at the moment, there was not much to show the British how.

The Soviets had been much embarrassed by the failure of a nation of more than two hundred million people to put down a nation of three million. From the beginning of 1940, they had assembled power against the Finns. They wanted to pierce the Mannerheim Line before the melting of the snow turned the area into a great bog. This year the thaw, which the Finns wanted early, came late—six weeks late—and that was enough time for the Russians to act. The Soviet offensive opened on February 1, with aerial bombardment of all bases and artillery massed for ten days of heavy work. After two weeks, the Mannerheim Line was broken, and the attacks succeeded in gaining ground. By the end of February, the Mannerheim Line was a shambles; no small force could withstand that much manpower and firepower without help, and the Finns had no help. By this time the Finnish troops were on the point of exhaustion, and the Russians were bringing in fresh troops constantly.

The sea aspect of the war, the First Lord of the Admiralty admitted with pardonable pride, was not going badly at all. In those months since the sinking of the *Royal Oak*, the navy had been working on the Scapa Flow defenses, and in February announced that the Home Fleet could return to Scapa as of March 1. The Germans gave them a fine welcome as they moved, dropping mines in the entrance to Scapa Flow on the night before the fleet was to come in, and so the fleet stood out to sea for twenty-four hours while the channel was swept, spoiling a very nice homecoming.

Scapa Flow had changed. A U-boat would have a hard time of it now trying to get in at all. The three main entrances were defended with booms and mines, and submarine nets. More blockships had been placed in Kirk Sound, and more were coming. A large military garrison guarded the base ostensibly against sabotage, and the antiaircraft guns were coming. Soon there would be more than 120 of them, with scores of searchlights and a whole system of barrage balloons to discourage the Luftwaffe from trying any low air attacks. Three squadrons of Hurricane fighter planes from nearby airfields were ready to move at a moment's notice, and they had radar which made it possible for them to fight at night.

So March arrived, a month full of surprises. If the war was still somnolent along the Maginot and Siegfried lines, not so in the sea, and in the Scandinavian area. The Finns at long last, given so many promises that were not kept, could not continue to fight. On March 12 the British cabinet fiddled and faddled with plans to land troops at Narvik and move toward Finland. All this was delayed until March 20, but it proved to be a wild dream, because on March 7, Minister Paasikivi went back to Moscow. Finland's resources were at an end. Her European friends had not acted. The Finns had no recourse but to seek an armistice if they were to hold the government together. The Russians laid down the terms, and on March 12 the Finns accepted them. Britain and France had again failed to come to the aid of an ally, and the ally had gone under.

The collapse of Finland started a whole new chain of events. First of all, it caused the fall of the Daladier government in France, because Daladier had come out strongly for assistance to the Finns. The first accomplishment of Paul Reynaud, the new French premier, was a joint Anglo-French declaration that neither country would enter into separate peace negotiations with the Germans. For the first time, the French government was unalterably (it seemed) committed to the war. This assertion came as a result of the meeting of the Supreme War Council of Britain and France, at which the Allies also agreed to mine waters off Norway to help stop the shipment of iron ores to Germany. The mining was to begin early in April 1940.

At the same time, the Germans were beginning to move in Scandinavia. They were as conscious of the need to protect their major source of iron ore for the furnaces of the Ruhr as were the British. During the next year the Germans were counting on eleven million tons of Swedish iron ore, of a total fifteen million tons their war industries planned to use. But there was another reason for German concern with her Nordic neighbors. In World War I the German navy had been seriously hampered by having no access to the wide ocean. To reach the Atlantic, the German ships had to travel through the North Sea and around Scotland or run the English Channel. Both areas were blockaded by the British then, as they were being blockaded now by the Royal Navy. The German naval war plan for 1940, then, called for the obtaining of bases in Norway, which would make it possible to reach the sea. Submarine bases would help establish a blockade of the British Isles. And in the 1930s the emergence of air power had added another reason, air bases from which the Luftwaffe could attack British targets.

So April—seven months after the British and French had declared war—was to be the month in which Germans would butt heads on the land with their Western enemies.

CHAPTER 18

The U-Boat Assault

Once the U-boat war was established, Admiral Doenitz began an analysis of his successes and problems, and came to the conclusion that not much had changed in the past quarter century in British antisubmarine defenses. It was true that the British had the asdic system, but Doenitz was not much impressed by it. The U-boat now moved silently underwater, and its torpedoes left no wake, as they had done in the 1914–18 war. Doenitz remained convinced that the U-boat was still Germany's most effective weapon against the British, and that given the three hundred U-boats he wanted, he would be able to force the British to end the war.

In the winter of 1940 Doenitz was eager to begin wolf pack operations with his U-boats, but his problem was a shortage of boats that precluded his having more than five or six boats for operations at one time. Gone were the halcyon days of September, when he could put twenty-one boats out into the sea, to await the coming of war. Those boats had to come back for reprovisioning and rearming and repairs oftentimes, and that meant time in the dockyards. So by November, the number of boats was down to a handful, and it had made itself felt in the sinking figures.

In October Doenitz had tried his first wolf pack operation. He had communications control with modern radio from Wilhelmshaven with which he could direct boats all over the world, and an intricate system of grids by which he could plot their courses and areas of operation to within a few miles. Six boats were available for this first wolf pack under Commander Hartman, of the *U-37*. But one boat, the *U-40*, made the error of trying to cut the distance to the Atlantic operating area by using the English Channel and was sunk there by a mine. This was the second U-boat loss in the channel, and the event taught Doenitz that the channel must be avoided, which it would be until much later in the war.

Of the five boats that set out for the area southwest of Ireland, two were sunk by the British and three survived. The three boats managed to sink at least three ships in one convoy, but then they were dispersed, having expended their torpedoes or being needed elsewhere. So the first wolf pack attempt was anything but a success.

In November 1939 Doenitz started a thrust into the Mediterranean but found the weather there so bad, and the shallow sea so treacherous to the big oceangoing U-boats, that this effort, too, failed. But in Doenitz's mind, the real reason for failure was inadequate numbers. Since he could not expect any results from the accelerated U-boat building program until late in 1940, he had to improvise, and take a patient attitude.

In January 1940, Doenitz had twelve U-boats ready to sail, but this month exceptionally bad ice conditions in the Baltic interfered. Several of these boats were involved in the final training program, which got crews and captains accustomed to one another, and the decision had to be made whether to sacrifice operations or training. Doenitz was eager to operate, so it was decided that the last stages of the training could be accomplished in the field. It turned out to be a mistake. In eleven attack operations, Doenitz lost four boats, three of them among those U-boats that had not had sufficient training. Once again, circumstances had worked against the U-boat force.

During the fall and winter, the little 250-ton Type II

U-boats had distinguished several captains with mining operations, and these were continued in the spring of 1940. Although the British were indefatiguable in sweeping for mines, the little boats could penetrate estuaries and harbors, and lay their deadly globes. The magnetic mine was a serious problem until degaussing ruined one of its major attributes. But the mining continued.

At the end of six months of warfare, Doenitz again made a major assessment of his situation. He was very pleased with the Type VIIC U-boats, 517 tons, which had been designed for attacks on Atlantic convoys. The boat had good diving qualities, and since she was small, was hard to see at night. The large Atlantic boats, Type I and Type IX, displaced 700 tons, and were harder to handle, but they had longer range and carried more torpedoes, which would make them suitable for work on the far side of the Atlantic.

By the spring of 1940, Doenitz had reason to be satisfied with his captains and his officers and men. They had received excellent training, and their enthusiasm for the difficult and dangerous task was unbounded. The problem was to organize the wolf packs with a technique of command that could be exercised from Wilhelmshaven, because that command post should have reports from weather, the Luftwaffe, and agents abroad about the British activities around the world. Quickly it became apparent that the reports from agents were unreliable, and after that, they were seldom considered, largely because the information was too old. One major difficulty for the U-boats was an inheritance from the days of peace. The boats had been forbidden to dive deeper than fifty meters, although they were constructed for much greater depths, and thus it was not discovered that certain weaknesses appeared in the engine exhaust valves and bedplates of the engines. The truth came in November, when the *U-49*, beset by destroyers, went down to 170 meters without damaging her pressure hull. Thereafter the U-boat skippers had a lot more confidence in their weapons.

But the greatest problem Doenitz encountered in the early days of the war involved the magnetic exploder of the torpedoes. After the first few days of war, submarine captains began arriving back in Wilhelmshaven with stories of "fish" that did not work, or exploded prematurely, and one captain told of a torpedo that blew up almost in his face, and damaged the bow of the U-boat. That could not be gainsaid, but generally the staff tended first to believe that the captains were covering up for inadequate performance. However, when captains like Prien, the Bull of Scapa Flow, returned to tell such stories, they had to be believed. For Prien was never one to exaggerate, and he thought he had indeed sunk another warship in an attack on a London-class cruiser, when all he had done was blow up her wake. So Doenitz began an investigation, but it was hampered by bureaucrats in the torpedo section of the navy, who claimed there was nothing wrong with the weapon, just something wrong with the men who handled it.

By January 1940, the problem had become so serious, it affected the morale of the U-boat service. Captains had shown that the torpedoes ran as much as two meters below the setting, which would put them below the keel of a destroyer or minesweeper and sometimes a merchant ship. The magnetic exploders were deactivated, but this meant that one of the greatest attributes of the torpedo was lost. Now a captain had to score a direct hit to damage a target, whereas if the exploders worked, he had simply to come near it and the torpedo would home on the steel hull.

At the end of the year, the "improved" magnetic exploders had been delivered and the captains were told to use them. But the improvement was not much, and at least 25 percent of the torpedoes fired failed to do any damage. Doenitz estimated that the difficulties had cost the U-boats at least three hundred thousand tons of enemy shipping.

Then in March came events that would put enormous pressure on the U-boats, and failures that would seriously damage morale once more.

CHAPTER 19

The War of Words

In the fall of 1939 the inactivity on the western front created serious problems for the German propaganda machine that had been impressing the world in the earlier days. As Propaganda Minister Josef Goebbels said about the weekly newsreel (which was one of his responsibilities that Hitler took very seriously), ". . . somewhat boring. We have no real subjects anymore." Goebbels was eager to promote German propaganda in the neutral countries and against France. Hitler still hoped to pull France out of the war, and Goebbels did what he could, setting up clandestine radio stations to broadcast defeatist programs to the French.

But his excesses kept getting in the way. When the cruiser *Belfast* struck a mine and was damaged, Goebbels sank her, and then had to retract. He waxed poetic about the successes of the U-boat war, even as the U-boats were failing to sink ships because of torpedo troubles. "Our U-boats are achieving fabulous successes against England," he wrote, and "Our U-boat successes are weakening England's position with the neutral countries." But whatever successes he was having in his propaganda were usually countered by a new excess, as on November 29, when the German press crowed about the Prien sinking of a British heavy cruiser, when none was sunk. It did not take many such reversals to convince the neutral press to take care in its writing of the headlines.

The Germans needed a string of successes to shore up their propaganda, and they were not getting them. When they did not get them, the overtones of terror from the occupied countries of Czechoslovakia and Poland began to make themselves felt even in Germany, and more in the neutral countries. Public enthusiasm for the war waned, and Goebbels became ever more frantic in his search for the positive. "Our press has become very bad recently," he wrote on December 3. "Because nothing in particular is happening, it seems to be full of boring material. I take energetic measures. We must have no lax habits here."

Public morale was shaky. There was talk by the economic managers of curtailing the Christmas celebration in Germany, but Hitler put a stop to that, with the enthusiastic support of Goebbels. It was dangerous to make the people tired of the war.

On December 10 Hitler complained about the weekly newsreel as being too negative. All Goebbels could say was that "if nothing is happening, we can film nothing." Hitler was feeling the need for activity to conceal from the people the desperate nature of the war he had undertaken.

So in the absence of any military activity on land or in the air, German propaganda turned to the war at sea for excitement, and again became overblown in its claims.

On December 15 Goebbels finally found something that he hoped to use for a ten-strike.

"Sea battle between *Graf Spee* and three English cruisers in the estuary of the La Plata. *Graf Spee* seems to have given a magnificent account of itself. The three English cruisers seriously damaged. No more detailed information yet. Churchill tries yet again to fool the public. But we immediately issue a clear statement."

That statement, which was blown up in all German media, indicated a great victory for the *Graf Spee*, but within twenty-four hours the world knew that she had been bottled up in Montevideo harbor, ''and so we tone things down in the press for a short while.''

Next, Goebbels was charging that the British used mustard gas in their fight with the *Graf Spee*. His irritation with the war in general caused him to start a different sort of campaign against the Allied leaders. Earlier they had been portrayed as comic figures. They were now to become sinister. And when he had indications of defeatism in Paris, he carefully kept all such reports out of the German newspapers. ''The German people must steel themselves for the struggle.''

The flow of information around Germany was disturbing, and Goebbels and Hitler set out to eliminate it. First Hitler forbade his Wehrmacht officials to listen to foreign broadcasts. By December he put a stop to general listening, by imposing heavy punishment. He planned to confiscate all radio sets outside Germany itself.

One result of the British victory over the *Graf Spee* at sea was the banning of all German-language foreign newspapers and the tightening of German censorship. ''This is necessary during these critical times.''

The New Year, 1940, began with the same uneasiness in Berlin ruling circles, the same propaganda line about the victory at sea, because there was nothing else to talk about, and a continuation of the lie Goebbels had been telling for four months about the sinking of the *Athenia*. Hitler was obviously very nervous about the plans for the attack on the western front, and threatening noisily to carry the war to the West in every way. In January Hitler spoke grimly about a future for Germany if she lost this war. He realized that the British were in to win, and he told Goebbels in a burst of pessimism that Germany could not survive if it lost.

''Real bravery only comes when there is no turning back,'' he said. ''It is then that one finds the courage for really momentous decisions. So long as there is still a way out, it is easy to lose one's nerve under pressure . . . We simply cannot afford to lose the war. All our thoughts and actions should be guided by this consideration.''

Hitler's growing nervousness communicated itself to those around him, and they shored themselves by overpraising the Luftwaffe, the U-boat war, and every aspect of success that seemed indicated. Hitler was already beginning to talk about wonder weapons that would win the war for him.

The leaders of Germany were all nervous these days. Hitler had finally made the decision to bypass the military commanders and deal through General Keitel, who became that winter the key figure in the German military machine. Goering, now given the responsibility for economic affairs, showed the greatest concern about the possibilities of the war in the West. "God help us if we should lose this war," he said, parroting Hitler.

The military hiatus that fall and winter of 1939–40 was welcomed by the generals, who had always claimed that they had been thrust into a war for which the military machine was not prepared. Hitler never accepted their arguments, but for one reason or another, he did keep postponing the date for attack on the West, and hoping that somehow at least France would fall out of the Allied partnership.

The hiatus continued through February, and into March. Only then, when the German leadership began to understand that the British were planning some sort of move against Norway, did they grow so nervous that they decided to act.

CHAPTER 20

Germany Plans a Takeover

As was illustrated in the affair of the German ship *Altmark*, which was reportedly searched by the Norwegian authorities and found to have a clean bill of health, but actually was not searched at all and had British prisoners aboard, Norway's allegiances in this war between Germany and France and England were very much mixed. Many Norwegians sympathized with England. But some also sympathized with Germany, and the key figure in this group was Vidkun Quisling a politician of the Nazi stripe, and Quisling had enjoyed a distinguished career, first as a professional soldier, then as defense minister. But he had veered to Nazism and founded a political party of that sort called the National Union, which was so unpopular that he could not even get himself elected to the Parliament on that ticket.

He had long been in touch with Alfred Rosenberg, the Nazi Party philosopher, and in the summer of 1939 at a convention in Lübeck, he asked Rosenberg for help. But no one in authority in Germany paid any attention to him, until Admiral Raeder began to get reports from his naval attaché in Oslo about Allied plans to land in Norway. At about this time Quisling arrived in Berlin and met with Rosenberg, who introduced him to Raeder. Out of all this came a plan for Quisling and his storm troopers, who were now being trained in Germany, to seize power in Norway at the same time that the German navy and army would appear at a summons from this new government.

At a meeting with Raeder, Quisling aroused the admiral's fears by telling of a British landing planned at Stavanger and Christiansand. Quisling was prepared to put the necessary bases at the disposal of the Germans. He had come to Berlin to arrange for just this. He told Raeder, Raeder went to Hitler, Hitler wanted to see Quisling, and on December 14, 1939, he did. And thus was set up the plan for the invasion of Norway by the Germans, with friendly assistance from the band of traitors.

Once Hitler accepted the plan, the next step was to find a commander of the troops to invade Norway. The man suggested by the army was General Niklaus von Falkenhorst, who had commanded troops in Finland in World War I. Hitler interrogated Falkenhorst at length, and was satisfied that he had the right man. He indicated that the *Altmark* incident had persuaded him to speed up his plans. The British were becoming too active for his liking.

With assistance of the Baedeker travel guide, which he bought that day, Falkernhorst put together a plan for invasion of the major Norwegian ports by five divisions of German troops. One division would go to Oslo, one to Stavanger, one to Bergen, one to Trondheim, and one to Narvik. So came into being the Weser Exercise.

Hitler's orders were precise:

> The development of the situation in Scandinavia requires the making of all preparations for the occupation of Denmark and Norway. This operation should prevent British encroachment on Scandinavia and the Baltic. Further it should guarantee our ore base in Sweden and give our navy and the air force a wider starting line against Britain.
>
> In view of our military and political power in com-

parison with that of the Scandinavian states, the force to be employed in the Weser Exercise will be kept as small as possible. The numerical weakness will be balanced by daring actions and surprise execution.

[The reason for this remarkable dependence on unknown factors was that Hitler knew he had already stirred up the army by his demands for troops for the Norway operation, and that he could not take all the troops he might need.]

On principle we will do our utmost to make the operation appear as a peaceful occupation, the object of which is the military protection of the neutrality of the Scandinavian states. Corresponding demands will be transmitted to the governments at the beginning of the occupation. If necessary demonstrations by the navy and the air force will provide the necessary emphasis. If in spite of this, resistance should be met, all military means will be used to crush it . . . The crossing of the Danish border and the landings in Norway must take place simultaneously.

Also, said the führer, the element of surprise was very important.

And so Hitler's Germany embarked on another adventure, one every bit as cynical and misleading as the last. The German people and the people of the world were to be made to believe, if Dr. Goebbels's propaganda agency could manage it, that only for the good of Scandinavia was the German might being pushed upon them.

There was some difficulty with the army and the Luftwaffe, which had not yet gotten the idea that Hitler was running the show and would do exactly as he pleased. General Halder and Marshal Goering were angry at not being consulted (particularly because the navy was in on the secret from the beginning). But these difficulties were overcome by Hitler in his discussions with the leaders. Then came another obstacle. The Finns suddenly surrendered to Russian force on March 12, thus depriving the British, and the Germans, of a major reason for putting troops into Norway. But although the Germans fretted over the reasons they would give the world for this action, the decision was made, and Hitler was determined to take Norway and Denmark.

So were the British now determined, but the problem was that the Germans had the head start and the better plan.

On April 2 Hitler ordered the Weser operation to begin at 5:15 A.M. on April 9. He also told his generals that under no circumstances should they let the kings of Denmark and Norway escape from their countries.

The first three German supply ships sailed for Narvik on April 3. The next day, through a leak in the German intelligence system, the Danish naval attache at Berlin was informed that the Germans in a few days would move against his country. He reported to Copenhagen—and he was not believed.

The following day, April 5, the Norwegian government was informed by its legation in Berlin and by the Swedes of a concentration of German troops and naval vessels in the North Sea, and of the imminence of German landings in Norway. But the Norwegian cabinet, when it had the report, did not believe. One reason for their skepticism was the German campaign of deception. The German ships were ordered to identify themselves as British, to answer signals only in English, and to claim to be British. They were given British call signs and identifying numbers.

An hour before dawn on April 9, the German ambassadors at Denmark and Oslo were to present to the Danish and Norwegian governments ultimatums demanding that they accept "the protection of the Third Reich."

The signs added up. On April 7 large German warships were seen moving up the Norwegian coast. On April 8 the newspapers reported on German soldiers rescued from the transport *Rio de Janeiro*, a German transport sunk by the British off Norway, and they said they had been en route to Bergen to protect it from the British. But still the Norwegian government did nothing.

On April 1 the rumors began to come in to London. On April 3 the British war cabinet talked over the reports from Stockholm about large numbers of German troops collecting in the north German ports. But no one seemed to worry much. They thought it was just German preparation to meet a possible British invasion.

And such an invasion was being planned in connection with the British idea of mining the Norwegian waters to prevent German ore ships from reaching the destinations. So as German troops were loading and moving toward Norway, so were British troops, but not in as great numbers or as well prepared.

The German preparations were thorough in every regard, and they dominated German military operations in all branches during the month of March. Admiral Doenitz, for example, was planning another wolf pack U-boat operation in the Atlantic and had eight U-boats ready for that purpose. But on March 4 he received orders from Raeder's staff to keep all his boats in German harbors in readiness for the attack on Norway. A few hours later, Doenitz went to Berlin for a meeting at which the plans for the invasion were laid out for him, and he was told that since the British might attack with strong forces on the sea, he must make all his U-boats available to support this operation.

The U-boats would cover the warships and transports after the landing. They would try to prevent enemy troop landings, and attack enemy naval forces operating against sea communications between Norway and Germany. To accomplish this, Doenitz was to move four boats to Narvik, two boats to Trondheim, five boats to Bergen, two boats to Stavanger, have nine boats ready to attack the British fleet coming from Scottish waters, four boats around Pentland Firth, and five boats around Lindesnes.

This disposition took every one of Doenitz's U-boats. All sailing stopped in early March, and all boats at sea were recalled. OKW was very nervous as the operation approached, and on March 11 Doenitz was ordered to put his boats in positions around Narvik and Trondheim. On March 14 decoded British naval messages showed unusual British submarine activity around the Skagerrak, and this bothered OKW, but then on March 16 the Luftwaffe reported an enormously successful air attack on the British fleet at Scapa Flow (which was highly exaggerated; only the old *Iron Duke* and the *Norfolk* were hit), so the fears subsided. Doenitz was ordered to move his boats to meet the eventuality of the British again abandoning Scapa Flow. The problem now was that the German naval general staff was calling the shots, and they did not understand U-boat operations. So boats were moved and boats were told not to move, on what seemed to Doenitz to be whimsy.

April 9 was the date set by Hitler for the beginning of his lightning move to take Denmark and Norway, and April 9 was just when it happened, with German precision. The U-boats were all in position set to repel any attempts by the British to land troops. The Germans did not expect any resistance. In the case of Denmark, they were right. But in the case of Norway, they were wrong. The Norwegians said they would not submit voluntarily, and that resistance had already begun. The Germans blustered, but by midmorning the king and government had fled Oslo for the mountains in the North.

At Narvik, where a Quisling follower, Colonel Konrad Sundlo, commanded the Norwegian garrison, the Norwegians surrendered without firing a shot. But the Norwegian navy had a different idea. Ten German destroyers appeared in the fjord that morning, and the two old ships in the harbor fired warning shots and demanded identification. The German commander, Admiral Fritz Bonte, answered with a demand for surrender. The Norwegians said no. The admiral called his negotiators back, and as their launch cleared the harbor, he ordered his ships to open fire, and they blew up one of the Norwegian ships— the *Eidsvold*—with torpedoes. The other ship, the *Norge*, started firing and was quickly destroyed, and along with it, about three hundred Norwegian sailors died. So by 10:00 A.M. on April 9, Narvik was in German hands, held by the crews of ten destroyers, and two battalions of German troops.

Trondheim, halfway along the Norwegian west coast, was assaulted at the same time by the Germans. The harbor batteries did not fire on the German ships, because of treachery, and the heavy cruiser *Hipper* led the ships into the harbor. The landing troops and the crews of four destroyers landed at the city's piers without resistance. Several forts held out for a few hours, and troops at the airfield held out for two days, but their fate was preordained by the presence of German troops and the absence of British.

At Trondeim the Germans gained a fine port for their submarines and an air base for the Luftwaffe.

Bergen, which lies three hundred miles down the coast from Trondheim, saw some resistance, as the batteries that guarded the harbor shot at the German ships. The cruiser *Koenigsberg* was damaged, and so was an auxiliary vessel, but the Germans landed and occupied the city before noon. That afternoon, however, fifteen British dive bombers came over and sank the *Koenigsberg*. And outside the harbor lay a British flotilla of four cruisers and seven destroyers, which could easily have overwhelmed the Germans, but their attack, just begun, was canceled when the Admiralty in London got cold feet and worried about mines in the harbor.

Actually the British Royal Navy had gone into action on April 7, when air reconnaissance reported a German fleet moving across the mouth of the Skagerrak. The Home Fleet, which included the battleships and battle cruisers, *Rodney, Repulse, Valiant*, and two cruisers and ten destroyers, was already under steam, and they left Scapa Flow at eight-thirty that night. The Second Cruiser Squadron, consisting of two cruisers and fifteen destroyers, left Rosyth later in the evening. The first Cruiser Squadron got ready to leave. The cruiser *Aurora* and six destroyers were ordered to leave the Clyde River and head for Norway. And, because of previous decisions, British destroyers already were laying mines off Narvik, under cover by a battle cruiser and a cruiser.

One of the minelaying destroyers, the *Glowworm*, got separated from the others that night of April 7 and ran into two German destroyers on their way to Norway, and began a fight. The cruiser *Hipper* appeared on her way to Trondheim, and got into the fight. The *Glowworm* then retired under a smoke screen, and when the *Hipper* penetrated it, the *Glowworm* rammed her, tearing a big hole in the side of the cruiser, but wrecking the British destroyer, which soon blew up.

So by April 8, the British had superior naval forces at sea, but confusing signals from the Admiralty prevented the fleet from doing its best. First they steered south, then they changed and headed for Narvik. The *Renown* group encountered the *Scharnhorst* and the *Gneisenau* off Narvik, and engaged, and made several bits on the *Gneisenau*, which put her guns out of action. She was screened by the *Scharnhorst,* and both ships ran north. The weather was very foul, with intermittent snow squalls, and the speed of the chase had to be reduced to twenty knots. The Germans finally escaped to the north, and the *Renown* gave up the chase. She had suffered two hits and was slightly damaged.

On the morning of April 8, British Admiral Sir Charles Forbes arrived with the main British fleet off Bergen. He prepared to send a force into Bergen to attack the Germans there. The Admiralty also told him to move into Trondheim, but to expect German resistance there. The admiral was worried about the German battle cruisers and postponed the Trondheim attack, but half an hour before noon, he sent four cruisers and seven destroyers toward Bergen, eight miles away. The weather was rough, and the reports from the air were disturbing. The planes reported two German cruisers in Bergen. This was reported to the Admiralty and Admiral Pound in London. The latter made the decision that it was too risky to send the battle force in to Bergen under the circumstances. Winston Churchill, the political chief of the Navy, agreed, and the attack was canceled on orders from London, thus subverting Admiral Forbes at sea, and causing the British to fail in their first confrontation with the Germans in Norway.

But the naval battle was joined, and that afternoon of April 9, planes of the Luftwaffe were over the British fleet in a series of attacks that sank the destroyer *Gurkha* and damaged the cruisers *Southampton* and *Glasgow*. The flagship *Rodney* was hit, but not much damaged. Then came the attack by the British carrier planes from *Furious* on the *Koenigsberg*, which sank her. After that, the *Furious* was sent to Trondheim, where the damaged *Hipper* was reported. The carrier steamed that way and her planes attacked Trondheim at dawn on April 11, but most of the German ships had left, and so the British found only two destroyers in the harbor. The attack was a failure, because the torpedoes grounded in shallow water before they hit the destroyers.

Several British submarines were off the Norwegian coast, and they sank the cruiser *Karlsruhe,* and damaged the pocket battleship *Luetzow* and at least nine German transports and supply ships during this Norway operation, but they lost three submarines in the process.

The operations of the German U-boats were a big disappointment to Admiral Doenitz. The constant second-guessing and movement by the naval general staff meant the skippers of the U-boats could never get set on an operative system here. On April 11 Admiral Doenitz asked for reports from his U-boats at sea around Norway. The results were appalling to him. Twelve torpedoes had been fired at enemy ships, and eight had exploded prematurely. The only explanation seemed to be that the magnetic exploder, even the changed one, did not work at northern latitudes. So again Doenitz ordered the U-boat skippers to return to impact firing.

On April 13 Doenitz quarreled with the naval general staff, who were intent on trying to cover every area of Norway with the U-boats. From April 15 his boats were concentrated at Narvik and Trondheim. But because of torpedo failures, they were sinking no ships. And the weather suddenly calmed, with glassy seas that made antisubmarine warfare more effective.

Lieutenant Prien, who was completely trusted by Admiral Doenitz, reported on April 15 that he had missed two big transports, of twenty thousand to thirty thousand tons, and at least one shot at a cruiser, because of torpedo failure.

So impact firing did not seem to help either. The trouble was that in the excitement about the discovery of the failures of the magnetic torpedo, the torpedo men had tried to move too fast, and had supplied the operational force with new exploders that failed at least ten percent of the time. But in the narrow Norwegian fjords, the submariners found, the incidence of failure was much higher.

On April 19 Doenitz was even more disturbed by another report. Of twenty-two torpedoes in the area, nine had failed, and they had also detonated good torpedoes in the same salvoes. The worst was that the torpedo was running to too deep, and targets drawing less than five or six meters could not be torpedoed—and this meant destroyers.

So that was the bad news. The German navy had no torpedoes that could be used in the north latitudes. On April 19 Doenitz withdrew all his U-boats from the northern Norwegian waters, where they were useless, to water farther south. But even then, Prien encountered the British warship *Warspite*, fired two torpedoes from less than two miles, set to run at eight meters. One torpedo exploded at the end of its run, and the other did not explode at all. Prien's U-boat was then attacked by several destroyers, which dropped depth charges all around him. Next day, farther south, Prien encountered a northbound convoy. He did not attack, because he had no faith in his torpedoes, but shadowed the convoy until joined by two other boats. But they came into the northern waters again, where the torpedoes would not work properly, and so the whole attack was ended in another failure.

The U-boats retired to German ports very shortly. Morale was shattered, the torpedoes still did not work properly, and Doenitz had a lot of work to do to put things in his U-boat corps right again.

On April 9, when it became world news that Germany had invaded Norway and Denmark, the French flew to London for a meeting of the Supreme War Council. They were inclined to blame the British for stirring up the animals with the mining of the Norwegian inner waterway, but Churchill soon set them right, pointing out that the German occupation was highly planned and executed with a skill that meant they knew precisely what they were doing. The war council learned that the French now expected the Germans to attack through Belgium and were prepared to move when they did. Obviously the "phony war" was not phony any longer in any sense.

Then the talk turned to Norway. The British reminded everyone that the original two divisions destined for Finland had been sent to France, so the only spare troops in England were eleven battalions, and two of those were sailing that very night for Norway.

The French-British council agreed to send "strong forces" to Norway. The French would embark an Alpine division in a few days. The British would send five more battalions in three days and then another four battalions.

On the morning of April 9 at Narvik, the Germans were in control, but when the British entered West Fjord, they were not sure of the situation. Up came Captain Warburton-Lee with five destroyers, the *Hardy, Hunter, Havock, Hotspur*, and *Hostile*. Norwegian pilots told him that six ships and a U-boat had passed in, and the entrance to the harbor was mined by the Germans. He reported that he intended to attack at dawn. The Admiralty offered no objections this time, and the captain did go into action. The five destroyers steamed up the fjord at dawn, and stood off Narvik. Three of the destroyers went in, and the other two stayed outside in reserve. The *Hardy* torpedoed the flagship of the five enemy destroyers in Narvik, and another German destroyer was sunk by two torpedoes. The British destroyers smothered the German ships in gunfire, and sank six German merchant vessels as well. The *Hotspur* and the *Hostile* came inside, and the *Hotspur* sank two more merchant ships. The British prepared to withdraw, victorious. But then three other ships appeared, and then two more. They were heavy German destroyers with guns larger than the British. Soon the bridge of the *Hardy* was hit and Captain Warburton-Lee was mortally wounded. The destroyer was soon beached. The *Hotspur* and the *Hostile* were damaged, the *Hunter* was sunk, but the fight went on as the British ships tried to get out to sea. The two damaged vessels and the *Havock* made it, and encountered the German supply ship *Ravenfels*, carrying ammunition. The *Havock* opened fire, and the *Revenfels* blew up.

On April 10 it was apparent to the British that the Germans had stolen a march on them by occupying all the ports on the Norwegian coast. Now the British must seal off Narvik and try to capture that port to stop the shipment of iron ore to Germany.

On April 12 planes from the carrier *Furious* made a dive-bomb attack on the ships in Narvik harbor. Two aircraft were lost, but the raiders claimed four hits on destroyers.

On April 13 the flagship *Warspite*, with nine destroyers and the *Furious*, attacked Narvik. The destroyers drove away one U-boat (perhaps Prien's *U-47*) and sank another one. A destroyer was discovered lurking in an inlet preparing to launch torpedoes against the battleship. When the British flotilla was a dozen miles from Narvik, they found five enemy destroyers. Then the fight began, with the *Warspite* firing her fifteen-inch guns. The Germans retreated, and some of the British ships went into Narvik harbor to complete the destruction of the German ships caught there and port facilities. Others went after three German destroyers and sank them in Rombaks Fjord. Of the eight German destroyers that had survived the attack on the ninth by the British destroyer squadron, all were destroyed without the loss of a British ship.

Admiral Whitworth considered the idea of landing a force of marines and sailors and occupying Narvik, but he was sure the Germans would rush heavy reinforcements and he did not want to risk the *Warspite* in these unfriendly waters for too long, so he decided against the attack. His decision was confirmed when a dozen Luftwaffe planes appeared at about 6:00 P.M. That night he withdrew, leaving two destroyers off the port to watch. He quickly recommended to London that the British send in an occupation force and take and hold Narvik before the Germans could recover.

On April 12 the first convoy of troops sailed for Norway. Major General Mackesey commanded the land forces, and Lord Cork commanded the naval forces. There was some confusion when Lord Cork decided to capture the port with naval forces because Mackesey had not shown up, but he was soon set right on that and waited for the army, and led the convey into Harstad, on the morning of April 15. The Twenty-fourth Brigade then landed. Lord Cork urged an immediate assault on Narvik, but the general said there were too many machine-gun installations and he refused. He seemed to have the idea that fighting was not in the plan. He opened his headquarters at the hotel in Harstad. He said it was impossible to land at Narvik, and not even naval bombardment would make it so. So the army stalled.

By April 13, King Haakon of Norway broadcast to his people, telling them that the Germans had made an attempt to kill him after he refused their demands, and indicating that the resistance should begin. His hiding place was secret: soon he would be in England.

The next day, the Germans issued a proclamation in the name of General Falkenhorst, claiming he had come as a savior of Norway from the wicked designs of the Western powers. He admitted that the Norwegian government had refused to cooperate with the Germans, and demanded obedience to German order so that "Norway will be spared the horrors of war." If the Norwegians did not submit, "I shall be forced to employ the severest and most relentless means to crush such opposition."

Then began what Winston Churchill called "the ramshackle" campaign to save Norway, started with too little and started too late.

On April 16 Lord Cork and General Mackesey met, but the general flatly refused to try to seize Narvik. He wanted to take two unoccupied positions on the Narvik road and hold them, waiting until the snow melted at the end of April or in May. Nobody asked the Germans if they would wait, but the answer was no. This attitude of the army, very much akin to the attitude in France, all meant disaster, because the Germans were already moving to fortify Narvik, and then that would be the end. The general was waiting for that small brigade of French troops, but Churchill was now determined that he who would not fight should not get them. Churchill was counseling immediate strong action, but he was not getting it.

As matters stood, the British effort in Norway, having started little and late, was bogging down fast.

CHAPTER 21

The Battle for Narvik

In a sense, the odds had evened by April 18. The Germans had outwitted the British by occupying Denmark and Norway so expeditiously, but the British had overwhelmed their naval forces, and sunk or wrecked ten of the most modern German destroyers with very little loss to themselves. The *Hipper* was badly damaged, the *Gneisenau* had been damaged, and the U-boat fleet was at the moment in shambles.

The British had moved swiftly to blockade the Norwegian coast, and the German fleet was in no position to contest the action. The British also moved swiftly to land a small force at Namsos, under General Sir Adrian Carton de Wiart, who flew into Norway on April 14. That admirable speed, however, was not duplicated in other landings here, or in the planning. A force of French Chasseurs Alpins, French ski troops, arrived to help, but they did not help much. They failed to obliterate traces of their landing, and the Germans were soon wise to it, and then the French, obviously untrained in weapons discipline, began firing weapons indiscriminately, which put the end to any secrecy whatever. General de Wiart moved to Verdael and Steinkjer, near Trondheim, and awaited reinforcement and an opportunity to attack. The Germans, aroused by the French didoes, bombed Namsos and destroyed the town. The French were of no use. They did not have their ski equipment in order, and their mules had not turned up. They could not move or fight. The British troops were equipped with fur coats, special boots and socks, and so much clothing that if they wore it all, they looked, said General de Wiart, "like paralyzed bears."

This Namsos occupation limped along. The Germans, with air superiority, bombed frequently. Three days after De Wiart's men had occupied Steinkjer and Verdael, the German navy came up and shelled those two places, and forced the troops out. They retired to positions north of Steinkjer. General de Wiart was waiting for a major naval engagement, as he had been told to do, when he proposed to take Trondheim. But no signal came. The naval attack was delayed, and soon enough De Wiart saw that with his force, he could not take Trondheim, and suggested to the War Office that he get out of there. They said stay, so he stayed. But to what useful end, no one ever explained.

French Prime Minister Paul Reynaud and British Admiralty Lord Churchill were completely in agreement on one matter: the need for speed in movement in Norway if all was not to be lost. But in this matter they faced the dilatoriness of their two governments, which had not yet recognized the need for immediate action in this modern war. The British and French generals were still thinking of war as it had been in 1914–18—a relatively leisurely matter.

The British and French together had about eight thousand troops in the area, as opposed to only five thousand Germans, and south of Namsos, the British and Norwegians had another five thousand troops, so the prospects looked good for the capture of Trondheim. But only for three days. The Allies did not move fast enough, and on April 23 the Germans reinforced Trondheim from Oslo. The Luftwaffe, which had moved up to Norwegian air bases, became more aggressive and more effective, and maintained control of the air over Norway. The Allied war council met again on April 27 in London. Still nothing was being done on the land, and now the opportunity to capture Trondheim had been lost. Finally De Wiart's force was evacuated by the navy in early May, after having accomplished nothing at all, and in the evacuation, the navy lost two destroyers. Trondheim was another disaster from the beginning, because of very bad planning.

But Narvik remained.

As Winston Churchill knew very well, the problem of the British army was a lack of aggressiveness, and General Mackesey had certainly shown this in Norway. Churchill's reaction was to secure appointment of Lord Cork, an aggressive naval commander, over all the forces in the Narvik area, army, air force, and navy. Churchill had hoped that by relieving Mackesey of administrative responsibility, the general would want to do something, and the something should be to attack the enemy.

"The result," Churchill wrote later, "was contrary to this expectation. He continued to use every argument, and there was no lack of them, to prevent drastic action."

The British had rejected the idea of an improvised assault on the town after their naval victory, and three days later, it was too late to do it the easy way. The Germans had brought in about two thousand troops and had organized the two thousand or so sailors from the sunken destroyers, and had quite a respectable force at Narvik. The first engagement of the war between British and German troops took place on April 21 at Lillehammer, north of Hamar. This was the first place that the Norwegian government had reached when the Germans occupied Oslo. King Haakon had then gone to the village of Nybergsund near Elverum. From there the king had issued a decision that he would not cooperate with the Germans, and called upon the three million Norwegians to resist the invaders. When the Germans learned this, they sent the Luftwaffe up to Nybergsund to bomb the village, and the fliers demolished it with explosives and incendiary bombs. The king had then moved up into the Gudbrands Valley, which led past Hamar and Lillehammer to Andalsnes on the coast, a hundred miles southwest of Trondheim. He would hold out as long as possible, but ultimately he would be taken by warship to England to go into exile.

On April 20 a second British brigade had landed at Andalsnes. This was Brigadier Morgan's 148th Infantry Brigade. But their supply ship had been sunk, and it had carried all their artillery and mortars. They had no artillery, antiaircraft guns, or air support, and the Luftwaffe bombed them day and night. They could not even land supplies. But they did meet a Norwegian unit at Dombas, a rail junction sixty miles to the east, and pushed southeast to aid the Norwegians who had been holding out against the Germans coming up the valley from Oslo. This Norwegian force was the main element of Norwegian military resistance, under General Ruge, the Norwegian commander in chief. This force was fighting rearguard actions against the Germans, who had three fully equipped divisions, with artillery and tanks, coming up along the road from Oslo toward Trondheim.

On April 24 the Fifteenth Brigade, which had been recalled from France, also arrived. The Germans were pressing hard, but General Paget, who assumed command of the Allied troops, extricated the troops, including Morgan's brigade, which had lost seven hundred men in the fighting, and some Norwegian units. One day most of the Allied troops hid in a long railway tunnel. Fortunately the railroad remained intact, and over that line the troops retreated a hundred miles to Andalsnes. There what was left of Morgan's brigade was taken back to Britain by cruisers and destroyers. On the nights of April 30 and May 1, the British forces were evacuated from Andalsnes.

The trouble with the British operation in Norway was that it was anything but planned. Thirteen thousand troops had been landed, but the Allies had no established bases in Norway, and were operating with slender lines of communication. Their position was much stronger at Narvik in the far North, because the Germans had not managed to make major reinforcement there. The task at Narvik was to clear the town and the district and then advance in strength up the railroad to the Swedish frontier. As Prime Minister Chamberlain and Admiralty Lord Churchill went to Paris to confer with the French Allies that week, the conversation shifted from the situation in Norway to the general war situation. The French were concerned because the German numerical superiority over the Western Allied forces was three to two, and they were afraid it would soon be two to one. They talked about the dangers to the Dutch and Belgians of a German attack, which they now expected soon. They were very conscious that to avoid annoying the Germans, the Dutch and Belgians had not taken any common measure of defense. If Germany advanced into Holland, they agreed at this meeting, the Allied armies would advance into Belgium, without notice, and the RAF would start bombing German installations in the Ruhr.

By the time the British leaders got back to London, the mess in Norway had grown more dense. The military was run by six chiefs of staff and their deputies, three ministers, and General Ismay of the army, all with their own ideas and the authority to meddle in the affairs in Norway. It made the sensible operation of the campaign almost impossible. Churchill managed to wrest authority from the prime minister and was appointed to preside over the chiefs of staff committee, with General Ismay as his assistant.

After the Namsos evacuation and the fighting of the 148th Infantry Brigade at Lillehammer, the British decided it was impossible to take and hold Trondheim, so Narvik was the focal point. But at Narvik the inferior German force held out and created a stalemate.

The British had been attacking at Narvik since April 16. On April 24 the battleship *Warspite* and three cruisers conducted a three-hour bombardment. But still the Germans held out. French and Polish troops arrived at Narvik, and Lord Cork pressed the attack there. The plan called for the British to land at the head of the fjord beyond Narvik and then attack across Rombaks Fjord. The Twenty-fourth Guards Brigade was to stop any advance from Trondheim. At Narvik three battalions of

French Chasseurs Alpins, two battalions of the French Foreign Legion, four Polish battalions, and a Norwegian unit of thirty-five hundred men were available for the attack.

To delay the northern advance of the German divisions toward Narvik, the British resorted to the most desperate and ineffective measures. They were desperate because they involved the use of untried units, special companies, quickly organized, called "commandos." Several of these companies were sent to Mosjoen, one hundred miles up the coast. Churchill wanted the Namsos force to go along the coastal road to Grong and fight rearguard actions, and then retreat on Mosjoen. This would give Colonel Gubbins, the commander of the commando units, time to get set for a stand. But, and this was why any measures seemed to be destined to be ineffective, the army commanders assured Churchill that the road was impassable. From London came requests that they at least send some of the French ski troops there. But the military men in Norway said that the Chasseurs could not traverse the road, so obviously the Germans could not either. The Germans traversed that same road in just seven days, Namsos to Mosjoen. So the Gubbins force was to retreat, to Bodo and to Mo. The army command was proving totally ineffective, and although the British had control of the sea, they did not have control of air, and that proved decisive.

No one could fault Lord Cork for lack of aggressiveness, but the opportunity missed at Narvik in the beginning was difficult to recreate. The six thousand Germans of the garrison were dug in and organized by the end of April, and a three-hour bombardment from the sea was not enough to soften them up. But when the French and Polish arrived, Lord Cork decided to press the assault on Narvik.

Meanwhile Britain was shaken by the failures and inaction of the war, and early in May the Labor Party demanded a debate on the war situation, which began on May 7, 1940. One speaker after another attacked Prime Minister Chamberlain. The debate became a debate of censure of the prime minister. When the vote came, the Tories won, but by a narrower margin than anyone had thought possible, and it was apparent that Chamberlain had lost the confidence of his own party members. Churchill told him to go on, to bull his way through, but Chamberlain had no heart for the fight.

After much discussion, Chamberlain proposed a National Government, representing all political parties, but the Labor Party balked. While all this was happening, on May 10 the Germans struck in the West, invading Holland and Belgium. Later in the day, Chamberlain recommended that Winston Churchill succeed him as prime minister, and by the end of the day, Churchill had presented himself at Buckingham Palace and was asked to form a new government.

On that day the war changed immeasurably, and so did Britain's official attitude toward fighting it. From this point on, there would be no more relaxation.

On May 10, even before Prime Minister Designate Churchill took office, he had taken the reins of power and responsibility. From that moment, Churchill's major responsibility concerned the new war shaping up in the West, but at the same time, the Norway campaign must be dealt with.

The first landing was finally made by General Mackesey on the night of May 12 at Bjerkvik, and contrary to army expectations, there was very little loss. Winston Churchill, as director of operations in Norway, had sent General Auchinleck to take over from the timid Mackesey, and he took charge of the operation on May 13. His instructions were to cut off the German shipment of iron ore and to maintain a presence in Norway. He asked in turn for 117 battalions of troops, two hundred antiaircraft guns, and four squadrons of aircraft. Only half that could be delivered, but even as the orders for the landing were issued, it was obvious that the war had suddenly changed so much that a total reevaluation was in order.

So by the first week in May, the situation in Norway was really hopeless, because of the failures of British leadership. As Winston Churchill put it—and he was the foremost proponent of positive action in Britain—"The superiority of the Germans in design, management, and energy were plain. They put into ruthless execution a carefully prepared plan of action. They comprehended perfectly the use of the air arm on a great scale in all its aspects. Moreover their individual ascendancy was marked, especially in small parties."

Churchill's assessment of the German planning was really too generous. He did not know that General von Falkenhorst had written his plans for the Norway assault out of a Baedeker travel guide, or that the German army and Luftwaffe had dragged their feet about supporting the operation because it was a navy show. Here Churchill failed to give the British navy credit it deserved for throwing a monkey wrench into the German plans, or how the Norwegian navy and coastal defense forces had done the same. In the planning stages, the Germans had really relied on the promises of Vidkun Quisling and had given him a large sum of money with which to bribe officials and the military. But when on the night of April 8 the German legation at Oslo had stood out on the quay at Oslo Harbor waiting to welcome the German fleet which was heading for the capital, they waited in vain. They were waiting for the pocket battleship *Leutzow* (name changed from *Deutschland*) and the heavy cruiser *Bluecher*, and other ships. Those ships had expected to come in triumphantly with no shots to be fired by Norwegians who had been safely bribed. But as the Germans reached the entrance to the fifty-mile-long Oslo Fjord, they had been challenged by the Norwegian minelayer *Olav Trygverson*. As noted, she had sunk a torpedo boat and damaged a cruiser. The German fleet had come on up the fjord, to a point fifteen miles south of Oslo, where the fjord grew narrow and the Norwegians had built a fortress called Oskarsborg. The Germans arrived just before dawn on April 9, to be greeted by fire from the fort's guns and torpedoes launched from the shore. The *Bluecher*'s magazine blew up and she sank, carrying down with her the Gestapo men who were to take over administration of the government if the king did not come to terms. The *Letzow* was also badly damaged but still floated. But ignominy—Rear Admiral Oskar Kummetz, commander of the German squadron, had to swim ashore, and so did the army commander who was riding in his flagship for the triumph. That certainly was no triumph of planning or of execution.

Churchill was right in his assessment nonetheless. The Germans willed success, they were confident and they plunged ahead, obedient to orders regardless of the odds. The British army leaders shared with the French a timidity born of the 1914–18 war, lest they make the wrong decision that would send thousands of men to their deaths. The best decision for them was no decision at all, and so the Germans moved and the Allies sat, and on May 10 the Germans struck like lightning in the low countries.

CHAPTER 22

The End in Norway

Winston Churchill, as the principal advocate of strong British action in Norway to hamper the German war effort, had hoped for a quick victory, but it was apparent in early April that he was not going to get it. The British army had no enthusiasm for the attack. By mid-April Churchill had managed to get the direction of military operations in Norway into the hands of Lord Cork, of the Royal Navy, but even this change did not solve the problem. On April 16 Lord Cork had undertaken the three-hour bombardment of the German defenses at Narvik. But alas, the dithering of earlier weeks had given the Germans a chance to dig in and get set, as well as to reinforce what had been a ragtag garrison after the smashing of the German destroyer fleet. And so, although the *Warspite* and three cruisers threw everything they had at the shore defenses on April 16, it was not enough power to dislodge the German garrison, and Lord Cork had to seek another solution.

The thaw came, and then French and Polish troop contingents arrived, so Lord Cork decided it was worthwhile to try to attack the town, moving up to the head of the fjord beyond Narvik with the nine battalions of Allied troops and the thirty-five-hundred-man Norwegian force. The assault was begun, but meanwhile, on May

10, the Germans unleashed their offensive against Belgium, Holland, and France, and an entirely new war situation confronted the British. May 10 was the day that Winston Churchill assumed power as prime minister, and immediately he had to make the hard decision about Norway. Britain did not have the resources, the troops or air force, to conduct two military campaigns simultaneously with any chance of success. Troops had actually been borrowed from the French front to use in Norway on the precept that there was nothing happening in France. But with the German breakthrough on the Meuse, which was complete in the second week of May, all resources had to be flung into the battle to save the French front if possible.

At Narvik the battle was going very well for Britain, after a slow start on the land. Getting the command authority out of the hands of the army and into the control of the navy had worked wonders. But now it had to be concluded, even though on May 24 the cabinet made the decision that the Norway expedition would have to be withdrawn. But to withdraw, they must have a port, and so they had to complete the capture. On May 27 the attack on Narvik began across Rombaks Fjord. It was conducted by two battalions of the French Foreign Legion under General Bethouart. It was successful, the landing was made without notable losses, and a German counterattack was beaten off without much trouble. Narvik was captured on May 28, and the Germans retreated into the Norwegian mountains, leaving four hundred prisoners of war in Allied hands.

But now the problems of withdrawal became very serious, because concurrently the British Expeditionary Force had been trapped on the channel coast by the Germans, and the Dunkirk withdrawal had begun. The Royal Navy had the responsibility of covering the Dunkirk evacuation, and the battle fleet had to be held in readiness for a possible attempt by the Germans to invade Britain in the confusion of the Allied defeat in France. Available at Scapa Flow were the battleships and battle cruisers *Rodney*, *Valiant*, *Renown*, and *Repulse*.

Fortunately for the British, the previous defeats of the German naval forces in Norwegian waters had so weakened Admiral Raeder's surface fleet that it was in no condition to offer serious opposition to the British withdrawal. In fact, no opposition from surface forces was offered at all as the convoys assembled at Narvik for the withdrawal.

In the first week of June, all the Allied troops, French and British, numbering twenty-four thousand, with their supplies and equipment, were loading aboard three convoys and getting ready to sail. The only opposition of note was from the Luftwaffe, and the only protection against the force was the naval air arm, since the Royal Force aircraft that could be spared from home defense duties were all employed at Dunkirk.

One squadron of Hurricane fighters had been landed at Norway for shore operations. It fought there until the end, and then the pilots flew their planes onto the deck of the carrier *Glorious* and headed back for Britain. The *Glorious* and the *Ark Royal* offered the convoys protection on the homeward journey.

Lord Cork's Norwegian naval force included the cruisers *Southampton* and *Coventry* and sixteen destroyers, plus service ships and patrol vessels. The cruiser *Devonshire* was also employed, but to embark King Haakon of Norway and his court from Tromso, where they had finally taken refuge. The Admiralty also sent the *Valiant* on June 6 to pick up the first convoy, escort it north to the Shetland Islands, and go back for the second convoy.

But the Norwegian evacuation was to see some German naval resistance after all. The German battle cruisers *Scharnhorst* and *Gneisenau* had been damaged in the earlier Norway operations and returned to Germany for repairs. On June 4 they left Kiel with four destroyers, to attack the British shipping in the Narvik area. Admiral Raeder had no inkling that the British were withdrawing; his dispatch of these vessels was to aid the beleaguered German occupation force. But on June 7 the Germans at sea knew that the British were withdrawing and decided to attack the convoys. On the morning of June 8 the

German force encountered a small convoy coming to Norway, a tanker, a trawler, the troopship *Orama*, and the hospital ship *Atlantis*. They sank all but the hospital ship, which they let alone to go on its way.

The *Hipper* and the destroyers then sailed into Trondheim, but the *Scharnhorst* and the *Gneisenau* stood out to sea, looking for more ships to sink. They found them within hours, the aircraft carrier *Glorious*, with all these Hurricanes aboard, and the destroyers *Acasta* and *Ardent*. The *Glorious* had been detached from convoy duty and sent on ahead to Scapa Flow. Why, no one seemed quite sure. The story was that she was low on fuel, but the convoy was not traveling at flank speed or near it, and investigation showed the *Glorious* had enough fuel to go with the convoy. In any event, the decision to detach her caused her destruction, for at four-thirty on the afternoon of June 8, the two German battle cruisers sighted her smoke, and closed. At a range of about fifteen miles, they began shooting their big guns. The *Glorious* was two hundred miles out ahead of the convoy, and thus could expect no assistance from the *Ark Royal* or the *Valiant*. Her four-inch guns were made primarily for antiaircraft fire and could not reach the enemy. The captain ordered the torpedo bombers launched for attacks on the enemy ships, but before it could be done, a shell hit in the forward hangar and started fires that destroyed the Hurricane fighters. The fires also spread and prevented the loading of torpedoes on the bombers. The shells from the two battle cruisers struck home again and again.

The two escorting destroyers did all they could to save their charge. Both made smoke and both fired their torpedoes at the enemy ships. Soon the *Ardent* was sunk by the big guns of the battle cruisers. The *Acasta* continued to fight, steaming full speed away from the German ships, making smoke to try to cover the *Glorious*. But the men aboard could see that she was sinking. They ducked back into their own smoke and fired torpedoes. They saw one torpedo hit and send up a yellow flash and a column of smoke and water. They ducked back into the smoke screen, came out, and prepared to fire torpedoes again. But this time the *Scharnhorst* was waiting for them, and when they emerged, the shells came thick and fast.

A shell hit in the engine room, and then there was an enormous explosion, probably the magazine going up, and the ship lifted out of the water. The captain gave orders to abandon, and the crew began going over the side. The ship's surgeon was still trying to help the wounded. The captain refused to leave the ship, and virtually no one else left it successfully. There was only one survivor of the destroyer.

The *Glorious* was glorious no more. She was listing heavily and burning as the destroyers were sunk. Soon the order was given to abandon ship, and the crew got off as best they could. The carrier sank twenty minutes later.

In all, nearly fifteen hundred officers and men of the Royal Navy died in this action, thirty-nine were rescued by a Norwegian ship, six were rescued by the Germans and made prisoners of war.

The *Scharnhorst* had been badly damaged by the single torpedo from the *Acasta*, and she went back to Germany to dry dock.

The *Valiant* was at sea during all this action, out to meet the convoy, and while she received one message from the *Glorious,* it did not make any sense, and the belief was that one of the first shells from the *Scharnhorst* had disabled the ship's radio.

The cruiser *Devonshire* was about one hundred miles away, carrying the king of Norway into exile. She received the message from the *Glorious* saying she was under attack, but that was all, and she did not make a signal lest by breaking radio silence, she bring enemy capital ships down on her.

On the morning of June 9, the *Valiant* met the hospital ship *Atlantis,* and the story of the attack by the *Hipper* and the other ships was revealed. The suspicions about the fate of the *Glorious* were aroused. Admiral Forbes set sail from Scapa Flow with the *Rodney*, the *Renown*, and six destroyers, and began search.

The damage done to the *Scharnhorst* also caused the *Gneisenau* to abandon North Sea operations and to return to Trondheim. The *Hipper* came out again briefly, but the convoys by that time had escaped.

On June 10 Admiral Forbes ordered the *Ark Royal* to leave the convoy patrol and join his squadron. Then he would take the *Rodney*, the *Renown*, and the carrier and his destroyers to the Trondheim area and start with a carrier attack on the two German battle cruisers bottled up there. The attack would be made in conjunction with attack by RAF bombers. The RAF bombers attacked on June 11, but did not hit anything. Next morning, fifteen Skua bombers from the *Ark Royal* attacked and came to disaster. They were too slow, and the Germans were warned of their coming.

Eight of the Skuas were lost.

Thus the Norway campaign came to an end with a final British naval disaster. But in retrospect, the naval campaign in Norway had a positive balance, for in fact, after Norway, the Germans could never again try to challenge the British fleet at sea. Beginning on April 9, the Germans had suffered one naval disaster after another. On that day the eight-inch gun cruiser *Bluecher* was sunk by the Norwegian coastal defense team near Oslo. The light cruiser *Karlsruhe* was sunk by the British submarine *Truant* in the Kattegat, while on its way to participate in the invasion of Norway. The torpedo boat *Albatross* was sunk off Oslo on April 9 in that assault on the Norwegian capital. The battle cruiser *Gneisenau* was damaged in action with the *Renown*.

The British had lost the destroyer *Glowworm* to the *Hipper* on April 8, and the next day lost the *Gurkha*, and on April 10 lost the *Hardy* and the *Hunter* in the brave attack on Narvik. But the *Hipper* had been badly damaged in the encounter with the *Glowworm*, as had the pocket battleship *Luetzow (Deutschland)*, first by shore batteries and then by a torpedo from the British submarine *Spearfish*. The light cruiser *Emden* was also damaged off Oslo by the shore batteries, and the gunnery training ship *Bremse* was damaged as well.

On April 10 the British at Narvik had damaged the destroyers *Anton Schmitt, Wilhelm Heidkamp, Hans Ludemann, Georg Thiele,* and *Bernd von Arnim.* Three days later, the British squadron destroyed those five destroyers and five more as well.

The Light cruiser *Koenigsberg* was sunk by the fleet air arm off Bergen on April 10; eight U-boats were sunk in the Norwegian campaign. Only the U-boat losses could be easily repaired by the U-boat building campaign, which Admiral Raeder was uneasily putting into effect at the expense of his surface fleet, knowing as he now did that there was no hope of challenging the British on the surface except with the odd raider. Admiral Raeder did not know it yet, but he was headed for trouble, because Hitler had been oversold in the 1930s on the surface fleet, and was going to be in for some severe shocks.

British losses at Norway included one carrier, two cruisers, one sloop, seven destroyers, and three submarines, while their allies, the French and Polish, each lost a destroyer and a submarine. The British suffered damage to six cruisers, two sloops, and eight destroyers.

But considering the disparate strengths of the British and German fleets, the losses to Britain were troublesome, but those to Germany were nearly disastrous. Never again in this war could Germany launch a destroyer action, with those ten new destroyers gone. And the damage to her battle cruisers and cruisers was such that her sea power was enormously diminished. The result would show in a few months when Hitler contemplated the invasion of Britain, and had to be told by Admiral Raeder that Germany did not have the naval strength to mount such an effort.

That spring of 1940 came two developments in the sea war, one in favor of the Allies and one in favor of the Germans.

The British victory came about when the *U-31* was undergoing trials in Schillig Bay in the Heligoland Bight that March. On March 11 the British Bomber Command ordered a reconnaissance mission of the area by a group of Blenheim bombers. They were armed with 250-pound bombs for attack on land targets and shipping. The bombs were not meant for submarines; the usual antisubmarine charge was a twenty-five-pound bomb.

In the bight, one of the Blenheims became separated from the others. It was trying to get through the overcast and came down to thirty-five hundred feet then ducked through the clouds to twenty-five hundred feet and surprised the *U-31*. The bomber attacked, using its camera at the same time. The U-boat dived, but the bomber dropped 250-pound bombs and scored two direct hits. The pilot circled and took photos of the oil and air bubbles rising to the surface.

When the Blenheim returned to England, Bomber Command studied the photographs, and then took actions that brought the anti-U-boat war into a new phase. For the first time, the British were confident that aircraft could be used successfully in a routine way to sink U-boats.

The German development was more complicated and at first seemed to be more important. When the Norway campaign ended, Admiral Doenitz was quick to move U-boat bases into Norway. He had not been idle in the period when the torpedo problem was being investigated. May had brought a satisfactory U-boat construction record so that for the first time, Doenitz had enough 500-ton and 750-ton U-boats to begin his wolf pack campaign in the Atlantic. But before he could start that, he had to reestablish the morale of the shattered U-boat service. This he undertook to do by sending his U-boat corps operations officer, Lieutenant Commander Victor Oehrn, out to sea in the *U-37* to show the captains that ships could still be sunk. At this point, the skippers had no confidence in their torpedoes.

Lieutenant Commander Oehrn used the standard electric torpedo, but closed down the magnetic exploders, using contact exploders instead. He came back from his cruise that spring with a record of eleven ship sinkings, for a total of forty-seven thousand tons of shipping. It was impressive, both to Doenitz and to his captains, and did much to bring back their confidence in their weapons.

By June, the U-boat men had that confidence and Doenitz had a plan of attack against the British. The U-boats now had access to the Norwegian ports (except Narvik) all along the North Sea, which gave them an enormously increased latitude for attack on British shipping. Bergen was already being converted to become a U-boat base. And to man his new oceangoing boats, Doenitz now had well-trained and dedicated crews such as that of Lieutenant Ott Kretschmer, who had earned his spurs in one of the little 250-ton boats, in which he had made nine successful patrols, mostly minelaying.

At the end of the first week of June, Admiral Doenitz launched his U-boat offensive. Lieutenant Lemp sailed from Wilhelmshaven in the *U-30* and moved to the west of Ireland and south to St. George's Channel. Lieutenant Commander Prien moved in the *U-47* to the Southwestern Approaches, as far south as Spain, and went into action. Soon he had sunk ten ships—sixty-six thousand tons of shipping.

Lieutenant Kretschmer's *U-99* sailed on June 17, and after one narrow escape from attack by a scout bomber, from the battle cruiser *Scharnhorst,* he had to scurry back to friendly waters for repairs. The German bomber had broken the lens of his attack periscope and knocked out his compasses. He did not have to go to Wilhelmshaven, but pulled in to Bergen for his repairs. But the damage was too serious, and finally he did return to base, before starting out again.

The June campaign was hugely successful, wiping out the memory of those terrible months for the German submariners when nothing had seemed to go right. The U-boats sank sixty-four ships that month, more than 260,000 tons. If Winston Churchill had earlier felt that the submarine threat was under control, he had new ideas after this month. Doenitz's boats sank ships on twenty-six days of the month. Because of the shortage of escorts, some ships were still traveling alone, and these were the principal targets of the new U-boat campaign.

Another factor working for the Germans these days was the shortage of escort craft that had continued, forcing the British to try a patrol system instead of escort. It did not work very well, as witness Doenitz's record, but it would take the British time to change. The patrol craft did not sink any submarines in June. The most effective British weapon was countermining, which cost the Germans some submarines later.

In June the British built escort craft furiously, even as they struggled to get their troops out of the trap in France. Sixty-seven destroyers were under construction, ninety-two corvettes and sloops, forty-three trawlers, and two hundred motor launches for harbor patrol. But before the British building program began to produce its best results, there were many cheerless days ahead for the Royal Navy, and what the U-boat men called a "happy time" for them. In the beginning the new Atlantic boats would cruise as "loners" and make significant scores, but soon Doenitz would be able to put his highly organized team system into play.

CHAPTER 23

Blitzkrieg
in the West

In the spring of 1940 the French and the British sat and
trained and planned for static defenses behind the Maginot Line and its extensions, with very little attention
to armored vehicles. The British did not have a single
armored division in the British Expeditionary Force, as
noted. The Germans were getting ready to fight a modern
war. The odd fact was that the total combined British
and French forces could mount four thousand armored
vehicles, while the Germans had only twenty-eight
hundred and only twenty-five hundred were available for
the offensive. But the British and French tanks were not
very effective, because they were split up among the
infantry divisions. The British Matilda tank was superior
to the German Mark III because it had stronger armor
and a two-pound gun as compared to the German 37-
mm gun. The French did not have any faith in their own
armor, although the Germans knew that the French tanks
were superior in armor and gun capacity, although
slower. But in France, even more than in Norway, it was
a question of confidence. The Germans massed seven of
their ten panzer divisions, five of them in the Sedan
sector.

General Heinz Guderian had distinguished himself in Poland with his panzer tactics, and in the fall of 1939 he first made some evaluations of the armored performance. The light divisions were changed into panzer divisions. The motorized infantry divisions were made more mobile by the elimination of one of their infantry regiments. The tank regiments were equipped with new panzer units, Panzers III and Panzers IV. Guderian was entrusted with the training of the Grosse Deutschland Infantry Regiment, and some panzer divisions, but his main job that fall and spring was to plan for panzer operations.

Guderian conferred with General von Manstein, who was developing his own plan for the invasion of the West and finally secured Hitler's support for it so that it was forced upon the conservatives of the army general staff. The real reason for the acceptance of the Von Manstein plan was that forced landing in Belgium by the plane carrying the generals' plan, which had apparently been compromised. The Von Manstein plan made use of the old plan. The German forces were divided into Army Group A and Army Group B. The latter, Army Group B, would make a great attack on the right flank, invading Belgium and Holland, as the Allies expected them to do. They would use three panzer divisions and parachute troops. As General von Mellenthin later wrote, "The advance of Army Group B would be formidable, noisy, and spectacular." It would also be deceptive, because the decisive role in the struggle was that of Army Group A. This group consisted of the Fourth, Twelfth, and Sixteenth Armies, and Panzergruppe Kleist. The Fourth Army would advance south of the Meuse River and cross at Dinant. But the main thrust would be delivered by Panzergruppe Kleist on the Twelfth Army front. This shock force consisted of the Reinhardt Panzer Corps, including the Fifth and Eighth Panzer divisions, Guderian's three-division Panzer Corps, and Wietersheim's Motorized Corps of five motorized divisions. They would confuse the enemy by crossing the mountainous Ardennes area, which was very difficult for tanks, and cross the Meuse at Sedan. Then they would turn west and push beyond the flank and rear of the French and British forces in Belgium.

This daring plan appealed to Hitler and was adopted in the winter of 1940, but the old-line generals continued to block the way of the panzer advocates. At war games at Koblenz early in February, Guderian proposed that on the fifth day of the attack, a thrust be made with armored and motorized forces which would cross the Meuse River near Sedan to break through the Allied lines and move toward Amiens. Army Chief of Staff General Halder said the idea was totally ridiculous. He said that a bridgehead should be established across the Meuse, but then the panzers must wait for the infantry armies to come and make the regular sort of unified attack that Halder was used to from World War I. Guderian spoke up in favor of his idea, but nothing was decided.

Guderian then went back to studies of the French fortifications made by the engineers, which strengthened his opinions about the need for a swift move. When new war games were held a week later. Guderian tried again, and was again rebuffed by Halder. But, said Guderian, the terrain in the Ardennes north of the Meuse was so difficult that it would take the infantry forever to move.

But, said the conventional generals, the Guderian way was very risky.

The argument continued until finally Guderian and General Von Wietersheim, commander of the XIV Army Corps and a convert to the panzer concept, said that under the circumstances, they had no confidence in the ability of the army to succeed. They were arrayed against the chief generals, above all Colonel General Von Rundstedt, who said he did not know anything about tanks, and preferred to follow the old ways. After much more discussion, it was decided that General von Kleist would be in command, but Guderian could take solace in the fact that his Panzer Corps would form the van of the attack through the Ardennes. He would have the Grosse Deutschland Infantry Regiment, and three panzer divisions, and a number of specialist troops.

So the games ended, with the traditional generals totally unconvinced that the panzer system would work, totally unconvinced that the Von Manstein plan of attack would work, and very disgruntled that Hitler was making up the rules for them.

Guderian went off on leave and then settled down to train his officers in what was to most of them an entirely new concept of warfare.

It was a trying time for Guderian, faced with the open opposition of the general corps. But one day Hitler held a conference of the commanders of Army Group A with Von Kleist and his generals. Everyone had his say; Guderian came last. He told how he planned that first day to cross the Luxembourg frontier, move through southern Belgium toward Sedan, cross the Meuse River, and establish a bridgehead on the other side so that the infantry corps following could cross over safely. They could move in three columns, he said, reach the Belgian frontier posts on the first day, and break through on the second day to reach Neufchateau, on the third day reach Bouillon and cross the Semois River, and on the fourth day reach the Meuse, and the fifth day cross.

Then what? asked Hitler. It was the first time anyone had asked this vital question.

Then, said General Guderian, he would continue his advance westward. The higher-ups would have to decide whether his objective should be Amiens or Paris. If they asked him, said Guderian, he would say drive past Amiens to the English Channel.

Hitler nodded.

General Busch found this talk of revolutionary warfare all very distasteful, and Guderian, an arrogant upstart, spoke up. "I don't think you'll cross the river in the first place," he said.

So the meeting broke up, with the traditional generals no more convinced than before.

As the Germans knew from the troop dispositions of the French and British, the indications were that the Allies expected a repeat of the Schlieffen plan of World War I, which Hitler had rejected. Belgian and Dutch forces faced Germany, from which they expected the attack to come. The French and British were strung out on the Maginot Line and its extension, and the Germans knew that the extension was weak between Montmedy and Sedan.

The mass of the French army and the British Expeditionary Force were located in Flanders between the Meuse and the English Channel, and studying the Allied order of battle, Guderian did not believe they had any conception of the sort of attack the Germans might launch. As for his own officers and men, he had imbued them with the vision: they would drive to the English Channel!

The German plan also called for a real attack on Belgium and Holland, to lure the French and British armies into Belgium, so they could be cut off by Guderian's panzer forces.

The Germans attacked Belgium and the Netherlands from the sky on May 10. By daylight, parachute troops had captured bridges around the Hague and Rotterdam that were vital to Dutch defenses and had also taken several airfields. By the end of that first day, the Dutch air force had been destroyed and the Dutch army rendered powerless. The German Eighteenth Army struck west in the southern part of the country, and broke the Dutch defense line along the Meuse River, or Maas as it is called in Holland. Queen Wilhelmina and her government left for England. The German Fifty-fourth Bomber Wing bombed Rotterdam, and killed nearly a thousand people and wounded nearly thirty thousand. It was part of a campaign of terror, and it worked; in order to prevent the destruction of another city the next day, the Dutch commander in chief surrendered all his forces.

The Germans also attacked Belgium that first day, along the Meuse River and the Albert Canal. On the second day, airborne troops captured the key fort of Eben Emael. The Belgian army retreated to the River Dyle.

As far as General Guderian was concerned, the concept of blitzkrieg included a high level of cooperation between the panzer units and the Luftwaffe. General von Stutterheim and General Loerzer were his contacts; General Loerzer's *fliegerkorps* (air group) would give close support. The critical moment was the crossing of the Meuse, they all agreed. And the way the support would come would be by constant attention and bombing and strafing to keep the enemy defenses off guard, rather than a concentrated bombardment attack by bombers and dive bombers. So it was all worked out satisfactorily before the operations began.

The German forces were called to the alert at one-thirty on the afternoon of May 9. General Guderian left Koblenz at four o'clock in the afternoon and arrived at his field headquarters near Bitburg that evening. The troops were drawn up along the Luxembourg frontier, between Vianden and Echternach.

At five-thirty on the morning of May 10, the units crossed the Luxembourg frontier. As Guderian had predicted, at the end of the first day, they had cracked through the Belgian defenses. In the planning, Marshal Goering had demanded that troops of the Grosse Deutschland Infantry Regiment be taken by transport aircraft behind the Belgian lines, to create confusion, and by the end of the first day, Guderian's panzers had made contact with these forces.

The Luftwaffe had various tasks assigned to it for this drive in the West. One was to knock out the air potential of the Netherlands and Belgium, which was not a hard task, because both countries barely had air forces at all. A second task was to protect Army Group A and Army Group B on their drives into the low countries and the Ardennes. The French air force was in a state of flux that spring, changing over from obsolete types of aircraft to more modern, and there was no uniformity, nor could many of the French planes stack up against the German fighters. The French air force's twelve hundred aircraft were soon knocked out of the air. The French squadrons were running only about 40 percent operational, and although the French aviators were skillful, they had the great disadvantage of obsolete equipment.

The British had been reluctant to expose too much of

their air force in France, and had about 420 planes there. The Luftwaffe had 2,750 aircraft at this point, enough to protect troop movements as well as attack the enemy air forces. The Germans had air superiority from the first day, even though they never did destroy all the Allied aircraft, particularly the British.

As with everything else connected with the British-French war effort, the air effort was confused in the utmost. The French and British air forces concentrated on attacking German troop movements, while the RAF in Britain bombed German targets in the Ruhr and other areas. Thus the whole air operation was highly dispersed, as compared to the concentrated effort of the Germans.

For the first two days of the campaign, the Luftwaffe shielded the Ardennes offensive from prying eyes. By May 12, the Luftwaffe reported superiority in the air, and then the German squadrons began attacking Allied transport and supporting the ground operations of the panzers. A basic element of this support was the bombing by the screaming Stuka dive bombers, which struck terror into the hearts of the French reserve troops who were holding the Meuse River line. On the first day of the attack, May 10, the Luftwaffe lost eighty-three aircraft, which was a very high figure, and the next day they lost forty-two more aircraft. It was an indication of the total support the Luftwaffe was giving the panzer forces.

Guderian's three columns were in various stages of advancement. The First Panzer Division had been held up by effective road demolition in the mountains. That night would be devoted to road repair. The Second Panzer Division was moving along, and so was the Tenth Panzer Division, which had run into French elements.

On the morning of May 11, the minefields along the Belgian frontier were penetrated, and by noon the repairs were finished and the First Panzer Division was moving forward again, tanks out front, heading toward Neufchateau. Soon Neufchateau fell after a short fight with the French and Belgians. That evening Bouillon was reached, as Guderian had specified, but the enemy managed to hold on to it that night. Except for this deviation, the panzer corps was right on schedule.

Von Kleist tried to divert the Tenth Panzer Division to meet a hypothetical attack by French cavalry. Guderian objected strongly and won his point: this diversion would have made it impossible to cross the Meuse on time. The advance continued next day, and in fact, the French cavalry did not appear.

Leaving the Grosse Deutschland Infantry Regiment in reserve at Saint Medard, the Guderian group on May 12 drove to Bouillon and watched the First Rifle Regiment launch an attack that carried the objective. The French had blown up the bridges over the Semois River, but the stream was fordable, so it did not make any difference. Guderian put his troops to repairing the major bridge, and then followed the tanks across the river toward Sedan. Soon the tanks were in trouble: mined roads. Guderian returned to Bouillon, where he ran into an Allied air attack. The planes were after his bridge, but they did not get it.

Later that day he checked his Tenth Division and witnessed an attack, was satisfied and returned to headquarters. Everything was going splendidly, from the German point of view. That day Guderian was sent for by General von Kleist to give him new orders. He was to thrust across the Meuse next day, May 13. Checking his troops, Guderian knew that the Second Panzer Division would not be ready to cross, because they had struck serious opposition. Von Kleist said send the others, and so Guderian agreed, but von Kleist wanted to use a softening-up carpet bombing which would slow down the Panzers. Guderian had an agreement with the Luftwaffe that they would act as his artillery, and so far it had worked fine. But rank had its privileges.

On May 12 the last of the French cavalry fell back behind the Meuse, and all the bridges in the Guderian sector were blown up. But the cavalry, which was supposed to delay the Germans for six days, had only delayed them for three days.

On the night of May 12, the First and Tenth Panzer

divisions had occupied the north bank of the Meuse and had captured Sedan. The next day, the attack went very well. Whatever happened between Von Kleist's headquarters and the Luftwaffe, Guderian did not know, but the Luftwaffe performed as he and Loerzer had agreed they would, with a constant air cover—emphasizing Stuka dive bombers that knocked out the French artillery on the other bank—and the results were excellent. That afternoon, Guderian, who liked to be up front with his troops, was one of the first to cross the Meuse.

On May 13 Prime Minister Winston Churchill of Britain made his first speech in Parliament. He was well aware of the rapidly deteriorating military situation in France, and he offered a glimpse of a grim future to Britain. "I have nothing to offer but blood, toil, tears, and sweat," he said.

The next day, mindful of the dropping of paratroops by the Germans on Belgium and Holland, the British formed the Home Guard of volunteers between the ages of seventeen and sixty-five pledged to defend the homeland. Suddenly in London the war seemed very close.

General Maurice Gamelin, the supreme commander of the Allied armies, had begun to recognize that the Ardennes thrust was the real one, but he was not much worried, even though the Germans had reached the Meuse. He did not expect them to try to cross until the German Twelfth Army Infantry arrived on the scene, which would be in five or six days.

General Erwin Rommel's Seventh Panzer Division was preparing to cross the Meuse at Dinant. The fighting here was furious, and French artillery fire was destroying many of the division's boats. Rommel needed a smoke screen, but he had none, so he ordered the engineers to set fire to a number of houses in the valley to create smoke. His Seventh Rifle Regiment got one company across the river but was stalled. The French fire was so great that the crossing equipment was destroyed and the crossing had to be stopped. Many wounded men were receiving medical treatment in a house by the demolished bridge. Rommel went back and got artillery support.

Then General Rommel drove back along the Meuse, to Leffe, a village on the outskirts of Dinant, where there was a footbridge, but it had been barred by the French with a steel plate. Here again, the crossing point a bit to the right had been inundated with fire, and the crossing had come to a stop. Some men had gotten across, but there were many wounded, and the debris of the crossing, damaged rubber boats and dinghies, lay on the opposite shore. The French fire was excellent and disabling; any man who showed himself got shot at.

Several tanks had reached the crossing point, but they had also run out of ammunition and sat, mute. Rommel had ordered other tanks up forward, and soon they arrived, followed by field howitzers. The tanks moved north along the riverbank, turrets turned left, closely watching the opposite shore and firing. Under cover of this fire, the crossing got going again. Engineers put up a cable ferry using several large pontoons. More rubber boats were launched, and they brought the wounded back from the far shore.

General Rommel took personal command of the Second Battalion of the Seventh Rifle Regiment, and directed operations. He crossed the river in a rubber boat, and joined the company that had been over since early morning. He saw two other companies up ahead, making progress in the bridgehead. He moved north along a gully to a forward command post, and heard that enemy tanks were coming. They had no antitank weapons, but he instructed the men to open fire with small arms; they did, and the French tanks pulled back into a small hollow a thousand yards to the northwest of the village of Leffe.

Rommel finally arrived at brigade headquarters on the west bank and found that the commander of the Seventh Motorcycle Battalion had been wounded, and his adjutant killed. The French had launched a counterattack and had caused many casualties. He needed to get more tanks to the west bank, and ordered them ferried over that night, but ferrying across the 120-yard-wide river was slow work, and next morning there were still only fifteen tanks on the west side of the river. More had to be hurried across.

It was a hard crossing for the Seventh Panzer Division, and many men were killed and wounded.

It was May 14.

At daybreak General Rommel learned that Colonel von Bismarck's regiment was surrounded by the French near Onhaye, three miles west of Dinant, and he decided to go to his assistance with every available tank. At 9:00 A.M. he sent the Twenty-fifth Panzer Regiment under Colonel Rothenburg along the Meuse valley with the thirty tanks available on the west bank, and they got nearly to Onhaye without meeting resistance. There they found Von Bismarck, safe and sound. The radio reception had been faulty; he had said he had arrived at Onhaye, not been encircled there.

Five tanks were assigned to support the infantry which would move to a wood a thousand yards north of Onhaye. Colonel Rothenburg led the five tanks, and Rommel followed close behind him. The tanks were 150 yards out in front, and following them were the thirty other tanks of the unit. Suddenly, as the tanks reached the edge of the wood, they came under heavy gunfire, from the west. Shells landed all around, and Rommel's tank received two hits on the periscope and the upper edge of the turret Rommel was wounded in the cheek by a fragment.

The tank driver throttled up and drove into the nearest bushes, but he did not see that it was a steep hillside, and the tank slid down the hill to the western edge of the wood. It stopped, canted over on one side, in open position for the enemy artillery, which was only five hundred yards away on the edge of the next wooded space.

General Rommel tried to swing the turret around to bring the tank's 37-mm gun to bear on the opposite woods, but the angle of the tank made it impossible. The French battery then opened fire on them, and Rommel decided to abandon the tank. The supporting infantry gave fire, but the lieutenant in charge was seriously wounded, and had to be rescued. They made their way down the hill, found two other tanks damaged, and then discovered the rest of the tanks. Rommel gave orders for them to move east. Rothenburg's tank had been hit, and the smoke candles it carried had been set afire, so it provided a smoke screen which prevented the French from hitting any more of the German vehicles. They regrouped, and the Twenty-fifth Panzer Regiment launched an attack that evening which was successful, and they occupied their current objective.

On the morning of May 14 the French Third Armored Division counterattacked with air support. But the French tanks moved slowly, and by the time they got up front, the German antitank guns were in place and part of the First Panzer Division came up. Seventy French tanks were destroyed, and a number of French aircraft were shot down by small-arms fire.

The Second Panzer Division crossed the Meuse near Donchery and began fighting its way up the southern bank. The air attacks from the British and French were met by strong antiaircraft fire, and at the end of this day, the Germans estimated that they had shot down 150 aircraft. That day Guderian sent the First Panzer Division across the Ardennes Canal to head west and break through the French defenses.

At this point the German aim was to cut the Allied armies in two, from their new bridgeheads across the Meuse at Sedan and Dinant. Forty-five divisions had been allocated to the thrust through the Ardennes, while only thirty divisions had invaded Holland and Belgium. The plan was succeeding brilliantly. British and French troops were still advancing into Belgium to meet the German threat to Brussels. "I could have wept for joy," said Hitler when he learned of this. "They have fallen into the trap."

At the end of May 14, it was apparent that the French resistance was about to collapse. French morale had been undermined in the months of inactivity, and now the dive bombing seemed to unnerve the soldiers. North of Meziers, General Reinhardt's two panzer divisions crossed the Meuse at several places as General Hoth's panzer corps surprised the French at Dinant. On May 14 Guderian's panzer corps enlarged the bridgehead.

On May 15 the Netherlands was conquered; the German Eighteen Army swung south to help the Sixth Army.

On May 15 General Rommel's Seventh Panzer Division was driving on Avesnes and crossed the railroad line a mile southwest of Solre le Chateau. Here is General Rommel's recollection:

> The people in the houses were rudely awakened by the din of our tanks, the clatter and roar of tracks and engines. Troops lay bivouacked beside the road, military vehicles stood parked in farmyards and in some places on the road itself. Civilians and French troops, their faces distorted with terror, lay huddled in the ditches, alongside hedges and every hollow beside the road. We passed refugee columns, the carts abandoned by their owners, who had fled in panic to the fields. On we went, at a steady speed, towards our objective. Every so often a quick glance at the map by a shaded light and a short wireless message to divisional headquarters to report the position and thus the success of the Twenty-fifth Panzer Regiment. Every so often to look out of the hatch to assure myself that there was still no resistance and that contact was being maintained to the rear. The flat countryside lay spread out around us under the cold light of the moon. We are through the Maginot Line. It was hardly conceivable. Twenty-two years before we had stood for four and a half long years before this selfsame enemy and had won victory after victory and yet finally lost the war. And now we had broken through the renowned Maginot Line and were driving deep into enemy territory. It was not just a beautiful dream, it was reality.

On May 15 General von Rundstedt's staff grew nervous and forbade any further advance by the panzers until the infantry divisions of the Twelfth Army could come up to protect the southern German flank. When Guderian and the other panzer commanders learned this, they raised a storm of protest. If the drive stopped now, the British and French would be given a chance to re-group, and the opportunity to strike to the sea would be lost. Guderian went to Von Kleist's headquarters to press the argument, and held several heated discussions with staff officers, until finally Von Kleist intervened and per-mitted the continued drive for another twenty-four hours.

While the French center was being broken at Sedan, another violent tank encounter developed in Belgium, when Hoeppner's panzer corps ran into more powerful French armored forces north of the Meuse near Gem-bloux. Hoeppner then moved along the line of the Sambre River, in order to keep in touch with the Von Kleist thrust south of the river.

Once across the Meuse, the Germans began to accel-erate. South of Sedan, General Huntzinger, who com-manded the Second French Army, had made the error of keeping his best troops in the wrong area. North of Sedan, General Corap's Ninth French Army had been whittled down steadily until it was hardly effective.

On May 16 Guderian's troops were still driving and reached Montcornet, where they met the Sixth Panzer Division, which had also reached the town. Three panzer divisions were poured through. That day Guderian's lead-ing units covered forty miles and were fifty-five miles past Sedan. That night Guderian announced his intention of continuing the drive the next day in the belief that the "hold" order had been rescinded.

May 16 was the day the French called *Le Jourde la Grande Peur*, the Day of Wrath. In Paris it was reported that the whole French army had fallen apart, and a great bonfire was made of the official archives at the Quai d'Orsay. The road to Paris was now open to the Germans. But the French did not understand that at the moment, the Germans were not interested in Paris. They were driving for the English Channel, to entrap both French and British armies.

But early on the morning of May 17, General Guderian received another summons to General von Kleist's head-quarters, along with the shocking news that he was to stop his advance to the sea immediately. Von Kleist berated Guderian for disobeying orders, to the point that Guderian asked to be relieved of command. The argument continued until General List came up and told Guderian he could not quit his command, but that he must obey the order to hold up because it came from OKW—which meant Hitler himself.

The German attack continued in the air and on the ground. The Allied airmen tried desperately to destroy the new bridges the Germans had put across the Meuse, but they suffered losses of 56 percent, and did not wreck the bridge, because the Germans had fighter superiority. By May 17, when the French evacuated the airfield at Charleville, the Germans moved right in—they were that well organized. JU 52s flew in parts, equipment, and ground personnel. So the German panzers halted, having reached the Oise River, seventy miles from Sedan. By the evening of May 18, the panzers reached St. Quentin, having been ordered again to advance and break the Canal du Nord line, where the Allies were trying to establish a front. Two British divisions occupied their positions on that line, but the French, who were supposed to come up to defend fourteen miles south of the canal did not show up at all. The two British divisions had no artillery; so that line was not going to hold for long. On May 19 German ''reconnaissance in force'' reached the old Somme battlefield. On the twentieth they reached Abbeville and the English Channel.

The Allies were in disarray. General Reinhardt's tanks cut through to Le Catelet, to find that General Giraud was there, trying to set up a counterattack; instead he found the French Ninth Army command post overrun, and Giraud escaped alone on foot, to be picked up by the Germans the next day.

This swiftness of the German advanace caused confusion on both sides. Hitler complained that the army had moved too fast and jeopardized the success of the operation. French Prime Minister Paul Reynaud fired General Gamelin, who had made so many wrong decisions, beginning with reliance on the Maginot Line, and appointed General Maxime Weygand to run the war. Weygand found immediately that he had very little to run; he had only eight divisions in reserve, and they were in Lorraine and had already been cut off.

On the nineteenth General Charles de Gaulle's French Fourth Armored Division counterattacked at Laon and was severly mauled. That night, Guderian's XIX Army Corps had reached the Cambrai-Peronne-Ham line, and the First Panzer Division received its freedom of movement, and prepared to advance toward Amiens to establish a bridgehead on the south bank of the Somme. The Second Panzer Division was to move to Abbeville and establish another bridgehead across the Somme.

Before he was fired on May 19, General Gamelin had issued orders for coordinated attacks from north and south on the Germans. The British commander in chief, Lord Gort, obeyed those orders, not having heard of a postponement ordered by Weygand. The British Seventieth Infantry Brigade was overtaken by the Eighth Panzer Division and decimated, so that by dark, only 250 men were left.

On the morning of May 20, General Guderian reached Amiens, which was taken by noon. The Germans had a bridgehead extending four miles. Now they were collecting prisoners so fast that the front line units found it hard to handle them. Guderian sent his Second Panzer Division to Abbeville that day, and that night one battalion of the Second Panzer Division reached Noyelles on the Atlantic coast, and now four hundred thousand British and French troops were trapped in the Dunkirk pocket. Lord Gort was talking to the War Office about organizing a British evacuation.

CHAPTER 24

The British Expeditionary Force

The British Royal Air Force was the most modern weapon the Western Allies possessed in France, although most of the RAF strength was hoarded back at home to protect the British Isles from the Luftwaffe. At the outset, the RAF was still modernizing, and the fighter contingent sent to France included two squadrons of biplane Gladiator fighters, long past their prime. But before the action began, these fighter planes had been replaced by sleek Hurricane fighters, at the time among the best fighters in the West, a suitable match against the German Me-109. Fewer, but better, were the new Spitfire fighters, which had the most sophisticated equipment of any fighter planes in Europe.

But the fact was that the French did not know this, because the real strength of the RAF was carefully concealed, even from Britain's closest ally. France, said the British, was full of spies and Nazi sympathizers, and not to be trusted with the real secrets, such as that of the radar chain that controlled the RAF and would be vital to the defense of Britain all too soon. So although the RAF had fourteen hundred modern fighter planes in May 1940, fewer than one hundred of them were stationed in

France, and when the Germans began to move on May 10, only about two hundred more were sent over. Later the French would claim that had the British committed their RAF to the battle in May, the Germans could have been stopped. Perhaps that was true, but it was similar to restating the relative strengths of armor: the French and British had more tanks and better tanks than the Germans, but they did not know how to use them. So the British had more air strength than the Germans, but they were not willing to use it to save France. As far as the British Expeditionary Force was concerned, one can only say that it was the victim of the British thinking of the times. After the end of World War I, the British army had been regarded as an imperial policeman, dedicated to the maintenance of order within the empire. It was full of superannuated, overweight officers hanging on to the jobs because there weren't many others in the depressed years of the 1930s. Horse-drawn transport was not eliminated from the British army until 1936. The army was not enlarged until the spring of 1939, and even then, the plans were fuzzy. The Territorial Army (the equivalent of the American National Guard) was doubled, on paper, to 210,000 men. But they trained only two weeks a year and on weekends. The outbreak of war brought the call-up of the Territorial Army, but not the training or equipment of it. Most units had no artillery or signal services, not even any modern machine guns. Some units did not have enough rifles to issue one per man. Conscription began only in April, 1939.

So a half-prepared British Expeditionary Force set off for France in the fall of 1939, under General Lord Gort. He knew what he had: he reported to the cabinet a month before the fighting broke out that his force in France was distinctly inferior to that in France during World War I. The five regular army divisions were not very well trained, and the eight Territorial divisions were not fit for modern warfare.

The chain of command for the Allied forces was theoretically simple, with General Gamelin of France in charge, but actually very complex, because Lord Gort had the right to complain to the War Office in London about matters of high strategy, and he did not always conform to the French orders. The result when he did not was confusion.

The British Expeditionary Force was part of the French First Group of Armies, under General Billotte, who took his orders from General Georges, the commander on the northern front, who took his orders from General Gamelin.

Billotte's army, including the BEF, was sitting on the French side of the border with Belgium, from the channel coast at Dunkirk, to the Luxembourg border and the beginning of the real Maginot Line. At the sea, the line was held by the French Seventh Army, and to their right, on the plains north of Lille, the BEF, and to their right, the French First, Ninth, and Second armies.

The BEF organization on the ground in France consisted of three corps on the Belgian frontier, one of them short a division, which had been sent to serve with the French on the Maginot Line. And as for equipment, as Major General Bernard Montgomery put it:

"It must be said to our shame that we sent our army into that most modern war with weapons which were quite inadequate, and we had only ourselves to blame for the disasters which early overtook us in the field when fighting began in 1940."

On the face of it, when this action began in the West, the two sides were evenly matched. The Germans had 136 divisions ready to fight, and the French, Belgians, Dutch, and British had 135 divisions. On the surface, the French Maginot defense line in the South, like highly touted Belgian forts in the middle and the Dutch water defenses in the North, seemed most formidable. But appearances were most deceiving. In the event, the Germans avoided the Maginot Line, cracked open the Belgian forts like sardine cans, and inundated Holland with airborne troops and bombs.

The major difficulty of the common defense was that the Dutch and the Belgians were trying to pursue two policies, to remain neutral, but also to shore up that neutrality with British and French support in case of trouble. But this dual policy led to all sorts of complications. The British wanted a joint defense plan, the Dutch and Belgians ignored the idea. The British wanted a look at the Belgian defenses, the Belgians refused to give it to them officially, gave it unofficially, but it was far from complete and not very edifying.

So what actually happened in the war the British and French thought they were fighting in May 1940?

Their reaction and plans were based on anticipation that the Germans would follow the pattern of 1914. On November 17, 1939, the Allied Supreme War Council had adopted Plan D, which supposed an attack through Belgium. The French First and Ninth armies and the British Expeditionary Force would rush to the defense line to be established on the Dyle River and the Meuse through Antwerp, Louvain, and Namur, and Givet to Mezieres. They had Belgian assurances that they would hold the line here, but no proof and not too much faith.

At the end of November, the Allies added a fillip to the plan. General Henri Giraud's Seventh French Army would move up the channel coast to a point north of Antwerp to help the Dutch if they were attacked. Thus the French and British would meet an attempt to outflank the Maginot Line.

Hitler remained almost manic-depressive about the attack on the West. He bullied his generals and kept forcing them to set outside dates for the attack, and he kept changing his mind at the last minute. It had gone on all during the winter of 1939–40 and well into the spring. On May 1 he set the date for May 5. On May 3 he put it off another day, because of weather possibilities. On May 4 he set May 7 as the day, and the next day postponed it until May 8. The generals, particularly in the field, were getting nervous. So, noting the intense German military activity, were the Belgians and the Dutch.

On May 7 the Hitler railroad train was scheduled to leave at four-thirty in the afternoon for his western field headquarters, near Muenstereifel, about twenty-five miles from the Belgian border. With him were Generals

Keitel, Jodl, and others of the staff of Oberkommando Wehrmacht, the supreme command of the German armed forces. But once again, Hitler changed the date for the attack, since the weather was not that good. Rumors were flying in Berlin about treason and anti-German activity in Italy.

On May 8 the Dutch got the wind up and began mobilizing. This upset Hitler further, and he decided he could not wait longer. Marshal Goering wanted the invasion postponed until May 10 because of the flying weather, and he came to Hitler with the proposal. Hitler was very impatient, he said it was against his intuition to postpone, but he did so anyhow, until May 10, but he said, not for a single day past that.

On May 9 Hitler finally said he meant it, no more postponements, and at 5:00 P.M., his train left Berlin. One more check on the weather—it would be fine the next day, said the weathermen—and the die was cast. The code word *Danzig* was sent to the commands. That meant attack.

It was Friday, May 10. Hitler and the OKW staff arrived at the field headquarters just before dawn. The day was bright and fine, and then the Germans moved. What the French and British, Dutch and Belgians, perceived was the movement, on a front 175 miles wide, from the North Sea to the Maginot Line; what they did not perceive was the even stronger movement through the Ardennes.

Perhaps the symbol of it was the lone German aircraft that flew over the "secret" British fuel dump at Bethune, in northern France, and with a single bomb, blew up three million gallons of British motor fuel. No antiaircraft gun shot at the pilot, because the dump was supposed to be top secret, and fire might give away the position. Similar bombing was going on all along the line, as the German Luftwaffe did its duty to support the army in its drive. The Germans moved in the low countries, just as expected, and the Allies did not know that they were also moving in greater strength through Luxembourg and the Ardennes. From Waalaven in the Netherlands to Chateauroux in Touraine, bombers hit fuel dumps and rail-heads, and German transports dropped paratroopers behind the Dutch and Belgian lines.

The Dutch really had no defenses, but the French sent two divisions by ship to the mouth of the Scheldt River. Another division, sent by road, failed to get through the German cordon. In two days it was all really over, and on the third day Queen Wilhelmina was taken by British warship to exile in England.

The Belgian army consisted of twenty-two divisions, some of them well equipped, but not to withstand armored warfare. It was agreed that the Belgians would defend Antwerp and the eastern part of the country, while the British and French would defend the west on the River Dyle, east of Brussels. The British and French were looking for a leisurely war, with the Belgians perhaps delaying the Germans for two weeks or so.

That morning of May 10, true to the plan, the Allied advance began. The British moved very quickly, as the Germans hoped they would. They surprised their Belgian allies, General Montgomery's Third Division moved to occupy a sector of the River Dyle at Louvain, which was also occupied by a Belgian division. The British moved up in the night, and the Belgians awoke on the morning of May 11 to find British soldiers with them. Montgomery saw the Belgian commander and asked him to withdraw this division and allow the British to hold the front. The Belgian refused. So Montgomery drew back in reserve. But soon the Germans came, and then the Belgians went into reserve and Montgomery took over the front.

On the left of the British was the French Seventh Army, and on their left, the Belgians, holding the line to Antwerp. They claimed there could not be a German breakthrough since they planned to flood the fields along the Dyle by opening the sluices. It looked to be a very comfortable situation, for the Germans would have to cross the flatlands of Belgium for eighty miles, which should take the two weeks allotted by the plans, at least. Three days to get ready, ten days to consolidate the defenses and set up communications, register the guns for fields of fire, and improve the works. Then let the Germans come!

But from the beginning, the British advance was troubled. The German bombing of the fuel supplies was very effective. The Belgians, conscious of the flood of history, insisted that Brussels be declared an open city to save it from bombing. That meant the British troops who needed to traverse the capital had to go through the suburbs, where they got lost. The German fifth column did its best to help them get lost, too, and signs were often taken down or pointed the wrong way.

When the troops reached the Dyle River, they discovered that it was not a river anymore. By opening the sluices to flood the fields toward Antwerp, the Belgians had reduced the Dyle to a small, sluggish stream hardly larger than a ditch. And where were the defenses? The British troops did not find them.

Lord Gort moved his headquarters into Belgium on May 11 without an intelligence staff, because he told his intelligence officer to leave them behind as dead weight. So the intelligence officer got his information from the British Embassy in Brussels, which got its information from the BBC, which got its information from the French, who were putting out glowing communiqués about the war.

It did not take the Germans two weeks to traverse Belgium and reach the Dyle. It took four days.

In Berlin and at Hitler's OKW headquarters, where the German military leadership was watching and waiting worriedly, General Halder, the army chief of staff, could see on the night of May 13 that all was clear for the von Manstein plan to work, as he wrote.

''North of Namur we can count on a completed concentration of some twenty-four British and French and about fifteen Belgian divisions. Against this our Sixth Army has 115 divisions on the front and six in reserve. We are strong enough there to fend off any enemy attack. No need to bring up more forces. South of Namur we face a weaker enemy. About half our strength. Outcome of Meuse attack will decide if, when, and where we will be able to exploit this superiority. The enemy has no force worth mentioning behind this front.''

On May 14, while the British artillery was still en route by train, scouting parties and motorcycle troops could be seen coming from the east. At 6:00 P.M. that day the retreat began, as the leading British units were ordered to withdraw from the east bank of the Dyle.

May 15. Confusion among the Allies. Ragged, retreating Belgian troops of the Tenth Division approached the British defenses on the Dyle, and were promptly fired upon, because there had been no intelligence about their coming. British intelligence was almost totally non-existent. What Lord Gort did learn on May 15 was that the BEF was engaged in battle with German scouting parties. On their right the French First Army was under attack. On their right, what had happened to the Ninth Army? The rumor was that it was smashed and running. The rumor was soon confirmed. The Ninth Army had gotten in the way of the German drive through the Ardennes and across the Meuse and was being rolled up by the Germans. Now the French First Army began to retreat to guard its flank, and when that happened, it was chain reaction. The British would have to retreat to guard their flank.

May 15. It was just five days after the beginning of the German twin-pronged attack, and they had forced their way through the French defenses on the Meuse, and were driving down the peaceful roads toward the mouth of the Somme River. Eight divisions of British troops were in Belgium, with engineers, artillery, and support troops. Also there were four more British divisions, but only half-trained and without adequate equipment and communications, and all sorts of special service personnel on the three-hundred-kilometer system that ran to the ports of Brittany.

Had there been some cogent organization of the BEF at this point, the retreating troops might have been organized, and regrouped and reequipped to fight the Germans. They certainly had the heart for it. But there was nothing, not enough transport, not enough weapons, and no clear view of what was really happening.

From Sedan the panzers were driving for the coast.

In Paris on the fifteenth the French cabinet met to consider the idea of moving south to Tours. Prime Minister Reynaud that day telephoned Prime Minister Winston Churchill, only five days in office, to ask for more troops and aircraft to stem the German tide.

But the British had no troops. They had scraped the barrel, and even brought troops from France for the Norway operation that was still very much in progress. Just a few hours earlier, Churchill had asked his war cabinet to send more aircraft to France. But Air Chief Marshal Sir Hugh Dowding, who had no faith in the French, was flatly opposed to weakening the defense forces he thought he would have to use soon to protect against the Luftwaffe's attacks on Britain, and he lobbied so that most of the war cabinet voted his way, and the prime minister lost the vote.

Aroused by the sense of urgency from France, Churchill decided to go to Paris to see for himself what was happening.

He met with Premier Reynaud, Minister of Defense Daladier, and General Gamelin, the army commander, and asked where were the reserves to throw into the battle. But there were no reserves, General Gamelin replied. Churchill was shocked. "I admit," he said later, "that this was one of the greatest suprises I have had in my life."

It was also a surprise, almost unbelievable, to Hitler. He could hardly believe it, and he suspected it was a trap of some sort. He conferred with his generals. The Luftwaffe had a report that the French were about to mount a great counterattack, to cut off the armored columns. On the map they looked very extended and very forlorn out there in front of the army. Hitler conferred with General von Brauchitsch and with General Halder. He was certain, his intuition told him, that the French were mounting an offensive from the south.

Later that day, Hitler conferred with General von Rundstedt. The general said he had the same feeling; "a great surprise counteroffensive by strong French forces from the Verdun and Chalons-sur-Marne areas,'' was his prediction. The specter of those defeats on the Marne in the last war rose before Hitler's eyes. He was very nervous and very irritable. He was afraid that the success would turn to dust in a moment. He worried, and the more worried he became, the more voluble he grew; the more irritated, the more screaming that went on. He said they had to stop the drive west, and to the southwest, and called for a thrust to the northwest. He told Brauchitsch and Halder that they had to immediately build up a flanking position to the south, paying no attention to where his armies were and how they were faring.

Because of the wrong guesses of the French military leaders, the million men in the North, along the Maginot Line, were effectively cut off from the battle. And that day Gamelin stepped down as commander, and two days later General Weygand took over, and Marshal Pétain, a relict of World War I, was recalled to the cabinet.

By May 19 the German thrust of the wedge of seven armored divisions was only fifty miles from the English Channel. On the evening of May 20 they reached Abbeville at the mouth of the Somme River.

Hitler's mood changed completely. He was all smiles and laughter. He started talking about the peace he would dictate to the Allies, the return of territory . . . all his dreams.

General Weygand decided on an attack south across the German thrust from the Meuse by combined Allied armies. But once again, there were almost insuperable obstacles. The worst was communications, nowhere better illustrated than in General Weygand's trip to the front lines on May 21.

The general set out by bomber early on the morning of May 21. The plane flew over the German lines and landed at a field near Bethune. There was supposed to be an RAF squadron there, but it had been recalled by the British to protect it from capture. So there was no transportation and the general had to hitch a ride into town, where he went to a café because it had a telephone.

His aide tried to get some headquarters on the line, and the general ordered an omelet. It was after 3:00 P.M. when he finally arrived at Ypres, the Belgian army headquarters. He was greeted by King Leopold of Belgium. Soon General Billotte, commander of the First French Group of Armis, arrived, and the naval officer in charge of the port of Dunkirk, Admiral Arioal. At last Lord Gort showed up, but by the time he came, Weygand had already left by torpedo boat for Cherbourg, and then by train for Paris. He had seen little and done less and been out of touch with his headquarters in Paris for more than twenty-four hours.

The Ypres conference did not prove anything. Weygand wanted to press for the attack across the German salient, to meet a force from the main body of the French army which had not been called into the battle, but King Leopold would not agree to the abandonment of Belgium, which this would entail. So no action was taken. Lord Gort headed back to his headquarters, and General Billotte started back for his. On a crowded road Billotte's driver crashed into a truck, and the general was badly hurt and knocked unconscious. He died the next day, leaving the French First Army Group without a commander, and because of communications and failure of top leadership, no commander was chosen for four days. During all this time the German advance continued, from Belgium toward the French frontier, and from the Somme north toward the ports on the English Channel, closing the trap made by the twin German advances.

So here was the BEF on the line, not having really met the enemy, but today to retreat before it did. The soldiers were shocked; they did not know of the panzer offensive that was outflanking the Allied armies hour by hour. So they were ordered off the Dyle River line. But now one of the major weaknesses of the BEF came into play: the shortage of motor transport. Even if the trucks could move through the jam of refugees coming along the roads, they soon ran out of fuel. So the troops began to march, and the marching columns of men added to the congestion of the road and made the situation worse.

For reasons that seem now obscure, the BEF had relied on the public telephone system of Belgium rather than laying its own communication lines. Now they began to use their radio network, but they had not tested it, and it did not work properly. They had batteries, but the batteries soon ran down, and the wireless trucks were useless. The field telephones soon became useless as they retreated faster than the communications men could lay cable.

The foul-up of communications was almost complete. For security reasons, at the company level, maps were taken away, and then no one knew where he was going. Orders were conveyed by officers in staff cars, or by motorcycle riders. Again trouble with the jammed roads full of horse-drawn vehicles, hand-drawn carts, Belgian field guns retreating, and staff cars from every service, passing each other on right and left—anything to keep going and get there. One antiaircraft battery communicated with its headquarters through the woman who ran a public bar across the road from the guns. She had a telephone.

Germans and their supporters were probably hooked up.

Some of the British troops did not even have proper ammunition for their small arms. On the line, food began to run out, and there were only three days rations in reserve. Looting became the rule as the supplies ran out, and British lorry columns could be seen full of beef and pork and chickens as they retreated.

The German Luftwaffe began to attack the columns on the roads. One attack on the 145th Brigade cost the unit almost 250 men, as lorries were smashed and run off the road. The survivors began to march. The wounded were left behind to wait for transportation. Soldiers stood in the road and fired their rifles at the Heinkels. They had no antiaircraft guns, and their machine guns would not traverse for antiaircraft fire. But the British did not bear the brunt of the air attacks, the French and Belgians did, just as they would bear most of the horrors of this war.

CHAPTER 25

The Netherlands Engulfed

While the British were trying to hold the Germans in Belgium, what was happening in the Netherlands, which in World War I had managed to preserve its neutrality?

The Dutch had again been very careful in their relations with Germany, so much so that when Hitler came up against the time factor in planning his attack, he found it very difficult to make a case for the invasion of the Netherlands and violation of her neutrality. It was done by the now typical Nazi trick of fabricating the evidence. One bit involved the capture of two British officers in the Netherlands who were charged as British agents, and the other involved the air space of Holland, which, the Germans said, had been violated by the British, without Dutch complaint.

So by May 8, the plan was in order. At six o'clock on the morning of May 10, a courier was supposed to deliver a personal note to Queen Wilhelmina of the Netherlands, saying that international developments had made it necessary for Germany to send troops across Dutch territory. Let the queen direct her army to permit the passage unmolested, and all would be well.

The Foreign Office courier had a visa from the Dutch

Embassy in Berlin, and he crossed the border on May 9, and intended to wait until early morning to fulfill his mission. But Admiral Wilhelm Canaris, the chief of military intelligence, and an enemy of the Hitler regime, had contrived to tip off the Dutch that something was afoot, and the courier was arrested at the border and his secret letter taken away. The Dutch had already been alerted and had begun mobilization of their resources, again through information supplied by Admiral Canaris.

So the Dutch had a few hours warning of the German intentions, for what little good it would do them. For the conquest of Holland, not really expecting the queen to accept the ''invitation'' offered by the German Foreign Office, the army and air force had set up a cooperative operation involving one panzer division, airborne troops, parachutists, and bombers.

As the Germans prepared to move, the Dutch did too, causing Hitler (as noted) to have another of his attacks of paranoia, and almost to call off the whole operation once more. So he conquered his fears, and set off by train from the small station at Grunewald. For security reasons it had been announced that Hitler was going to visit Hamburg, and the train headed that way until darkness fell, then reversed direction and traveled to Euskirchen, near Aachen, and then Hitler traveled by car to Felsennest, the headquarters built for him by the Todt Organization. This was his first visit to the war headquarters; ultimately he would have two such aeries, one for the western front and one for the eastern. Bunkers were blasted out of solid rock in the mountains, with separate windowless rooms for the chief officers of the German military. General Keitel had a room next to Hitler's, and General Jodl was not far away. Five minutes walk down the forest trail was the office, equipped with the latest in communications. From here Hitler would direct the lightning operations that would end in the fall of France. Indeed, from the Holland operation to all the rest, Hitler was totally familiar with the plans of his armed forces, even down to the combat assignments of the regiments. For months he had known precisely how this operation in the West would go. In October 1939 he had summoned all the army group commanders involved and had discussed the coming operations with them individually. As General Keitel had written later:

"With each one he had discussed all the details, sometimes asking awkward questions, and showing himself to be remarkably well informed on terrain, obstacles and the like, as the result of his penetrating study of the maps. His critical judgment and suggestions proved to the generals that he had immersed himself deeply in the problems inherent in executing his basic orders, and that he was no layman."

At his aerie, Hitler was particularly interested in the situation developing in Holland. This was not the first occasion on which the Dutch had indicated an awareness of German intentions. On January 16, 1940, they had also suddenly canceled leave for all the armed services and given other indications of concern; Propaganda Minister Goebbels had put this down to the discovery of the German war plan, and to British agitation.

Now however, it was much more serious. Word came that night that the Dutch had begun opening their dykes and flooding the countryside. Roadblocks were going up over all of Holland. People were being evacuated from the cities. Marshal Goering's Luftwaffe was responsible for much of the activity that would occur in Holland. He now expressed his concern about the plans for bombing Holland, because there was obviously going to be resistance, and his supply chain was not as strong as he thought it could be, so he asked for at least two days delay before conducting military operations in Holland.

But Hitler said no. He could not delay until the twelfth or thirteenth. There had already been too much delay.

Hitler did not know that Admiral Canaris had warned the Dutch, but did know what the warning had done. The first move on May 10 was supposed to be the capture of the Dutch airfields near the Hague. Once that was done, the German troops would occupy the capital city and capture Queen Wilhelmina, and keep her, as guest or hostage or whatever one wanted to call it. She would be hostage to the peaceful behavior of her subjects.

But now the Dutch infantry, warned, were ready for the German paratroops. Among the first bits of news Hitler received about his first day's fighting was the unpleasant note that the two German regiments assigned to the capture of the three airfields had failed; many of the Germans had been captured, and the Dutch infantry, supported by artillery that could not have been in place had Holland not been warned, had cleared the airfields of Germans. The plan to capture Queen Wilhelmina had failed: the whole German war plan had gone seriously astray.

General Georg von Kuechler, commander of the Eighteenth Army, set out at dawn on May 10 to cross the Dutch border and drive deep into Holland. The key to his success had to be landings by paratroops to capture the bridges he would have to pass en route; if the bridges were destroyed, his effort might fail or at least would be seriously delayed. And delay brought the specter of Allied reinforcement of the Dutch. The distance was one hundred miles. General von Kuechler had to reach the Dutch heartland, and the cities Utrecht, Rotterdam, Amsterdam, and Leyden.

Marshal Goering's Luftwaffe did its job well. One company of airborne troops landed on the river in Rotterdam in seaplanes, and seized key bridges. Other units dropped from the air, and did the same. The Dutch were simply overwhelmed. They rallied and tried to recover possession of the bridges and destroy them, but the German paratroops hung on, until the morning of May 12, when Kuechler's panzers arrived after smashing through the Grebbe-Peel line, which the Dutch had expected to stand for a week. Here was another illustration of the enormous change that the panzer concept had brought to twentieth-century warfare.

The key Dutch bridges lay south of Rotterdam over the Niuwe Maas (New Meuse) and two estuaries of the Maas (Meuse) at Moerdjik and Dordrecht. If they could be destroyed by the Dutch, then Kuechler's force could be delayed, perhaps in time for the British and French to send reinforcements, the Dutch believed. The Dutch really had no conception of the shortage of troops for such purpose. The BEF had no such reserves; only the French might act. Queen Wilhelmina that day issued a personal appeal to King George VI by telephone. Please send planes, she asked, to bomb the Germans. But King George had no aircraft to send her. Several Dutch ministers waited on Winston Churchill in his first day of office as prime minister, and he had no aircraft to send them, and the RAF would not risk any of its aircraft thus.

The French did their best. General Giraud's French Seventh Army hurried along from the English Channel and reached Tilburg on May 11, but the French had no air support (the British failure again). They had no armor, antitank guns, or antiaircraft guns, and were soon pushed back to Breda by the Germans. Had the British come through with bombers and fighter bombers, this German blitzkrieg might have been stopped temporarily, for what good it would have done. But, as could be seen by the tempo of the battle elsewhere, the respite even so would have been brief.

The failure of the French to reinforce the Dutch opened the way for the German panzers to cross the Maas bridges and, on the afternoon of May 12, to arrive on the south bank of the Nieuw Maas River, across from Rotterdam. Here the Dutch held them, by sealing off the bridges at the northern ends. So on May 13, Holland was still holding out, and the Germans had not captured any major city. The Germans, who had expected to be in the Hague by now, were dispersed around the villages. Rotterdam was holding out.

Hitler did not like this at all, because he had other uses for that panzer division in France. From the aerie on the morning of May 14, Hitler issued a war directive noting that the Dutch resistance was much more effective than he had expected.

"Political as well as military considerations require that this resistance be broken speedily."

Marshal Hermann Goering said that the way to break

the resistance was by a saturation bombing of Rotterdam. And Hitler agreed to it.

The Luftwaffe was already deeply involved in the Dutch campaign; because the general staff had stipulated the use of paratroops to capture the Dutch bridges, General Kurt Student, chief of the paratroop Seventh Division, had to have air transport for his men. The Germans had neglected· in the years of peace to build a force of air transport planes, so JU 52 bombers had to be used, and for that purpose, the Luftwaffe training command was raided to secure new combat crews. Nearly four hundred JU 52s were engaged. Now more bombers would be diverted from the support of the panzer divisions to plaster Rotterdam. (This cannibalization of the training command was to have its negative effects starting the next year with the Battle of Britain, when the training of German pilots and aircrews fell off sharply.)

On May 14 the Germans on the bank of the Maas from Rotterdam sent a staff officer from the XXXIX Corps across the bridge under a white flag to negotiate with the Dutch. He warned that unless Rotterdam surrendered, the city would be bombed. Embarrassingly to him and his superiors, as negotiations were· under way at German headquarters, German bombers appeared in large formations and struck the heart of Rotterdam, killing more than eight hundred persons, wounding thirty thousand, and destroying the homes of seventy-eight thousand people. Most of the casualties were civilians. It was the first such bombing in the Western world (although the Japanese had already bombed several Chinese cities), and it was so quick and so devastating that it shocked the world and brought to the people of Britain a grim realization of what they had to expect in the future. The Luftwaffe had bombed other cities, including Paris, but the targets had been military. This Rotterdam attack was terrorism pure and simple, akin to the bombing of Warsaw during the Polish campaign, but more concentrated and more deadly.

So Rotterdam surrendered, Queen Wilhelmina and her government were picked up by two British destroyers and taken to Harwich on the east coast of England, and on the night of May 14, General H. G. Winckelmann, the Dutch chief of staff, saw there was no further hope in resistance, so he ordered the Dutch army to lay down its arms the next day, and at 1:00 A.M. on May 15, he signed the instrument of capitulation. The Germans had gained another colony.

CHAPTER 26

The Fight at Arras

If General von Rundstedt had one fear during the German rush across the Meuse to the English Channel, it had to be that the Allies would counterattack and cut the narrow corridor of his panzer forces. He described it later:

"A critical moment in the drive came just as my forces had reached the channel. It was caused by a British counterstrike southwards from Arras on 21 May. For a short time it was feared that our armored divisions would be cut off before the infantry divisions could come up to support them. None of the French counterattacks carried any threat such as this one did."

The nightmare was very real. The German panzers had been surging across France at the rate of fifty kilometers a day, cutting a path that divided the Allied armies of the northern front from the main body of the force that defended France. But the strip on which they moved was very narrow, and both flanks were open. Von Rundstedt realized that the Allies might attack this lifeline either from the north, from the south, or worst of all, from both directions at the same time. This matter had been considered all along, as far back as the war games in Germany in the winter, but the panzer generals had held that the stakes were worth the risk, and they counted on the inability of the French and British to organize such a counterattack on short notice. It was a question of hours, not days, that the great danger would exist.

The French were very much aware of the opportunity, and General Gamelin had hopes of achieving such a smashing blow at the German corridor. But the French armies were thoroughly disheartened or broken by this time. The only possibility of such a counterbreakthrough existed in a force of two battalions of British tanks, supported by two battalions of British infantry.

On May 15 the French began to have difficulties on the right of the British Expeditionary Force. The German breakthrough had come on the front of the Ninth French Army, and the British had known nothing about it for many hours, because of faulty communications between the two armies. There was no British liaison officer with the Ninth French Army.

Lord Gort had compounded the problem by depriving himself of the services of his intelligence officer, Major General Mason-MacFarlane, by putting him in command of a detachment enjoined to protect the right rear of the BEF. The general took with him his senior staff officer, which left Gort with no one experienced to handle the difficult task of keeping up on information with increasingly disorganized French high command.

As noted, the British had come to France without an adequate force of tanks. They had only the Fourth and Seventh Royal Tank Regiments, two battalions of tanks in all, and these were treated with kid gloves. When the BEF came into Belgium, the tanks went by train. They were then ordered back to meet the German panzer drive across the Allied rear. A train was marshaled again, but the Luftwaffe bombed it, and so it was not used. False reports, again faulty intelligence, sent the tanks rushing around the countryside, wasting fuel and wearing out the tank treads. Ultimately the tank groups arrived back at their starting point under their own power, the British headquarters at Arras.

On May 18, when the tanks returned to Arras, they had covered 120 miles without access to repair and overhaul. About a quarter of the tanks were out of service by this time, and the operating force consisted of fifty-eight Mark I tanks, which had only machine guns as weapons. There were also sixteen Mark II (Matilda) tanks, each of which carried a machine gun and a 37-mm gun.

At the time that the tanks arrived at Arras, Lord Gort was organizing. The tanks joined what was called "Frankforce," named for Major General Franklyn. Lord Gort just then was being pressed by the French to mount a joint counterattack southward, but he had dismissed the idea as unrealistic until on May 20 Prime Minister Churchill decided that such a counteroffensive should be made, and so instructed the War Office. Lord Gort got his orders, and he gave the job of organizing the assault to Frankforce. To support the two armored battalions, General Franklyn assigned one battalion of the Fifth Durham Light Infantry and another battalion from the Eighth Durham Light Infantry.

These infantry battalions were territorial Army Battalions, recruited from the depressed areas of Northern England, and hardly trained at all, even though they had been in France for months. They had spent their war so far digging trenches, at which they were quite skilled, coming from the coal pits and the shipyards. The platoons were commanded by second lieutenants, either fresh from grammar school, or old "retread" lieutenants, veterans of the First World War. The noncommissioned officers were either grizzled veterans of the first war, or youngsters no better trained than the privates. Most platoons did not have a platoon sergeant. The two battalions had no radios, no artillery, and about half the usual number of automatic weapons. They were, in other words, not only ill trained for the job at hand, but ill supplied and ill armed.

Lord Gort's orders to General Franklyn called on him to defend Arras, and then block the roads to the south of the town, thus cutting off the German communications from the east. In other words, they were to cut the German column and isolate the forward part of it from its services of supply.

When Franklyn had his orders, he made contact with the French—General Prioux of the Cavalry and General Altmayer of the French Fifth Corps. At their meeting also in attendance was General Billotte, who nominally was in command of the French First Group of Armies, and thus of Lord Gort and the BEF. General Franklyn did not know who Billotte was, and the language barrier confined their interchange to a handshake.

That meeting was held on May 20, and the Germans were pouring out of their cornucopia toward the channel ports. General Franklyn and General Altmayer tried to work out a joint plan. Altmayer was arranging an attack to the south for May 21, by the French Third Light Mechanized Division, which had 250 heavy tanks. But later in the day, General Altmayer told General Franklyn that the attack would have to be postponed, because the French troops were not ready.

General Franklyn was having problems getting ready, too. There were not enough trucks to transport the infantrymen, so they had to march, and because their officers were as inexperienced as the men, they had trouble with blisters on the march. Many men fell by the wayside, but General Franklyn was determined to attack, French or no French.

On the morning of May 21, the British attack was led by motorcycle scouts, and at 11:00 A.M., plunged forward to cross and break the German line. The infantrymen had spent the night at Vimy Ridge, and were supposed to march fifteen kilometers in two and a half hours. They did not make it.

The first target for the tanks appeared near the village of Duisans, but it turned out to be a detachment of French tanks the British were firing on. Then the tanks moved on and seven of them arrived at Achjicourt, on the southern edge of Arras, just missing the German tank spearhead which had passed through, avoiding French-held Arras, and heading toward the main road at Le Touquet on the shore. Behind the tanks were the mechanized infantry that accompanied the panzers, riding in unarmored trucks. The Germans had antitank guns, but they were ineffectual against the heavy armor of the British tanks. One British tank took fourteen hits without being stopped.

But the apparent victory soon turned around. Lieutenant Colonel Fitzmaurice, commanding the Fourth Battalion, was in a light tank when it was hit by a shell from a field gun, and Fitzmaurice was killed. Lieutenant Colonel Heyland, commander of the Seventh Battalion, tried to line up his tanks to attack the German flank, and when his wireless did not work because of dead batteries, he got out of the tank to make hand signals to his men and was killed by machine gunfire.

The loss of the battalion commanders was fatal, because of the lack of training of those under them. And twenty of the seventy-four tanks broke down from lack of maintenance in recent weeks.

The Germans were also having their problems. These were troops of the Totenkopf Division, of the SS, and despite their name (death head), they were not tough soldiers, but young Nazis, and the officers were not trained soldiers. The British noted that they were not good fighters: many of them surrendered instantly, and others lay facedown on the ground, simulating death.

It was four o'clock in the afternoon before the tired British infantry finally arrived on the scene, and again they ran into French tanks which opened fire on them. The French also were accused by Germans (supported by the British stories) of massacring a large number of the SS troops after they surrendered. Apparently more than four hundred Germans were killed by the French and the British infantry thus, for one British record showed that more than four hundred prisoners were taken, but none of them ever reached a prison camp. One officer of that Seventh Tank Battalion captured a German noncommissioned officer and took him to the rear, to turn over to the infantry. But the British infantrymen were so threatening that he drew his revolver to protect his prisoner from his own men. The officers behaved thus, but by the end of May 21, all the senior officers were dead and the eight infantry companies were all commanded by second lieutenants. (The compliment was returned later, when units of this same SS Death Head division massacred around two hundred British prisoners.)

The apparent British victory was not long in coming unstrung that day. Behind the German infantry in their trucks was another element of German armor, led by General Erwin Rommel, who was traveling with his aide, Lieutenant Most. Here is Rommel's account of the action, from his diary.

"The enemy tank fire had created chaos and confusion among the troops in the village, and they were jamming up the roads and yards with their vehicles instead of going into action with every available weapon to fight off the oncoming enemy.

"With Most's help I brought every available gun into action at top speed against the tanks . . .

"I personally gave every gun its target. With the enemy so perilously close, only rapid fire from every gun could save the situation.

"Although we were under very heavy fire during this action, the gun crews worked magnificently. The worst seemed to be over and the attack beaten off when suddenly Most sank to the ground behind a 20-mm antiaircraft gun close beside me. He was mortally wounded and blood gushed from his mouth . . ."

The secret of the German success was twofold: the superiority of German weapons, particularly the 88-mm gun, which the British saw here for the first time, and the Luftwaffe's Stuka bombers, which Rommel called up for help. The 88s had velocity to pierce the armor of the Matilda tanks, and soon these were being knocked out of action.

The British called on their RAF for help to fight off the Stukas, but it didn't come, because the RAF, sensing defeat, had already moved its bases back across the English Channel, and British communications were so poor that no message ever arrived at RAF headquarters asking for help. So the British, outgunned on the ground and harried from the air, moved north, leaving half their tanks disabled or wrecked on the battlefield. The Germans, who pursued them, ran into the French Third Light Mechanized Division, which was preparing to attack in the morning, and the fighting lasted all night. The French tanks had thick armor, and the German shells did not pierce it. They rescued the British infantry from disaster and launched their own attack the next morning, May 23. But they had lost the element of surprise, and the German Luftwaffe was watching them. Soon the heavy German artillery was called up, and brought into play, and the French attack fizzled out.

The major result of the battle of Arras was to confirm the worst fears of the German high command about the potential for disaster inherent in the panzer attack when the tanks get out far in front of the supporting infantry and leave their flanks exposed. General Von Kleist, the commander of the panzers, became very nervous. General von Kluge, the army commander, wanted to stop everything and hold. General von Rundstedt was inclined to agree, until the flanking infantry could be brought up.

But the failure of the Battle of Arras was that it ended French-British cooperation on the southern front. Lord Gort had not believed in the attack, because he thought the battle of France was already lost and the only thing to do was to get out as quickly and as efficiently as possible. Only because of Winston Churchill's direct instructions as prime minister had Lord Gort even committed the small force that went into battle.

When the Allies failed to halt the Germans at Arras, that was the end of the British effort to conduct any offensive operations. From this point on, they would be on the defensive, trying only to escape the German trap that was closing tight around them.

The Channel Ports   237

CHAPTER 27

The Channel Ports

The German surge toward the channel ports continued after the abortive British attempt to cut the German corridor at the Battle of Arras. On May 21 General Heinz Guderian received orders to continue his advance north against those ports, with the Tenth Panzer Division heading for Dunkirk, by way of Hesdin and St. Omer. The First Panzer Division was to move on Calais, and the Second Panzer Division on Boulogne. But Guderian lost control of the Tenth Panzer Division, and so the assault on Dunkirk had to be delayed.

Units of the XLI German Army Corps reached Hesdin on May 21, and the Sixth Panzer Division took Boisle. Guderian's new drive began on the morning of May 22, and at 8:00 A.M., his troops crossed the Authie River heading north. Everyone was moving with more caution now that the Arras battle had shown what might have been. Guderian had to leave elements of his two remaining divisions back to secure the Somme bridgeheads, until the infantry of General von Wietersheim's XIV Army Corps could catch up and take over that duty.

On the afternoon of May 22, the Germans ran into strong resistance south of Boulogne. They faced mixed units, French, British, Belgians, and Dutch, and the superior organization of the Germans won their way through, but they did suffer seriously from air attack, because the Royal Air Force was now doing its best to protect the retreating British troops and get as many of them home again as possible. In spite of the heavy air attacks, the Second Panzer Division got to Boulogne that day.

After considerable argument, Guderian got back control of his Tenth Panzer Division, and decided to send it to take over the Calais assault, while the First Panzer Division moved on Dunkirk. On May 23 the First Panzer Division moved toward Gravelines, while the Second Panzer Division was fighting around Boulogne. It took some time to penetrate the old town walls, but this was done that day, and fighting began in the harbor area.

On May 24 the First Panzer Division reached the Aa Canal, and put bridgeheads across it at four places, and the Second Panzer Division took control of Boulogne. The Tenth Panzer Division was also moving ahead in the Calais area. This day, too, Guderian got a new element to his command, the Leibstandarte Adolf Hitler SS Division, which he ordered to advance in the Dunkirk area, and at the same time ordered some troops of the Second Panzer Division to move that way as well. The Tenth Panzer Division by this time had encircled Calais. That day, also, the XLI Army Corps put a bridgehead over the Aa Canal at St. Omer.

The full effect of the British attempt to cut the German line at Arras was now felt: Von Rundstedt and his lesser commanders were worried, and now Hitler issued a momentous order. He stopped the left wing of the German army at the Aa Canal. One reason for this decision was Marshal Goering's boast to Hitler that he could handle the situation and wipe out the British forces converging on Dunkirk with his Luftwaffe alone. So the order came down:

"Dunkirk is to be left to the Luftwaffe. Should the capture of Calais prove difficult, this port, too, is to be left to the Luftwaffe." Guderian was speechless, but there was no gainsaying an order from OKW, so he told his panzer divisions to sit on the banks of the Aa Canal and take a rest.

Actually, Hitler's orders were not precisely obeyed. General Sepp Dietrich, commander of the Liebstandarte Division, ordered his men to cross the Aa anyhow, and they did, taking position on the far side. But they went no farther.

On May 24 the Germans captured Boulogne and were fighting in Calais. The British there resisted stoutly. When the German commander made a demand for their surrender, Brigadier Nicolson said, "The answer is no, as it is the British army's duty to fight as well as it is the Germans'."

So the Germans renewed their assault and on May 16 captured the city. The British surrenderd and the Germans took twenty thousand prisoners, four thousand of them British and the rest French, Belgian, and Dutch, most of whom had been locked in cellars by the British, because the others wanted to quit fighting.

On May 26 General Guderian wanted to move on Dunkirk, but renewed orders from OKW denied him the privilege. They were stopped within sight of the city, and Guderian watched the Luftwaffe attacking.

By May 25, with the encircling panzers waiting in sight of the city, the Germans had closed the trap and the Luftwaffe was to show what it could do. Goering's aircraft had already been bombing the quays, and Goering boasted that they had been made unusable. The French were prepared to make a stand here, and General Blanchard, who commanded all the Allied armies on the northern front, ordered all the troops to stand and fight. "The bridgehead will be held with no thought of defeat," he said.

But the British were now thinking of nothing but escape. A headquarters for evacuation was set up by Admiral Bernard Ramsay in Dover Castle across the English Channel. The evacuation was to be called Operation Dynamo. Admiral Ramsay had modest hopes, that he might be able to move out forty-five thousand men in two days, and thereafter the Germans would close the ring.

So in deepest secrecy, keeping the plans from their French allies, Ramsay's staff got to work.

On May 14 the BBC had reported on an Admiralty call to all owners of pleasure craft from thirty feet to one hundred feet long to get in touch with the Admiralty. Rear Admiral Taylor was sent to the port of Sheerness to collect crews and vessels, in behalf of the Royal Navy, and a small vessels pool was established. A rescue fleet began to assemble. Soon some ninety boat owners fishermen, and skippers were signed up for temporary duty with the Admiralty at the pay of three pounds for a month. The Admiralty compiled lists of retired naval officers and petty officers who were capable of operating civilian boats in crisis.

On May 16 the matter took on a more lofty tone when Prime Minister Churchill flew to Paris in response to messages from Premier Reynaud. He found the French government in a state of paralysis and despair, and when he returned to England next day, he began thinking about withdrawing the French government from Paris and the BEF from France. The matter was taken up by a select committee of Parliament, and the idea of the evacuation began to grow. Adding to it came reports from Lord Gort's headquarters to the effect that cooperation with the French was proving impossible, and that Gort himself was out of touch with the BEF. His communications with the French were virtually nonexistent by this time.

Although the governments had agreed that Lord Gort's BEF was to be subject to French orders, on May 17 Gort had refused to accept French orders. "I am not prepared to lose my force," he said then. He declined formally to take instructions to make a stand with the French, refused to fight, and prepared to withdraw.

At midnight on May 18, General Billotte came to Gort's headquarters, and said that he was exhausted and that he could do nothing against the German panzers, unless the British would help. Gort refused, and when Billotte left the headquarters, he reported three options to London:

1. Counterattack against the Germans coming through Belgium.
2. Counterattack in the opposite direction against the Germans in France.
3. Run for the channel ports of Boulogne, Calais, and Dunkirk, ready to get out of the channel area as best they could.

So that word reached London, and what Gort planned was to take the third option and run. By May 19 this plan was actually in operation, with liaison officers sent to London to make arrangements for evacuation through Dunkirk. On May 19 all headquarters troops not needed for fighting were sent by train to Dunkirk to await evacuation. This was before the Germans had reached Abbeville, a week before they began the drive on the channel ports.

When the word of this plan got to the government, many of the political leaders were shocked, and some said horrified, at this bald-faced move to abandon the French allies. The chief of the Imperial General Staff, General Edmund Ironside, said that of course, the British would never evacuate their force completely.

When a Labour Minister of the war cabinet referred to the French as "these bloody allies," General Ironside reminded him that the British had really offered the French nothing but token support, "that we had made no army, and that therefore it was not right for us to say 'these bloody allies,' it was for them to say that of us."

Prime Minister Churchill also failed to share the general war office feeling that the French had let the British down, knowing that it was quite the other way around. So General Ironside was sent to France "to put some backbone into Gort," and he tried to get the British to attack, but Arras was the only attempt, and it was a miserable failure because of the ineptitude of the troops involved.

Ironside arrived in France. General Gort alibied. Ironside went to see General Billotte and made promises that the British would amend their ways and fight, but he really could not control affairs or events, and so his promises were hollow. The Arras fight failed, so did a French move the next day, and the Allies were as good as helpless.

Meanwhile at the War Office, the evacuation effort was gaining steam, and the generals watched as the Germans reached the mouth of the Somme, and Dunkirk became their focal point. The evacuation really began with the movement of railway troops and others whom the French called *les bouches inutiles* (useless mouths), and many persons who could have held rifles or served usefully suddenly disappeared into the returning supply ships that crossed the channel back to England. It was a measure of the defeatism that had suddenly descended on the British Expeditionary Force and of the disaster the German blitzkrieg had brought to the Western Allies.

NOTES

1   The Roots of War

Any good encyclopedia will give a reader the bare facts of the Versailles Treaty. To discover what it meant to various countries is another matter. The German position is revealed fully by Hitler in his *Mein Kampf* and by Dr. Josef Goebbels in his writings. William L. Shirer's *Rise and Fall of the Third Reich* also gives a good picture of the Germany that greeted the treaty. In a fictional mode, Erich Maria Remarque's works give a picture of the astonishment and gloom the treaty brought to Germany.

2   The War Machine

The story of the German army in the 1920s is well documented by J. W. Wheeler-Bennett's *The Nemesis of Power*. Shirer deals with it also in *The Rise and Fall of the Third Reich*. Various biographies of Hitler and Allan Bullock's *Hitler: A Study in Tyranny*, tell of Hitler's early relationship to the political army. Field Marshal Keitel's memoirs tell the story of the fall of Generals von Blomberg and von Fritsch. The career of General Heinz Guderian is detailed in his *Panzer Leader*.

3   The Luftwaffe

The several books about the Luftwaffe noted in the bibliography tell the story of the rise of this German air force from the ashes of the Old Imperial Flying Corps. C. G. Grey's study has some special merits, because as a writer on aviation, he was in and out of Germany all during the 1920s and 1930s, yet saw the developments from a British point of view. Shirer's study is more political, and Leonard Mosley's biography of Hermann Goering gives more about the reich marshal's work and influence. In 1988 I spent some time at the German military archives in Freiburg im Breslau.

4   The Navy

The books by Admiral Raeder and Admiral Doenitz are useful in the study of the German navy. Van der Porten's *The German Navy in World War Two* and C. D. Bekker's *Defeat at Sea* provided much material for this chapter, as did studies of mine at the British Public Records Office of Royal Navy Admiralty papers and the Naval History Center in Washington.

5   The Man Who Wanted War

Several years ago I wrote *Hitler's War*, a study of the German dictator's conduct of World War II. In that connection I made heavy use of Field Marshal Keitel's memoirs, and Hitler's own works and the various biographies of Hitler. Shirer gives a running picture of the road Hitler trod as he planned his war. Shirer is particularly good at describing the inner machinations and the contrast between the German dictator's public posture and his private machinations.

6   Advancing on Poland

The story of the German attack on Poland is told by Winston Churchill, by Field Marshal Keitel, and by General Heinz Guderian. The political environment of the period between the Munich conferences and the attack on Poland is very well detailed by Shirer. The British reactions and actions are told by Winston Churchill, and Sisley Huddleston gives a clear picture of France of the period. No one, of course, says very much about the British and French failure to actually do anything for the Poles.

7 The Last Crisis

The story of Goering's machinations to try to keep England out of the war is told in various biographies of the reich marshal and by Shirer. The British side is detailed by Churchill. Keitel deals with the situation at some length, and particularly with Hitler's many changes of mind about the timing.

8 Hitler Starts His War

The story of the attack on Poland comes from General Guderian's personal account, from the Keitel book, and from the Shirer book. Von Mellenthin contributes a slightly different view, from the standpoint of a panzer staff officer.

9 Raeder, Doenitz, and the Sea War

The movements of the German naval commanders are told by themselves, Grand Admiral Raeder in his book, and Admiral Doenitz in his. Von der Porten gives a good overall view of the starting of the naval war. The references and narrative about raiders in World War I comes from my own studies made for several books about the German navy in that period. The material about the U-boat war comes from materials in the Admiralty section of the Public Records Office in Kew, in the suburbs of London.

10 A Minor War Becomes Major

The study of the French situation is from Churchill, Huddleston, and Keitel. Raeder's remarks come from his autobiography. The story of the sinking of the *Athenia* comes from materials in the Public Records Office in Kew. The account of the blitzkrieg in Poland is from Guderian for the most part; but partly from Shirer and Keitel.

11 U-Boat Attack

The material about the U-boat war is from studies made at the Public Records Office in London, particularly in the Admiralty files, which were first employed in several books I wrote about the U-boat war of 1939–45. Winston Churchill gives the account of his own work as First Lord of the Admiralty in his book about the opening days of the war.

12 Navies

The study of the operations of the Royal and German navies comes from materials in the Public Records Office at Kew, and from the German naval records, and from Admiral Doenitz's autobiography.

13 Readying for Battle

Hitler's speeches, as published, are the source for part of this chapter. Sisley Huddleston's book was very useful, as was Shirer and materials collected in Germany for my book about Goering's war, which was published in 1989 in London. Churchill gives the British point of view. Keitel details the army's work. The material about the sea war comes from Doenitz, Raeder, Churchill, and various books about the U-boat campaign.

14 Hot War at Sea, Cold War in France

The material about the British Expeditionary Force comes from Nicholas Harman's *Dunkirk, the Patriotic*

Myth, published by Simon and Schuster in 1980. The story of Prien's sinking of the *Royal Oak* is from the Doenitz book, and from the German records, and from *The U-Boat War in the Atlantic*, a compilation of German records made by Lieutenant Commander Andrew J. Withers of the Royal Navy and published by Her Majesty's Stationery Office in 1989. The story of the *Graf Spee* and the *Deutschland* is from Von der Porten. Other tales of the war at sea are from the Churchill book and materials I collected in England about the battle cruiser HMS *Hood*.

15   The *Graf Spee*

The story of the *Graf Spee* comes from Churchill and Von der Porten and Shirer and the Raeder book.

16   The Battle of the River Plate

The story of the last fight of the *Graf Spee* comes from Von der Porten and Bekker and from Morison's *Battle of the Atlantic 1939–43*. Churchill tells it from a particularly English point of view.

17   The Fruits of Conspiracy

The relationships between Russia and Germany are well described by Shirer and by Churchill. The latter was one of the prime movers of the attempt to shore up Finland and at the same time to stop the German importation of Swedish iron ore. The story of the loss of the German war plans comes from Shirer and Keitel. The story of the *Altmark* is from Von der Porten. The story of the U-boat war is from the Withers book and Bekker.

18   The U-Boat Assault

The study of the German torpedo situation in the spring of 1940 comes from various records at the Public Records Office in Kew, and from the German naval records as

printed in the Withers book. Doenitz devotes considerable space to the problem, and so does Von der Porten.

19   The War of Words

The Goebbels diaries were a basic source for this chapter, and Shirer has a considerable amount of material
about the propaganda minister's activities.

20   Germany Plans a Takeover

Shirer, and Harold Deutsch's *Hitler and His Generals*
(University of Minnesota Press, 1974), and Churchill
were the sources for this chapter about the plans and
invasion of Norway. Keitel's memoirs were also useful.
Doentiz describes the use of the U-boats in the campaign,
and Raeder talks about the navy. I also used materials
from the Admiralty section of the Public Records Office
in Kew. I also used Wolfgang Frank's *Sea Wolves*, published in America by Rinehart and Company.

21   The Battle for Narvik

Winston Churchill, who supervised the British Norway
campaign, is a principal source for this chapter about the
battle for Narvik. Doenitz and Raeder also tell their sides
of the story, and Keitel gives the OKW point of view.
Shirer concentrates on the Norwegian traitor Vidkun
Quisling.

22   The End in Norway

Oddly enough, the British were winning the battle of
Narvik when the German breakthrough in France caused
them to withdraw their forces, because the army was
spread so thin it could not cover both fronts. Churchill
describes the end of the campaign. Admiral Raeder tells
of the German naval problems.

23 Blitzkrieg in the West

General Heinz Guderian led the XIX Panzer Corps on its breach of the Allied lines, starting from the Ardennes and breaking through at Sedan. Flower and Reeves's *The Taste of Courage* tells the story of General Rommel's fight in quotations from his papers. Keitel gives the "big picture." Huddleston and Churchill describe the activities of the French.

24 The British Expeditionary Force

The story of the BEF is told well in *Dunkirk*. Keitel adds some dimensions to it, as does Flower and Reeves's book. Shirer has some material, as does Guderian. Churchill gives the British point of view.

25 The Netherlands Engulfed

Keitel tells the story of Hitler's activity as the hot war began in the low countries. Guderian tells of the German troop movements. From research for my book on Goering, I got material about the Luftwaffe at this stage of the war.

26 The Fight at Arras

The British made only one stand at this stage of the campaign; at Arras they tried to slice through the German panzer column and halt the advance, cut the forward elements off from their supplies. Flower and Reeves tell part of that story, and *Dunkirk* tells more of it. Guderian sees it from the German point of view, as does General Rommel, another who made his reputation in this panzer operation.

27 The Channel Ports

The Channel ports fell swiftly after Arras. First Calais and then Boulogne. Only Dunkirk remained, and it was saved only because Hitler personally intervened and ordered Dunkirk to be left to the Luftwaffe. Goering had been boasting about the power of his air force, and Hitler believed him. The Polish campaign had shown how effective the Stuka dive bombers could be, but that was against the Polish air force, not against the powerful Spitfire and Hurricane fighters of the British, who responded with force here on the channel coast. But suddenly, as Churchill tells it in his book, the whole Allied effort came unraveled, and the British ran for the channel and a chance to get home. The Germans had already won a stunning victory, even though Hitler had prevented it from becoming complete and destroying the British Expeditionary Force.

BIBLIOGRAPHY

I am indebted to the U.S. Library of Congress for bibliographical materials, and to the Bundesarchiv of the German Federal Republic at Freiburg and the British Office of Public Records at Kew.

Arnold-Forster, Mark. *The World at War*. New York: Stein and Day, 1973.

Bekker, C. D. *Defeat at Sea*. New York: Henry Holt and Co., 1955.

Churchill, Winston S. *The Gathering Storm*. Boston: Houghton Mifflin Co., 1950.

Doenitz, Karl. *Zehn Jahre und Swanzig Tage*. Bonn: Athenaeum-Vrlag Junker und Duennhaupt, 1958.

Faber, Harold, eds. *Luftwaffe. A History*. New York: Times Books, 1977.

Flower, Desmond, and James Reeves, eds. *The Taste of Courage*, vol. 1. New York: Harper and Row, 1960.

Goebbels, Joseph. *The Goebbels Diaries*. Translated and edited by Fred Taylor. New York: G. P. Putnam's Sons, 1983.

Gorlitz, Walter, ed. *The Memoirs of Field Marshal Keitel*. New York: Stein and Day, 1966.

Grey, C. C. *The Luftwaffe*. London: Faber and Faber, 1944.

Guderian, Heinz. *Panzer Leader*. New York: Ballantine Books, 1957.

Hitler, Adolf. *Mein Kampf*. New York: Reynal and Hitchcock, 1939.

————. *My New Order*. New York: Reynal and Hitchcock, 1941.

Huddleston, Sisley. *France, The Tragic Years*. Boston: The Americanist Library, 1965.

Irving, David. *The War Path*. New York: Viking Press, 1978.

Mellenthin, F. W. von. *Panzer Battles*. Norman, Okla.: University of Oklahoma Press, 1956.

Montgomery, Bernard Law. *Memoirs*. New York: World Publishing Co., 1958.

Morison, Samuel Eliot. *The Battle of the Atlantic 1939–43*. Boston: Atlantic Monthly Press, 1975.

Mosley, Leonard. *The Reich Marshal*. London: Weidenfeld and Nicolson, 1974.

Murray, Williamson. *Luftwaffe*. London: George Allen and Unwin, 1985.

Pope, Dudley. *73 North. The Defeat of Hitler's Navy*. Philadelphia: J. B. Lippincott Co., 1958.

Porten, Edward P. von der. *The German Navy in World War Two*. New York: Thomas Y. Crowell, 1969.

Shirer, William L. *The Rise and Fall of the Third Reich*. New York: Simon and Schuster, 1959.

Raeder, Erich. *Struggle for the Sea*. Translated by Edward Fitzgerald. London: William Kimber, Ltd., 1959.

Taylor, Telford. *Munich: The Price of Peace*. Garden City, N.Y.: Doubleday, 1979.

Wheeler-Bennett, J. W. *The Nemesis of Power; The German Army in Politics, 1918–1945*. New York: St. Martin's Press, 1964.

INDEX

WORLD WAR II
Edwin P. Hoyt

STORM OVER THE GILBERTS: 63651-4/$3.50 US/$4.50 Can
War in the Central Pacific: 1943
The dramatic reconstruction of the bloody battle over the Japanese-held Gilbert Islands.

CLOSING THE CIRCLE: 67983-8/$3.50 US/$4.95 Can
War in the Pacific: 1945
A behind-the-scenes look at the military and political moves drawn from official American and Japanese sources.

McCAMPBELL'S HEROES   68841-7/$3.95 US/$5.75 Can
A stirring account of the daring fighter pilots, led by Captain David McCampbell, of Air Group Fifteen.

LEYTE GULF   75408-8/$3.50 US/$4.50 Can
The Death of the Princeton
The true story of a bomb-torn American aircraft carrier fighting a courageous battle for survival!

WAR IN THE PACIFIC: SOUTH PACIFIC   76158-0/$4.50 US/$5.50 Can

WAR IN THE PACIFIC: TRIUMPH OF JAPAN
                                           75792-3/$4.50 US/$5.50 Can

WAR IN THE PACIFIC: STIRRINGS   75793-1/$3.95 US/$4.95 Can

THE JUNGLES OF NEW GUINEA   75750-8/$4.95 US/$5.95 Can